Praise for *From Suffering to Peace*

"Mark Coleman's wise and clear words draw on his decades of experience teaching mindfulness meditation. *From Suffering to Peace* is an excellent guide to the depth and breadth of these ancient practices, giving a clear path to bring these principles into every facet of your life. I highly recommend it to anyone interested in deepening their understanding of mindfulness."

— **Troy Aikman**, Pro Football Hall of Fame quarterback and FOX Sports broadcaster

"As popular as mindfulness has become in the culture, many do not realize that it's more than simply a way to reduce stress. It's a profound practice that leads to the highest states of awakening and freedom. Mark Coleman has written an invaluable book that expands the simpler applications of mindfulness practice to reveal its full potential. In addition to giving the reader a clear understanding of the power of mindfulness, *From Suffering to Peace* offers a treasure trove of practices that allow the reader to develop and realize its true promise. A real gem!"

— **James Baraz**, coauthor of *Awakening Joy: 10 Steps to Happiness* and cofounding teacher of Spirit Rock Meditation Center, Woodacre, CA

"This book reveals how mindfulness enables us to manifest our full potential for living from an awakened heart and mind. Mark Coleman's writing is fresh and engaging, deep and inspiring!"

— **Tara Brach**, author of *Radical Acceptance* and *True Refuge*

"Mark Coleman's new book was a revelation for me, even after having a meditation practice for nearly three decades. While I've often thought of mindfulness as a means of turning off my brain, Mark helped me see it's more about turning on my awareness, which can often act as a gatekeeper for reactivity and judgment. Reading this book will help open the door to your growth and freedom."

— **Chip Conley**, *New York Times* bestselling author of *Emotional Equations* and hospitality entrepreneur

"This eloquent and brilliant compendium is astounding! Mark Coleman has the bravery and deep wisdom to tackle complex and challenging topics — such as the true nature of mind habits, stress, relationships, aging, and loss — bringing clarity and ease to them. He guides us, through embodied attention, to easily access the 'jewel of awareness' within us. Mark helps us shift out of our default state of self-absorption to experience joy within a quieter, more peaceful mind. You will find in these pages precious life lessons from Mark's journey and from the many students whose lives he has touched and guided over thirty-five years."

— **Elissa Epel, PhD,** professor and mindfulness researcher at University of California San Francisco and coauthor of the *New York Times* bestseller *The Telomere Effect: A Revolutionary Approach to Living Younger, Healthier, Longer*

"This is as clear, comprehensive, and practical a guide as you will ever find for fully understanding and integrating the power of mindfulness into every aspect of your life. Drawing on wisdom and insights from decades of experience as a meditation practitioner and mindfulness teacher, Mark Coleman offers the reader life-changing tools that promote flourishing, lasting peace of mind and freedom. In a meaningful and heartful way, this book delivers on the 'true promise of mindfulness' and may well change your life."

— **Rich Fernandez, PhD,** CEO of the Search Inside Yourself Leadership Institute and former director of executive education at Google

"Mark Coleman, a deeply experienced and kind mindfulness teacher and practitioner, has written yet another clear, accessible, and inviting book. He warmly invites readers to bring mindfulness — the genuine practice and not its watered-down, popularized versions — into all aspects of their lives, by addressing misunderstandings, showing ways around obstacles, and revealing its power in dozens of compelling examples. Mark has brought us a wonderful, refreshing, inspiring, and very personal text that will be useful for many people, new and experienced, on the path from suffering to peace."

— **James Flaherty,** founder of
New Ventures West and Integral Coaching

"*From Suffering to Peace* provides a beautifully clear wide-angle lens on the transformative power of mindfulness in our daily lives. In the same way that he has explored and loved the natural world, through his many years of practice and teaching Mark Coleman has discovered the inner beauty and spaciousness of our hearts and minds. In this comprehensive work, Mark shares the many insights and practices that so deeply inform its title."

— **Joseph Goldstein,** author of
Mindfulness: A Practical Guide to Awakening

"In turbulent times, we must develop inner peace from the inside out — and Mark Coleman shows us how. Step-by-step, like a wise friend who is also a world-class teacher, he offers practical tools and penetrating insights for lasting well-being in a changing world. Full of encouragement and heart, this book has great depth and breadth, and it is a sure guide to that highest happiness, peace."

— **Rick Hanson, PhD,** author of *Buddha's Brain:
The Practical Neuroscience of Happiness, Love, and Wisdom*

"Like mindfulness itself, this book is helpful and kind. It is straightforward, comprehensive, and wise."

— **Jack Kornfield,** coauthor of *A Path with Heart* and
cofounding teacher of Spirit Rock Meditation Center, Woodacre, CA

"This book is a direct transmission of wisdom from one of the most wellrespected dharma teachers in the field. His ability to integrate kindness into traditional practices of mindfulness, insight, and equanimity is a true gift, and this book is sure to transform the lives of many."

— **Kristin Neff, PhD**, associate professor in the department of educational psychology at the University of Texas at Austin

"*From Suffering to Peace* is a comprehensive and accessible look at mindfulness practices that lead to living wisely and with peace. This is an important, useful, and thoughtful book for the often chaotic and distracting times in which we live."

— **Sharon Salzberg**, author of *Lovingkindness* and *Real Happiness*

"*From Suffering to Peace* offers the wisdom of reflection, the effectiveness of years of teaching, and the rigor of deep personal practice to help guide us toward greater happiness and well-being. This illuminating book invites us into a new way of living that has the power to transform our individual and collective lives."

— **Shauna Shapiro, PhD**, professor at Santa Clara University

"Mark Coleman is a wise, kind, and compassionate teacher. This new offering will be very helpful for both new and experienced practitioners."

— **Bob Stahl, PhD**, coauthor of *A Mindfulness-Based Stress Reduction Workbook*

"This comprehensive guide to mindfulness rounds out the field in an extraordinary way. Moving far beyond mindfulness as a stress reduction technique, it shows us the depth and breadth of mindfulness teachings — including how they can make an impact in the world. Highly recommended for all practitioners."

— **Diana Winston**, director of mindfulness education at the UCLA Mindful Awareness Research Center, author of *The Little Book of Being*, and coauthor of *Fully Present*

From Suffering to Peace

Also by Mark Coleman

Awake in the Wild:
Mindfulness in Nature as a Path of Self-Discovery

Make Peace with Your Mind:
How Mindfulness and Compassion Can Free
You from Your Inner Critic

From Suffering to Peace

The True Promise of Mindfulness

MARK COLEMAN

New World Library
Novato, California

 New World Library
14 Pamaron Way
Novato, California 94949

The material in this book is intended for education. It is not meant to take the
place of diagnosis and treatment by a qualified medical practitioner or therapist.
No expressed or implied guarantee of the effects of the use of the recommenda-
tions can be given or liability taken.

Certain names in this book have been changed to protect privacy.
Permission acknowledgments on pages 293 and 295 serve as an extension of the
copyright page.

Text design by Tona Pearce Myers

Library of Congress Cataloging-in-Publication Data

Names: Coleman, Mark, date, author.
Title: From suffering to peace : the true promise of mindfulness / Mark Coleman.
Description: Novato, California : New World Library, [2019] | Includes biblio-
    graphical references and index.
Identifiers: LCCN 2018052577 (print) | LCCN 2019004292 (ebook) | ISBN
    9781608686049 (e-book) | ISBN 9781608686032 (print : alk. paper)
Subjects: LCSH: Peace of mind. | Mindfulness (Psychology) | Conduct of life.
Classification: LCC BF637.P3 (ebook) | LCC BF637.P3 C64 2019 (print) |
    |DDC 158.1--dc23
LC record available at https://lccn.loc.gov/2018052577

First printing, May 2019
ISBN 978-1-60868-603-2
Ebook ISBN 978-1-60868-604-9

Printed in Canada on 100% postconsumer-waste recycled paper

 New World Library is proud to be a Gold Certified Environmentally
Responsible Publisher. Publisher certification awarded by Green Press
Initiative.

10   9   8   7   6   5   4   3   2   1

To all practitioners and teachers of mindfulness meditation past and present, and to the awakening of hearts and minds that unfold from these liberating practices

• • •

The ultimate value of life depends upon awareness and the power of contemplation rather than upon mere survival.

— ARISTOTLE

Contents

Preface

The Mindfulness
Landscape Today

When Siddhartha Gautama first taught about mindfulness 2,600 years ago in northern India, he probably had no idea how these teachings and perspectives would spread around the world in the twenty-first century. The Buddha originally taught these practices as a vehicle for ending suffering and finding peace, genuine happiness, and a living freedom amidst any and all circumstances in life. Today, how these meditations are taught and developed in therapy offices, hospitals, school classrooms, and boardrooms may perhaps differ from the scope of his original intent, yet they continue to have a profound impact on tens of millions of people in every walk of life all over the world.

Indeed, mindfulness seems to be everywhere, and it is not difficult to see why. It can help develop focus and self-awareness. It can improve your well-being and ability to work with a wide array of challenges, from addiction and anxiety to ADHD. Extensive research now affirms that mindfulness practice results in better emotional regulation, improved attention, and an enhanced ability to work with pain. People everywhere are now discovering what meditation adepts across Southeast Asia have known for millennia, that mindfulness practice can help cultivate awareness and grow the heart of compassion, for both ourselves and others.

As a result, almost every week I hear of some new application for mindfulness. It's being taught in schools, from kindergarten to university, and integrated into an array of organizations, from NBA teams to corporate offices. It's practiced by the military, athletes, surgeons, therapists, programmers, and first responders. It has been featured in countless publications, as well as in numerous podcasts, books, and TV and radio programs. Mindfulness programs are helping people across their entire life spans, from supporting pregnant mothers with childbirth to assisting hospice patients with the challenges of dying.

This movement of mindfulness from cloistered monasteries into research labs, hospitals, schools, prisons, and organizations is helping unprecedented numbers of people worldwide. Yet this rapid, modern proliferation of interest also raises questions and concerns. Given the vast amount of information about and hype surrounding mindfulness today, how do we know we are getting an accurate guide to this subtle subject? Even researchers can overstate what mindfulness can do, and the media, in their zeal to identify the next "big thing," can tout mindfulness as the panacea for all personal and social ills. Given the meteoric growth of mindfulness and its reach into every layer of society, it is vital that the depth, limitations, and potential of the practice are clearly and accurately conveyed.

Mindfulness is a vast and complex body of teachings and practices that has been studied and cultivated for millennia, primarily within Buddhist traditions across Asia. Simply put, this matrix of teachings guides us in how to live a wise, ethical, and compassionate life. In this context, the core intention of mindfulness is to use the clarity of awareness to help ourselves and others find genuine freedom from suffering and to live with a kind responsiveness to life.

My hope with this book is to provide a comprehensive, clear understanding of the depth and scope of these ancient teachings as well as to shed light on their contemporary applications. That requires leaving no stone unturned as we explore our mind, body, heart, and world and discover what causes our pain and stress and what truly supports a life of well-being and peace. Throughout the book, as a support for this inquiry, I provide key meditations, reflections, and practices to help develop a real understanding of this quality and practice.

I began my own study of mindfulness in 1984 in England, before anyone I knew talked about meditation, let alone practiced it. In fact, when I told people I meditated, they thought I was either weird or antisocial. They looked upon what I was doing as navel-gazing, a cop-out from society, or at best a complete waste of time! But despite the dismay and judgments from friends and family, I persevered, even though this was neither easy nor socially acceptable.

Luckily, given the scant information about meditation available back then, I had few preconceptions to wade through. Also, I had the good fortune to train with an array of highly skilled meditation teachers in Asia, Europe, and the United States. I became passionate about my studies and underwent years of intensive, silent, mindfulness meditation retreats as a way to explore the practice deeply and intimately. As hard as that may sound, that immersion in deep contemplative solitude was one of the happiest periods of my life. It was that in-depth exploration that provided a solid foundation for learning to share these teachings.

And there is nothing like teaching to really get to know and understand a subject. For the past twenty years I have had the good fortune to teach mindfulness practices in Buddhist meditation retreat centers around the world. However, I soon realized there were many people who would never step foot inside, nor seek out, a traditional meditation venue. The need for a bridge between the ancient discipline of mindfulness and contemporary culture was clear. So in 2004, I founded the Mindfulness Institute as a way to reach those people and offer programs in an array of settings, weaving neuroscience and emotional intelligence into mindfulness-based courses.

With that intention, I have had the pleasure to lead a wide variety of mindfulness programs, and to see their effectiveness, in places as diverse as the UN in Africa, at tech companies like Google in Silicon Valley, in traditional businesses like Ford Motors, and with nonprofits like the Nature Conservancy. It has been equally illuminating to teach mindfulness in hospitals, universities, and prisons to psychologists, educators, doctors, and inmates and see just how impactful this practice can be for everyone, regardless of their circumstances. In response to our increasing tech-focused culture, I have also explored how meditation can be taught online, and so I created practices for apps that allow access to meditation digitally, including for the *New York Times* and many others. This is now quickly becoming the primary way for people to access meditation tools.

Teaching in this way has given me a distinct vantage point to see the significant impacts of mindfulness in society. I have had the good fortune to have a front-row seat in this grand social experiment, to see how people from all walks of life, from engineers in Silicon Valley to aid workers in Senegal, have found genuine personal transformation through learning meditation and engaging in mindfulness practice.

This book is a continuation of this exploration. In it, I return to the foundational principles of mindfulness while aiming to help you understand this transformative practice within our contemporary context. By outlining the full scope of mindfulness, I place it within its traditional framework, a complete path that leads from suffering to freedom, from reactivity to peace. While I draw on the wealth of mindfulness teachings and practices from the ancient Buddhist tradition, my goal is to present this rich body of work — much of it developed by monastics living in a feudal, agrarian culture as far back as 500 BC — in ways that are relevant and accessible to twenty-first-century life. I seek to both honor this rich and vast tradition and adapt these practices to the needs and demands of our own era.

Throughout this book, I trust you will discover how mindfulness is so much more than simply "focus" or attention, which is how it is often mistakenly described. Mindfulness refers to the depth of awareness we bring to our whole life, and in so doing we transform ourselves and the way we live in the world. Mindfulness supports us to live an intentional, meaningful life with presence, insight, and compassion. It is an extraordinary voyage, and I welcome you to take this journey with me as we explore the beautiful path of mindfulness together.

Introduction

Understanding Mindfulness

When I started meditating, I was a troubled young man. I was a punk rocker, had a white mohawk, and reveled in both the antiestablishment grit of that anarchic scene as well as the wild music. I was living and going to college in East London and was active in the lively squatting movement that helped people occupy the plethora of empty and abandoned state-owned houses. I had a lot of anger inside about the inequality created by capitalism, and I raged against England's oppressive class system. The rundown, working-class neighborhoods where I lived further entrenched my frustration. That was my outer struggle. Inwardly, I fared no better. I also turned my anger toward myself. I had a wicked inner critic; I was plagued with self-judgment and a lot of self-hatred. Looking back, I can see that angry young man was both deeply unhappy and confused about the source of his own suffering.

One day, the ceiling collapsed in the old Victorian house where I was squatting, leaving decades of dirt, dust, and debris strewn across our living room and kitchen. My stoned housemates didn't seem to care, which didn't help matters. In that moment, something snapped. Deep inside, I intuited there had to be a better way, a way not just to cope with the inner and outer challenges of life but also to flourish. The pain inside compelled me to look for answers. I quickly realized that my political interests in anarchy and socialism would not address my inner struggles. So I started to read any spiritual books I could get my hands on. I frequented second-hand bookstores for works on Kabbalah, mysticism, Christianity, and more, but I was stumbling along in the dark without a light to guide me.

As luck would have it, I ended up squatting in a Buddhist housing association property. Rather than evict me, they kindly suggested I take my confused self to their meditation center just around the corner in Bethnal Green in London's East End. Perhaps they hoped I would sort my head out there. I had no idea then that I was going to find keys that would help unlock secrets for working with the pain I was busy running from. It's not that meditation practice removed my sadness, anger, and confusion. At least, not immediately. It just gave me a lens and some tools for working with them. These tools were literally lifesaving, and they are skills that have served me well ever since.

As I learned then, we all can, through the practice of mindfulness, access the jewel of awareness, which can positively impact our well-being. This happens by becoming more aware of, and disengaging from, negative patterns of thinking and cycles of blame and reactivity, which just compound our distress. Through mindfulness, we can discern which choices and behaviors are skillful in any given moment and which just deepen stress and suffering.

Of course, back then, I was just taking baby steps in learning how to live well. But ever since that time thirty-five years ago, I have been studying and integrating these practices and teachings on mindfulness. This path has allowed me to find clarity, wisdom, and some peace in the midst of whatever I am going through, even with challenging emotions and stressful life circumstances. And with practice, anyone can do the same.

These are just a few of the fruits of mindfulness practice. Many other beautiful qualities can arise through cultivating attention, like calm, joy, and spaciousness, although ultimately, the goal of mindfulness isn't to feel or be any particular way. Rather, we develop a clear awareness, which provides insight about ourselves and reality. This not only supports a deep inner freedom but allows us to respond more wisely and compassionately to whatever life presents. My hope is that this book shares some of the important lessons I have learned along the way that will support you in your own journey.

So, What Is Mindfulness?

Ask ten meditation teachers "What is mindfulness?" and you may get ten different responses. The conversation about this complex and subtle theme is not new. Debates over this topic have occurred for centuries, across cultures, and within contemplative traditions. How would you answer that question?

When I ask students in my classes and retreats "What is mindfulness?" I hear a wide variety of responses. Some are more accurate than others, but often they reflect enduring misunderstandings about what it really is. People will say that it means "paying attention" or "being calm and focused." Or they remark that it's "thinking clearly about things," or "being free from thoughts." Others say it's about "letting go." All these answers contain kernels of truth, but none capture the essence and breadth of this quality. Hearing the many ways it is either misconstrued or its depth misunderstood inspired me to write about it.

Simply stated, mindfulness is clear awareness. It is the clear knowing of experience, a nonreactive, noninterfering quality of attention. But it is also much more than that. Having studied and cultivated mindfulness as a practice and a way of life for most of my adult life, I have seen firsthand what a multifaceted jewel it really is. It can impact every arena and every moment of our lives. Exploring the many dimensions of mindfulness, both in theory and in practice, is what this book is all about.

The word *mindfulness* is an odd word in itself, as it sounds like one's mind must be full of something. It was originally used by scholars in the eighteenth century to translate the Indian Pali word *sati*, which literally means "recollection" or "remembering," to mentally take note of an experience. In this context, one could say mindfulness is the conscious knowing of experience, to fully cognize something, which allows for recollection. For example, if you are not present to reading this book right now, how will you fully take note of and remember what you have read? *Sati* also refers to bearing something in mind. For instance, we bear in mind our breath when meditating, or we bear in mind our footsteps when walking along a rocky path.

The idea of being present is not something that is foreign to our experience. Even the name of our species, *Homo sapiens*, refers to being wise or being aware, to knowing that we know. In that way, mindfulness returns us to our birthright, or at least to our potential, to this innate quality of wise knowing. And it is through developing clear awareness of our moment-to-moment experience that we begin to cultivate wisdom and discernment. That is particularly true when we do so with a curious, reflective attention. A more complete definition that I like to use is that mindfulness is an awareness of our inner and outer experience with an attitude of curiosity and care, in order to develop wisdom and understanding. Caring attention, as I will discuss throughout, is necessary for being able to stay present for even the most difficult experience.

In this era when mindfulness has become popularized and perhaps its depth or scope diminished, it is important to reflect on why it can be so impactful in our lives. It isn't just "paying attention." It's the ability to know what is happening without our normal reactions, commentary, and judgment. It is the capacity to meet experience without trying to fix, change, or control it. To capture this characteristic, some refer to mindfulness as "bare attention." That is, it is the awareness of experience without the smoke screen of concepts, labels, and thoughts that can occlude our immediate perception.

To demonstrate this, try this simple mindfulness exercise: Hold up one of your hands, and for a few moments, simply look at your hand and become aware of all its aspects. Get to know your hand as if for the first time. For example, feel your hand's weight, its heaviness or lightness. Observe its size and shape, the colors, lines, contours, and veins. Feel the skin's texture and temperature. Does it have a smell? Can you feel it from the inside, noticing the muscles and bones, the pulse of blood and tingling of energy?

As you do this, notice if critical thoughts or reactions arise. For example, do you start to judge if your fingernails aren't clean, or how old and wrinkled the skin may look? If so, simply recognize these thoughts and return to just being present and observing your hand in a neutral way. Continue doing this for a few minutes, and be aware of whether you can remain in this simple observational mode or if judgments, associations, and reactions distract you from simply attending.

Mindfulness allows us to know the immediacy of experience directly as it is, along with an awareness of how we react to that experience. It allows an intimacy of attention that provides a deeper perception, one that goes beyond our initial concepts and opinions about an event. Knowing the difference between having a clear awareness of something versus thinking and reacting to it is an important element of the practice.

One reason mindfulness is hard to define is because it is not just a state of mind. It is also a way of cultivating awareness and a wide variety of attention training techniques. It is easily mistaken for the qualities that arise when we meditate, like calmness and focus. These qualities are simply some of the fruits of the practice. So understanding mindfulness is like getting to know the many facets of water, which has a variety of forms, properties, and expressions. To define water as simply fluid or wetness, to reduce it to ocean, ice, clouds, or rain, simplifies what it is and misses the scope of its potential. Similarly, to reduce mindfulness to simply attention or one of its related qualities misses its multifaceted nature.

Mindfulness is a clear awareness of moment-to-moment experience. To cultivate this, we can engage in any number of meditative practices. The technique of observing your hand is just one small example. The meditation at the end of this introduction is another, and I present many more in later chapters: walking meditation, open awareness practice, body scan, and so on. As you read this book, I strongly suggest you explore these meditations. An ongoing mindfulness practice helps train your mind to become deeply attuned to what is happening right now. There are many diverse ways to formally practice mindfulness, and yet what unifies them is they all develop awareness.

This can be done in any moment, anywhere. For example, right now, look out a window. Pay attention to whatever you see. Take in the whole panorama, and then focus on one particular thing: the leaves on a tree, a particular cloud, the bricks of a building, a telephone pole, the moon, and so on. Be aware of both *what* you are seeing and *that* you are seeing. And notice how you respond to what you observe. All this happens in a simple moment of mindfulness. And it's trickier than it sounds, as you may notice. Moments of clear attention can quickly get lost within and beneath the many other thoughts, judgments, and distractions that arise.

Mindfulness, as research shows, improves our focus, but it

provides impacts that go beyond a concentrated attention. These practices, as I will explore, help develop beautiful related qualities like clarity, wisdom, patience, resilience, empathy, compassion, and equanimity. Practiced to its depth, mindfulness can help us live with ease amidst the turmoil of life and discover a genuine inner freedom. This is the true peace we are so often seeking. To help people realize this is one of my intentions for writing this book.

The Benefits of Mindfulness

Studies have shown that we spend much of the time on autopilot, going about our day without being very present. In a 2010 study at Harvard, psychologists concluded that our minds are thinking about something else, rather than being present to the task at hand, 47 percent of the time! That means, for almost half of our waking life, we are not really here. No wonder there is an explosion of interest in mindfulness practice, which helps counter such habits. In that distracted mode, we miss so much of the precious and important moments of life.

We also mistakenly assume we see things as they are, but the truth is we usually don't perceive clearly at all. We filter our experience with all kinds of bias, judgments, and preferences. We swim in a river of likes and dislikes, ceaselessly running after one shiny thing and rejecting other less-pleasing experiences. This creates a never-ending push-pull conflict with life that all too often leads to unnecessary stress.

However, this doesn't need to be the case. Through training in awareness, we can learn to observe both our experience and the often turbulent reactions we may have to it. Over time, this clarity enables us to be less driven by our knee-jerk impulses and thus make wiser choices in our lives. This freedom from reactivity is one of the potent outcomes of mindfulness practice. It is why the practice was originally taught and developed, as a way to break free from the painful reactive cycles we so often find ourselves in.

For example, my client Jenny, by her own admission, worries a lot. She gets particularly anxious about her sixteen-year-old twin daughters, who are starting to date and go to parties. If they come home later at night than they promised, her mind whips into a frenzy of terror, imagining all kinds of catastrophic scenarios, fantasizing about terrible things that might happen to her beloved children. Yet she also knows that her daughters are street-smart, responsible kids who aren't reckless and don't use drugs. On nights when they return home late, what Jenny's mind does with all of that conflicting data is the difference between her peace of mind and a mild panic attack. Through mindfulness practice, she has learned to recognize and not buy into the scary thoughts her mind creates, and she is therefore able to be more grounded and steady even in this anxiety-provoking situation.

Another important facet of mindfulness is clear comprehension. This quality helps us discern not just what is happening in the present but what thoughts, speech, and actions are skillful or helpful and which result in pain or stress. With this clarity, we can learn to act in ways that support well-being and cease to engage in actions that cause unnecessary harm — in the same way we quickly drop a hot pan we pick up accidentally on the stove. We can't always avoid pain, but we learn to hold on less and to not pursue things that cause unnecessary anguish.

In this way mindfulness helps foster discernment and wisdom. The poet William Blake summed up this principle rather well when he wrote these oft-quoted words about how we skillfully or unskillfully relate to pleasure: "He who binds to himself a joy / Does the winged life destroy / He who kisses the joy as it flies / lives in eternity's sunrise." It is the clarity of awareness that reveals how our desire to hold and keep what brings us delight can be the very thing that causes us to experience pain and loss. Experience is ephemeral and always changing; all joys eventually fade. But we only multiply the hurt if, in folly, we grasp after pleasure. Rather, as Blake says, we can appreciate joy when it arrives, knowing its presence is fleeting.

Such a light way of being with experience is a perfect example of what awareness makes possible. Without that clarity and wisdom, we so easily get caught in the pain of attachment. The reverse is also true. We sometimes despair when pain arrives, forgetting that it, too, is fleeting, and our reactivity to it only extends our distress. When Jenny imagines worst-case scenarios, this just compounds the anxiety of her daughters' late return. By learning to simply be with her own unpleasant feelings, Jenny can save herself all manner of unnecessary woes.

By bringing direct awareness to any aspect of experience, we can develop clarity and insight. This, in essence, is the deeper purpose of mindfulness — to help us understand and know experience, ourselves, and reality just as they are. The wisdom that arises from this can facilitate a freedom from a painful contention with life. We will explore this theme extensively in later chapters.

How does this work in practice? Take an everyday scenario: being stuck in traffic. Whenever I drive to work in the San Francisco Bay Area, I often encounter traffic, which can threaten to make me late. If I'm aware, I can sense the tension in my gut and shoulders as soon as I see the cars ahead slowing down. I can also observe my self-judgments, such as critical thoughts over why I didn't leave earlier or anticipate the morning traffic. I may notice that my anxiety and tension increase as I anticipate the frustration of my clients if I'm late for our meeting.

These inner reactions just compound my stress. However, if I remain unaware of these reactions, they are more likely to grow, and I am likely to feel even more burdened. Instead of just being late, I will arrive at the office anxious, irritated, and ill-prepared to work with anyone. However, if I become aware of being triggered — of the tension in my body, of my racing thoughts and worry, of my impatience and self-judgment — I can make wiser choices about the best course of action. Mindfulness does not make the traffic go away, although we wish it would. Instead it provides tools to recognize stress and reactivity and to find skillful ways to work with them. And the good news is this skill is immanently portable. We can practice it anywhere, even in our morning commute!

Another useful analogy is to think of mindfulness as a gatekeeper. In the same way medieval towns had a sentry who prevented harmful forces from entering, awareness helps us guard the mind from unwholesome or painful states. In this case, the main thing we are guarding against is ourselves, from our own reactivity, judgments, and negativity.

Like traffic, everyday life is full of innumerable things we don't like or don't want to have happen. Our children may suddenly get sick, or we may hear about some injustice in our national politics. Our boss may suddenly dump a difficult project on our desk late on Friday afternoon, or a loved one may receive a troubling medical diagnosis. Whatever the reason, out of the blue, unexpected events may trigger resentment, panic, despair, and overwhelm. But with awareness, we can recognize when such difficult states overtake us. That clarity creates a pipeline of information that helps us understand how best to handle such eruptions.

As with traffic, that knowing does not necessarily keep reactivity from occurring, but it allows us to recognize it and find space in relation to it. This clear awareness gives us the opportunity to choose a healthy response. Such "wise action" might be to release a painful habit of anticipating the worst outcome, like Jenny did, or it might be to simply stop resisting an unpleasant reality, like traffic, back pain, or a child's illness, and do whatever is necessary or constructive to cope with it.

Being mindful means that, over time, we become less tossed around by our reactions or resistance to the things we dislike and don't want but have no control over. This allows us to not waste so much energy fighting the things we cannot change. This supports the stabilizing quality of equanimity, since we learn to be with experience just as it is, whether we like it or not, with a nonreactive attention.

For instance, consider another example, this time of a positive experience: When I get up in the morning, I love to meditate and listen to the dawn chorus of birdsong. Sometimes, though, rather than simply listening, I become gripped by a longing for the beautiful singing to go on forever, or I become irritated when the noise of the garbage truck drowns out the sweet melodies. Either way, my pleasure is replaced with frustration.

However, when I'm aware, like the poet Blake, I enjoy the song while it lasts and remain at ease when it goes or when something interrupts it. Mindfulness allows me to be present to the sweetness of the chorus *and* the sour sounds of traffic. This awareness helps me avoid contracting in negativity against unwanted noise, which I can't do anything about anyway. This simple but subtle shift in attention is a key principle to how we relate to all experience — and it allows us to release the struggle to either hold on to or resist anything in life, the ups and the downs, the joys and the sorrows.

The following story from Karen, a meditation student from Virginia, further illustrates how this practice of mindfulness helps develop wisdom in the midst of the messiness of life, no matter how hard it gets:

Like many others I have had very dark moments with a difficult divorce, being a single mom, and also having a strong idealistic tendency to think I could somehow find a perfect state of "happiness." Over the years I tried a variety of spiritual practices and teachers, but nothing really seemed to help me cope with my patterns of reactivity, which still played out and brought me deep frustration and unhappiness.

When I discovered mindfulness practice, it seemed as though I had finally found something that did not set me up to search for some ideal state. Instead it showed me a depth of awareness in which I could be kind, happy, and at ease in my ordinary life under any circumstance. Therein lies the peace and happiness I have longed for all my life. The pain of the divorce didn't magically disappear. Neither did the challenges of being a single parent. However, mindfulness did give me the capacity to be present, accepting, and patient with whatever life threw at me. That has been an invaluable gift.

In each of the four sections in this book, I explore the full breadth of mindfulness, which includes bringing a close attention to four key areas in our life: to our body, our mind, our heart, and the world we live in. I will discuss how, through the arc of practice, we learn to bring awareness to these key facets of our experience. As we practice this over time, we slowly discover how mindfulness is a vehicle for insight and wisdom that helps free us from suffering and to live with genuine well-being and peace. Each chapter is always followed by a practice, a way to implement and cultivate the specific quality or aspect of mindfulness being discussed. Many of the practices contain more information to augment and illuminate the chapter contents.

• PRACTICE •

Mindfulness of Breath

Perhaps the simplest, most commonly known, and most accessible way to cultivate mindfulness is through awareness of breathing. Mindfulness of breath is for many the easiest and most readily available practice, since it can be done anywhere, anytime, with minimal instruction or experience. Yet it is also a meditation that can have profound depth and subtlety.

The breath is a barometer for our inner emotional and physical life. By attending to the movement, depth, or tension in the breath, we gain a sense of our inner experience. We can observe how the breath changes in subtle ways depending on what is happening in our mind, heart, and environment. Touched by a moment of joy, we gasp. Overcome by fear, our breath is held tight. No matter where we are, we can learn to attune to the breath as a support for staying in our body in the present moment.

Begin by establishing a posture where you can sit with ease, one that is upright and yet relaxed and alert. Close your eyes and become aware of your body and its posture. Then shift attention to your breath. Try to let the body breathe itself, which it does quite naturally without our interference. Then simply attune your attention to all the various sensations of the inhale and the exhale. Stay curious where you feel the sensations of breath most clearly, like the movement of air in the nostrils, the tickle of air in the back of the throat, the expansion and contraction of the upper chest and ribcage, and the gentle moving in and out of the diaphragm and belly area. Notice how each breath is subtly different from the one before. Be aware of the changing sensations of breathing as well as the stillness of the pause between breaths.

Naturally, your attention will become drawn to other experiences, like sounds and physical sensations, and to other thoughts. When that happens, acknowledge those things and then shift attention back to the breath. No need to judge or become disheartened when you become distracted, even when this happens many times. Mindfulness practice is training, a discipline to develop present-moment attention. Little by little we become more focused and attuned. Continue to let your awareness become absorbed into the sensory experience of breathing, receiving each breath with curiosity, as if you were feeling it for the first time.

After about ten minutes or so, bring the meditation to a close and notice the impact of the practice. Observe what was interesting and where the challenges were in staying present. Know that this is a practice, to be developed over time, with patience and curiosity. Eventually you can extend this meditation to twenty or thirty minutes to support a deeper concentration. Remember, you can take this practice anywhere, since the breath accompanies you in every instant.

• • •

· SECTION 1 ·

FINDING PEACE
IN THE BODY

Chapter 1

Living with
Embodied Awareness

There is more wisdom in your body
than in your deepest philosophy.
— FRIEDRICH NIETZSCHE

I still remember the first day I stepped foot into a meditation center in East London back in 1984. I walked in clumsily, with my white mohawk, my gaudy post-punk disheveled attire, feeling out of place and not knowing what to expect. There I was, a figure of agitation, not comfortable in my own skin, restless and impatient. What I saw stopped me in my tracks. It wasn't as if anyone was doing anything special. People were simply going about their day: arranging books in a library, sweeping the meditation hall, and preparing flowers in the entrance way. However, what took my breath away was the quality of presence in which they moved. There was an air of grace or dignity in how they went about their activities. They exuded a sense of relaxed ease that was quite unfamiliar to me. I didn't quite know what it was, but I knew they were on to something, and I wanted to experience it myself.

The scene felt so ordinary I could have easily overlooked it. In retrospect, I realize that part of what I was witnessing was embodied presence. People who are at home in their own skin, who are connected to themselves and their physical experience, embody a sense of ease, groundedness, and connectedness. The appearance of my over-caffeinated, anxious, angry self in that meditation center was like a storm meeting a serene ocean. It has taken me many years to begin to grow my own way into that beautiful, embodied quality.

One of my favorite pastimes is to watch modern dance. I relish how trained dancers move in their bodies, turning their bodies into living dynamic sculptures. Their movements are artful expressions of living with mindful embodiment. It's as if their bodies are filled with presence, which of course they are. Even seeing a dancer simply walk across the stage can be spellbinding because of how present they are within their own skin. They are poetic reminders of how to move, live, and breathe with an embodied presence that is alive, graceful, and vibrantly here.

Of course, we don't have to be a trained dancer to discover this. Anyone can learn to inhabit the body with awareness. Right now, as you are reading, what do you sense in your body? Become awake to every physical sensation: of your skin against your clothing, of your body against your chair. Can you sense the warmth of your belly and feel moisture on your skin or the wetness of your eyes? With mindfulness, we can be present to our ever-changing inner landscape and its shifting tides. We can sense the fluid energy of the body, which can be experienced as vibration, tingling, expansion, contraction, spaciousness, or pulsing electricity. One of the mysteries of embodied attention is that as soon as we call to mind a particular part of our body, it comes alive with sensory stimuli.

Our bodies are a canvas upon which emotions, feelings, and moods are painted. Emotions are physiological phenomena; we feel them in the body. Right now, attune to the radio broadcast of your body's mood. Can you name what you are feeling? Can you feel the impressions that emotions make in your body? Take a few moments to become intimate with your heart's terrain and where you may feel particular emotions in your chest, belly, or other part of your body.

As well as being host to a whole panorama of beautiful feelings like joy, love, and awe, our bodies also contain emotions that are not so easy to be with, like anxiety and sadness. As much as our bodies can be a source of delight and pleasurable sensory experience, our bodies also hold painful and difficult sensations, which is why we so often tune out from our somatic landscape. However, even if what we feel is unpleasant, with mindfulness we can bring attention to it and stay curious, exploring whatever may not be easy to be with.

Unfortunately, in today's world, our attention is often scattered, distracted, and anywhere but in our bodies. We are less like modern dancers and more like Mr. Duffy, the protagonist in James Joyce's short story "A Painful Case," who "lived a short distance from his body." Smartphones, computers, and video games keep us lost in our heads. We focus on screens and digital devices that often seduce and mesmerize us, taking us away from the physical sensory present. This makes the practice of mindfulness even more necessary, as well as more challenging, because in its fullest sense it is an embodied awareness that requires us to inhabit our bodies.

I luckily had access to a sense of embodiment early in life, as many kids used to. I was born before the computer revolution, and as a child, though I enjoyed Space Invaders and TV, these were no competition for playing outside. I had the good fortune to grow up near the woodlands and seashore of my native Northumberland in northern England. I remember a childhood of skinny-dipping in streams in summertime, swimming in the cold North Sea breaks, and lying in the middle of vast golden fields of wheat, engulfed by the warm smell of grain and the buzz of flies. From an early age, I learned that nature invites us into our physicality and into the pleasure of opening one's senses to the richness of the natural world.

Nature still remains my daily portal to an embodied presence. Every day I make sure to go outside, whether to gaze at the morning sunrise, to kayak on the San Francisco Bay, or to hike among redwoods and eucalyptus groves, inhaling their fragrant scents. The physical sensations of being outdoors — warm air on my skin, soft ground underfoot, bright sunlight on the water, rich smells of sea air — help me inhabit my own body. This is the reason I do so much of my meditation outdoors and why I lead people on nature meditation retreats. Inhabiting our senses is a natural, accessible support for embodiment.

Our bodies are home to trillions of cells, with nerves and exquisitely refined sensors that can attune to an infinite variety of sensory experience. These sensations always reside in the present, which is why our bodies are perfect portals to mindfulness. By becoming aware of any one of our five senses, our attention immediately orients to what is happening in *this* moment. To appreciate the dawn chorus of birds, the sunset, the taste of a strawberry, or the tingling of fear in our belly, we must connect in an immediate way with our surroundings and physical body.

Not surprisingly, there is a growing body of research on the impacts of mindfulness and its relationship to the body. In a 2008 study, researchers found that, after only eight weeks, participants in a mindfulness course reported a heightened ability to observe sensations in the body. So the good news is that even if you feel disconnected from your physical experience, anyone can develop this skill.

The body with its refined sensory apparatus also improves our ability to handle difficulties, so that we can stay aware and connected even when we feel pain or are under duress. The following story from Anne, a meditation student of mine, illustrates this. Anne's husband, Tom, was diagnosed with lung cancer and a massive brain tumor. Tom had surgery to remove the tumor and underwent intense chemotherapy. Though he was miraculously spared from death, he still has cancer and requires routine tests to monitor its growth. Anne shared with me the anxiety she feels before getting his test results: "The sinking feeling in the pit of my stomach, heart racing, gulping in breaths, dizziness, and thinking that I might be losing my mind." However, rather than run from these feelings, Anne has been practicing embodied awareness, which has helped her cope. As she wrote, "These feelings still come, but I'm not afraid of them anymore."

Here's how she describes the experience of traveling with Tom to get his results:

> We are on the bus, and Tom interlaces his beautiful strong hand in mine. I sense the warmth in his fingers. I notice all the places where our bodies are touching as we sit side by side. We are hip to hip on this bus journey and always heart to heart. I close my eyes. I breathe deeply into this feeling of connectedness and then that becomes the emotion. Love. The anxiety has subsided and it has been replaced with love. How did that happen?
>
> It happened because I leaned into the discomfort. I allowed myself to physically feel it. Not the story (the catastrophizing and the "what ifs"), only the feeling. That's the thing with emotions. They must be felt... in your body. If you avoid, numb, or block them, they don't go away. That clenched stomach, the sweaty armpits, the racing heart — I have learned to embrace them. Stay with it. Don't rush to move on. When negative thoughts try and break in, gently come back to the body, to the breath,

to the feeling itself — not the story. Then there's a shift.
There's always a shift. That's how this whole mindfulness
thing works.

Our body is like a fine-tuned instrument, but it requires our
attention to fully realize its potential. Mindfulness is our ally here,
in that we learn to turn toward our physical experience, lean into
it, and feel from within this ever-changing topography. The body
is also a source of intuition and emotional information that can
serve us in the choices and decisions we make. But to optimize
that capacity, we have to attune to this inner knowing, which often
whispers its secrets and perceptions to us as subtle sensations in the
gut or to our heart. Sadly, if our heads are swirling in thoughts, lost
in past conflict or future worries, this knowledge will go unheard.

In a similar way, embodied attention can be a doorway to revelation. We tend to think of insight arising only through the mind,
with our thoughts, ideas, and perceptions, but the body is also a
powerful vehicle for understanding deeper truths. Sages and mystics throughout the ages have described how attuning to physical
experience supports this. For example, if we need to grok more
deeply how fleeting everything is, no matter how joyful or excru-
ciating, we need only turn to the ceaselessly changing nature of
our own body, breath, and sensory landscape to help awaken us to
this elemental fact.

Any sensation is short-lived, and often that's what makes it
precious. If a taste or delicate fragrance endured perpetually, we
would become immune to it. That's why silk flowers become bor-
ing after a time. Even the hottest orgasm, or the most intense pleasure, passes no sooner than it arises. Thus, as the poet William
Blake instructed, to relish the gifts of pleasure, we must learn not
to hold on to them, but to simply appreciate them, knowing they
will pass. This allows us to let go no matter how sublime sensations

are and frees us from the futility of chasing after every fleeting experience.

Attending to the body also reveals the mysterious selfless nature of bodily experience. Sensations, pleasures, and painful experiences come and go ad infinitum, despite our wishes! We don't own them, can rarely control them, and can neither hold them at bay nor grasp them indefinitely. The endless waterfall of experience teaches us how the body has a life of its own. We are simply guests within our own skin. Becoming intimate with this through an embodied attention, we cease to resist this river of change. Knowing this helps us access a sense of peace within our own body amid the broader changing circumstances of life.

• **PRACTICE** •

Walking Meditations

Many practices and techniques can help develop embodied awareness. I find that mindful walking is an expedient method to attune to the body, and here I provide two different types of walking meditation.

Sensory Awareness Walking Practice

For the first, I advocate walking outdoors in the most natural setting you can find, so that all your senses are engaged. You might choose a local park, along a beach, in woodlands, around your neighborhood, or beside farm fields. Simply start walking, without a destination, and open up to your senses. Become aware of and attuned to every sight, sound, smell, and sensation. Be present to touch: in the soles of your feet, on your skin, and the kinetic movement of your body.

Become curious about the physical world around you. What

pulls your attention? What uplifts your heart and draws your curiosity? Is it the billowing clouds forming in the sky or the silent spaces between leaves? The trickling sounds of water, the soft air against your skin, or the rich smells of the forest after a rain? When thoughts inevitably arise, or if your mind wanders or you space out, notice this and gently redirect your attention to a direct physical, sensory experience. As you keep returning to the present, notice how that touches your heart and affects your mood, energy, state of mind, and overall sense of well-being.

Continue this process for at least ten to twenty minutes. Then, as you transition back to your home, office, or the next activity, try to continue being aware of the physical, sensory world as a support for moment-to-moment mindfulness.

Walking Meditation

This walking meditation can be done anywhere, inside or outdoors, but ideally in a place where you are alone. Rather than focusing externally, focus internally while walking first one way and then back, taking twenty to thirty slow mindful steps in each direction. As you finish taking thirty steps or so in one direction, pause, then slowly turn around and recommit to staying present to the changing physical sensations of walking as you set out to take more mindful steps in the other direction. Keep walking like this, up and down, as a support for present-moment attention.

While walking, finely attune to the sensory experience of your movements, and as your mind drifts, which it naturally will from time to time, bring your attention back each time to the body. To help sustain attentiveness, focus awareness on the soles of your feet. As each foot moves with each step, feel all the sensations as you lift and place your foot on the ground. Attune to the muscles and bones of the feet and legs as you walk. Keep your gaze downward and your attention focused on your physical, bodily experience, no matter what other sights, sounds, people, and objects you may notice. Let your fascination be oriented to your inner world of movement and sensation, rather than to what is around you.

These practices, once developed, will enable you to stay grounded and present in your physical sensory experience as you walk anywhere, such as while shopping, in your home, on a hike, or even at work. They enable you to develop a continuity of mindful attention that's always accessible. Whenever you walk, simply bring awareness to your physical experience. Your morning walk to the bus or your daily stroll with the dog could be your new venue for cultivating mindfulness!

• • •

Chapter 2

Listening and Tending to the Body

Your body is a temple but only if you treat it as one.
— ASTRID ALAUDA

Matthew, a gentleman in his late sixties, is someone I have know since childhood who was once notorious for not taking care of himself. He preferred to drink beer over water and thought green vegetables were for herbivores, not humans. At one time, he loved to play soccer, and yet he severely disregarded his body, treating it as little more than an appendage to move him around the soccer pitch or to and from the pub. He had trouble holding down permanent employment.

Then, in his midforties, Matthew developed pain from years of bad circulation in one foot. This was made worse by smoking, drinking, and his poor diet. However, he ignored both the pain and the signs that it needed medical attention. Eventually, the pain got to be too much, and he went for treatment, but unfortunately he reached out too late. The infection and circulation problems had festered so long that gangrene had developed, and his leg needed to be removed from the knee down to stop the damage from spreading. This tragedy was particularly sad given that it was preventable, if only Matthew had listened to the signals of his body and taken appropriate action.

Unbelievably, Matthew did not learn his lesson and failed to start taking care of his body. Some years later he developed a similar circulation issue in his other foot, and astoundingly, he neglected the warning signs from that infection, too. Once again, he developed gangrene in the remaining leg, and the limb had to be removed from the knee down. What a double tragedy!

However, the good news is that, after this second surgery, Matthew listened to this wake-up call and began to change his old habits. He quit smoking, and though he couldn't go back to playing soccer, he developed a lifelong passion for coaching high school soccer teams, even into his late sixties. He later found a decent job and became happily married, all of which transformed his previous life of neglect.

I'm often in awe of the level of disregard people have for their own bodies. Some mystics say that the body is a temple, yet we often treat it as a chemical dump or a garbage bin. We expect high performance and optimal functioning, as if our bodies were sports cars, yet we give them dirty fuel and little maintenance. We neglect our need for adequate sleep, healthy food, and exercise, and then we complain when our bodies don't work properly! I've coached clients who worked sixteen-hour days for months, even years, in high-demanding corporate jobs, and eventually collapsed with fatigue and became unable to work at all. Others starved themselves with inadequate nutrition or ignored their need to rest because they thought self-care equals being lazy.

Mindfulness reveals our relationship to experience and in particular to our own body. We often only pay attention to the body when it hurts or is hungry and tired. Then when the body does grab our attention, we treat it like an annoyance. Yet as with anything, if we want our body to be well and to thrive, it requires careful attention, maintenance, and care. This cannot be done without awareness. With careful attention we can track our physical experience so we can learn to live in harmony with our body and stay attentive to its needs. In the same way we lovingly care for our children, pets, and things we cherish, we need to care for our body, our physical home, without which nothing is possible.

When I first started practicing meditation, I was also hopelessly disconnected from my body. Trying to sense my body as my mindfulness teachers instructed felt like trying to explore an unfamiliar, unknown foreign land. As a young student, I thought I could ingest copious amounts of alcohol and drugs and still have my body perform fine the next day. My habitual approach was to push my body, work too hard, and override my own need for rest and replenishment. These patterns ran deep and were supported by the culture I lived in.

In England, when I was growing up, any limitation of the body was judged as weakness, and the common response to any difficulty was to "toughen up" and just "get on with it." After I came to the United States, I absorbed the prevailing unhealthy work ethic, which encouraged people to work long hours and ignore imbalance or fatigue. However, it doesn't have to be this way. Once I started to hear my own wake-up call — after feeling the negative fallout from ignoring my body's needs — I slowly discovered through practice how invaluable self-awareness is for listening to the body's needs and learning to live within its limits. Research now suggests that, not surprisingly, cultivating mindfulness leads to healthier choices and actions, especially in relation to our body. In one 2010 study, researchers found that increased practice of mindfulness in everyday life predicted people's engagement in healthy activities, such as physical exercise, eating fruits and vegetables, and improving self-efficacy — all of which support a healthier body.

What is your particular relationship to your body? Do you treat it in the same caring manner you would treat a friend, a loved one, or a beloved pet? Do you have an intimate connection to your body and its needs, or do you ignore them? Do you listen to your physical limits and heed the signs that tell you when to rest, sleep, or eat? Mindfulness of the body can help develop this sensitive attunement. It helps us listen to the body's needs and challenges. The reality of being human is to be embodied, and bodies are vulnerable to aging, sickness, and ultimately death. This physical vulnerability cannot be avoided, and so learning to tend to our body becomes a beautiful path of self-care.

For instance, Jenny was a successful corporate executive in London. She had been a marketing consultant for several European corporations for twenty-five years. During that time, she had juggled international travel while raising a young family, but she eventually divorced and became a single mother, which added to her stress. As she buckled under the stress of one particularly challenging job, she started to feel her life force draining. She found it harder and harder to refuel, and the demands of her corporate job and of parenting did not allow her any respite. So she just kept pushing through because that was her habit. Up till then, pushing past her limits had allowed her to succeed.

Then, in her late forties, after years of pushing her body too hard, she finally crashed after one time too many. She became overwhelmed with chronic fatigue, where every muscle ached, and she barely had enough energy to pull herself out of bed to say good-bye to her daughters as they left for school. This was humbling, and it forced Jenny to radically shift her sense of identity. She went from an always competent "go-getter" to someone who had to slow down, rest, and do very little. She had no choice. Her body had pulled the plug. However, as often happens when life shakes us enough to listen, Jenny slowly picked up the pieces of her life and learned how to connect with her body and live within its capacity and limits. This meant letting some things go, changing jobs, doing less, and learning to nourish her body and spirit. Gradually, her strength returned. And after learning to cultivate a mindfulness practice, she eventually developed the self-awareness to stay attuned to her physical needs.

As the examples in this chapter show, when we fail to listen to our body, calamities can happen. Yet these are avoidable if we learn to attune to the body and hear its broadcasts. The challenge is that we often don't like what it has to say, so we ignore it, suppress the messages, and carry on as if whatever is wrong will just go away. As we all find out eventually, the body bats last. It will always have the final word. When we listen, we can save ourselves so much hardship. But it requires humbly accepting the body's limits and honoring its capacity and needs.

• **PRACTICE** •

Body Scan — "Head, Shoulders, Knees and Toes, Knees and Toes"

A body scan is a practice that supports embodied attention. This technique helps develop a fine-tuned awareness of each part of the body. It brings awareness to areas of our physical experience that are often inaccessible, are simply ignored, or go unnoticed. In short, the practice is to slowly move your attention through each part of your body, starting from the top of the head and continuing down your face, neck, shoulders, arms, hands, torso, hips, legs, and eventually to your feet and toes. This may take up to twenty or thirty minutes to do once, or you might do several sweeps through your body that each take only five minutes. Take time to be curious about each part of your body and about the subtle sensations that lie within each area.

As you begin, note where you feel sensation and where there is an absence of felt experience. Then at times direct your attention to outer sensations — like the feel of your skin, the touch of clothing, and so on — and at times to inner experience, like temperature, tingling, vibrations, pressure, heaviness, itchiness, and so on. As your awareness moves through your body, pay attention to any sensations of discomfort, contraction, or pain, and notice if you can be present to that experience. See if it is possible for those places to soften or if you are able to relax any contraction around them. Stay curious and sensitive with awareness, as if you were a biologist exploring the body experientially for the first time. See if you can let yourself be surprised by what you find. Shift from visualizing the various parts of your body to sensing the actual immediate sensations.

Once you have directed your attention through the body, then be present to the experience of the body as a whole. Notice if the body feels more alive or vital as a result of your awareness of it. As you end the practice, see if you can feel this quality of attunement and embodiment throughout your day.

• • •

Chapter 3

Working Carefully
with Physical Pain

To live a life beyond suffering and pleasure and include them both
in great measure is what my life is about.
— DARLENE COHEN

Darlene Cohen was a courageous meditation teacher who suffered from a debilitating form of degenerative arthritis for some decades. Her life was an inspiring example of how we can turn to meet our physical pain with a kind mindful attention, however hard that journey is. Her writings and teachings were testament to her finding joy and ease despite the terrible suffering she endured. Her book *Turning Suffering Inside Out* is a beautiful expression of that journey. Her arthritis was her teacher and also her ally in learning how to surrender to the truth of the moment, no matter how challenging. And with that practice, she grew in patience, wisdom, and compassion.

Her life serves as an inspiration for all of us to develop a wise and sensitive relationship to our body. Cohen wrote: "People sometimes ask me where my own healing energy comes from. How in the midst of this pain, this implacable slow crippling, I can encourage myself and other people.... It comes from the shadow.

I dip into that muck again and again and then am flooded with its healing energy." Cohen stands as a role model for how to lean in to our particular circumstances no matter how unwanted or difficult. I know for myself and for many people I have worked with, physical pain is often what forces us to grow, to open, and to find the courage to face the hard stuff in life. As much as we do not want pain, and would not wish it on our worse enemy, the crucible of that struggle is where we tap into resources and capacity we did not know we had.

I've suffered off and on for years with chronic back pain, which has only gotten worse with age. As much as I try to take care of my body and exercise regularly, my body, like all bodies, is subject to wear and tear, aches and pains, and at times chronic conditions. No one is immune. Everyone has a particular burden to carry. So I'm always curious how each one of us shows up to meet our particular physical challenges — with openness and kindness or with resentment and reactivity?

The invitation as a human being is to learn to face what comes with this physical form. Whatever pain or condition you struggle with — arthritis, fatigue, psoriasis, sporting injuries, or anything else — can you welcome it with an open and kind attention? This is the orientation of mindfulness practice, which helps us reframe difficult experiences from being a burden into being a chalice of growth and understanding. In working with our own pain in this way, we learn to open our heart to ourselves and broaden compassion for all those who suffer physically.

Take a moment now to reflect on how you face pain or other hard stuff in life. Mindfulness practice trains us to open to the conditions of this moment with a receptive awareness, yet typically, our first impulse is to do the opposite. Ajahn Chah, a beloved Thai meditation teacher, summarized our usual orientation to pain: "By running away from suffering, we run toward it." That is so often our go-to strategy. We try to escape pain in whatever way we can, through distraction, avoidance, and numbing ourselves. We get lost in our digital devices, stay busy, or drown our feelings with entertainment or alcohol. And who can blame us? Hanging out with discomfort and physical pain is hard.

However, the body doesn't let us run away. We can avoid pain for only so long before it catches up with us. And the longer the avoidance, the greater the suffering in the long term, as Matthew's story in the last chapter proved. So it behooves us to learn to gracefully turn toward and face the reality of any physical challenge. This is the lesson Darlene Cohen wrote about: "It's staring defeat and annihilation in the face that's so terrifying; I must resist until it overwhelms me. But I've come to trust it deeply. It's enriched my life, informed my work, and taught me not to fear the dark."

Another common reason we resist and avoid pain is the belief that if we feel the difficulty, we will be quickly overwhelmed and dragged into a well of suffering and despair. Yet it is the very running away that often adds to our stress and prolongs our misery.

Mindfulness, on the other hand, helps develop a capacity to stand in the midst of challenging experience and develop the skill to bear witness to that truth. By staying in the present moment and not being driven by anticipatory thoughts of future pain, we have more resources to deal with any difficulty. Indeed, not buying into catastrophic thoughts helps us remain steady in the midst of the pain. Research has shown that mindfulness practice helps reduce anticipatory fear of something negative or painful. This can spare us from a lot of anxiety about what is to come. It also allows a much quicker recovery from a difficult experience by being present for what is happening now, rather than being lost in the painful memory of the past.

Similarly, a 2008 pain study considered older adults with chronic low back pain who took part in an eight-week mindfulness

meditation program. The increased body awareness of participants led to better pain-coping skills, in part through the use of
"conscious distraction." Conscious distraction sounds paradoxi-
cal, but it simply means averting one's attention to something less
painful or difficult. This allows a sense of ease and restoration in
the moment, and it increases one's capacity to deal with pain when
it returns. This is an invaluable skill to learn when one has chronic
pain. I use it often when my own pain levels are high; at times, it
is more skillful to shift the attention elsewhere to bring temporary
relief, which allows a relaxing of the nervous system.

What does it look like to actually turn toward pain? It means
to simply turn the light of awareness toward the experience. This
means we take time to feel, sense, and inhabit the unpleasant and
difficult sensations with a soft, curious attention. It requires some
courage to lean into the physical difficulty and to feel all the nuances of that tender experience. By doing so we sense how pain
isn't a monolithic experience, which the label "pain" implies. It is
actually an ever-changing flow of sensations — pulsing, vibrating,
stabbing, and searing, along with pressure, density, heat, and tightness — all swirling together.

One thing we discover is that pain does not endure forever. It
is always a shape-shifting dance of experience, ebbing and flowing
depending on all sorts of factors, many of which are out of our
control. Pain may not go away for a long time, but it rarely stays
the same for more than two moments.

What is important to understand is how our experience of pain
is influenced by the quality of our attention. If we meet pain with
resistance and fear, or with an agenda to get rid of it, it often feels
worse because we grip in contraction against it. If we meet pain
with a sense of surrender, of softening the contraction or the tight
muscles around it, this can increase a sense of space or ease, even
when the difficult experience continues. This lessening of reactivity

is possible, but it requires perseverance and patience, which is why meditation is referred to as a "practice." Practice requires practice! For example, Joey, a woman who was on disability leave from work, came to a mindfulness-based stress reduction class I was teaching. Her physician referred her to the course, as she had suffered from chronic neck pain for over ten years, and no amount of surgery or medication had helped. Her life was tormented by this malady and by the feeling of being a victim of pain. Through the practice of mindfulness, Joey was invited, like all participants, to see if she could be with the pain, in her case the sensations in her neck, with a kind, curious, nonreactive attention.

At first she said this was impossible. All she felt was hatred toward the searing sensations, along with fear about the situation worsening. She also felt, as many do, a lot of resistance and tightness around the source of the pain, as if her whole body was bracing in fear and anger around the difficulty. However, after about five weeks, she came into the class excited to report her experience during a meditation session at home. For the first time in a decade, she had been able to soften her defenses around her neck injury and simply feel the center of the nerve pain, which was an intermittent throbbing. Although this awareness did not make the pain go away, it gave her the first relief in a very long time. She saw that the pain was not some permanent monolithic mass of unpleasantness but a pulsing wave of sharp sensations that came and went.

In that moment, Joey realized that fear, contraction, anger, and resistance just compound her pain. When she softened enough to meet her experience with kind attention, she felt the pain ease. As she stopped fighting and blaming, she also stopped adding to her distress. Steadily, through practice, she developed important tools to find some ease in the midst of difficulty, which became an important metaphor for other struggles she faced in life.

• PRACTICE •

Attuning to Pain with Kind Attention

The next time you are in physical pain or feel discomfort in your body, try this meditation, which is an invitation to explore pain with mindfulness. Settle your body into the most comfortable posture you can, either sitting or lying down. Close your eyes and allow your body to rest at ease. Try to release any tension you are holding in your jaw, belly, facial muscles, and shoulders. In general, invite your body to relax as much as possible.

Then gently shift your attention to the felt sensations of whatever discomfort or painful experience is present. Try to release the concept or label of "pain," and instead connect with the direct physical experience. Can you sense the periphery of the painful area? Can you feel the center of it? What are the sensations like? Notice what happens when you bring your awareness to this area. Does it change the experience, making it grow in intensity or fade? Keep exploring this area as if this were the first time you had ever felt this, and sense all of the changing nuances of the experience.

In particular, notice the "unpleasant" or painful quality of the sensation. This might be a quality of sharpness, pressure, pinching, stabbing, or searing heat. This unpleasantness is what we react to and try to push away, reject, or resist. Yet the more we can accommodate the unpleasant sensations, however difficult, the more we can find a steadiness of presence with them. From the perspective of awareness, these are simply temporal experiences, nothing more, nothing less.

However, our preferential mind seeks to get rid of what we dislike, and this contention, simply put, adds stress to the situation. So notice if you relate to your pain with hatred, fear, or resentment. Do you hope you can meditate it away? If you observe any aversion or resistance toward the pain, bring attention to that reaction. When we hold any experience in the light of awareness, we become less caught up in it. Rather than being swept up in resisting the pain, shift attention to feel the painful contracted nature of resistance itself. Feel how that very reactivity can add more stress on top of pain. When we see that process, it makes it easier to release the reaction.

However, if you find it too difficult to stay with the pain or you feel too reactive to it — which can happen when we hurt too much or have become too weary — switch your attention to something less difficult. For example, feel your breath, listen to sounds inside or outside, or attune to a place in your body where there is no pain, possibly in your hands or feet. Seek a refuge to rest the attention. Or you can simply shift your posture if that helps alleviate the tension. This allows some ease to the nervous system, which is necessary to stay resilient when working with chronic pain.

If there is nowhere in your body that is a calm refuge, then open your eyes for a moment and take in something uplifting, such as the sky, a flower or plant, or anything that is beautiful in or outside your room. In that way you can regulate your reactivity by turning awareness to that which brings ease or lightness. Once a sense of balance is reestablished, then you can again sense the pain but from a more spacious perspective. You may find you need to move your attention back and forth many times from the difficult stimulus to something pleasant as a way of staying balanced in relation to the pain. Utilize this principle throughout your day as a support for finding greater ease whenever physical pain or unpleasant sensation arises.

• • •

Chapter 4

Finding Refuge in
Transience and Uncertainty

No person ever steps in the same river twice,
for it's not the same river and he's not the same person.
— HERACLITUS

In 2017, I taught a mindfulness and emotional-intelligence leadership training for employees from an organization in Sonoma County. They were in the midst of dealing with a lot of posttraumatic distress. What were then the worst fires in Northern California history had recently devastated their county, killing many residents, incinerating over six thousand homes, and leaving thousands homeless.

During the program, Jane, who lived in Sonoma, told a particularly moving story. She had been evacuated when the fires quickly approached her neighborhood and had only minutes to gather any precious belongings. Many days later, when Jane was allowed to go back to her home, she discovered that her whole neighborhood had been lost. As she walked up to her house, there was not a single thing left. It had been razed to the ground. However, she noticed a rock engraved with the word *Faith* still lying where the front door had once been. She picked up the charred rock, a gift from a friend, and the metaphor of that word inspired her to begin to put the pieces of her devastated life back together.

No one would doubt the universal principle of change. The rupture in Jane's life is but one small example of how it manifests. It is a key teaching common to philosophy, science, and spirituality. The Greek philosopher Heraclitus pointed this out twenty-five hundred years ago: "Nothing endures but change." Indeed, transience is the only constant, and uncertainty the only certainty. Given that, how do we find peace in this changing world? What can we rely on given the flux and flow of every living thing and every experience we love and hold dear? This is the dilemma we face. Nothing endures, but we still feel an urge to hold on to and control our experience so it doesn't change or leave. My friend, who lost his wife to cancer, described this paradox beautifully. Not long after her death, he said: "I have completely let her go, and I totally want her back."

Though most people acknowledge and accept the reality of impermanence, it takes a wise person to live in alignment with this law. Most of the time, we resist it or ignore it. Despite all evidence to the contrary, we easily fall into the trap of expecting things to continue the way they are or have been, only to be caught off guard or annoyed when life upends that assumption.

Even though I know deeply how things change, I still forget this in simple ways all the time. For example, I can get annoyed when a scratch appears on my new car, or I can be surprised when the beautiful orchids I cherish begin their inevitable deterioration after their long months of bold bloom. I may feel shock when a favorite old shirt suddenly develops a hole, or feel resistance when a beloved friend moves to a different city, as if I'd assumed they would stay nearby forever.

That everyone gets taken aback by change in small ways is almost as enduring a truth as change itself. But our resistance to the bigger changes in life is what becomes more problematic. Do you resent signs of aging, like graying hair and lines etched more deeply around your eyes? Do you resist slowing down to accommodate your older, less supple body? Do you protest when your perfectly healthy body gets sick or you receive an unexpected medical diagnosis? Do the ups and downs of the stock market and economic uncertainty fill you with anxiety and resentment? The ways we resist change are innumerable, even though we know it is hopeless and even painful to do so.

These are natural responses to our human predicament, to vulnerability. We live in a changing world and an unreliable body; we live with uncertain relationships, a fluctuating economy, shifting social norms, and rapidly advancing technology. We never know when disaster will strike, whether that's a life-threatening diagnosis to a loved one, a forest fire that rips through our house, or a sudden economic crash that guts our retirement savings. No wonder we are anxious and restless. No wonder the brain, in an attempt to survive this turmoil, developed a negativity bias, which is always scanning for perceived threats. Where do we find peace and ease amidst these ever-shifting realities?

Susan, an independent-living specialist, teaches an "adjustment to vision loss" course to individuals and groups. A significant part of the class is teaching mindfulness meditation. Losing vision is an extremely difficult, fearful experience that affects all aspects of a person's life. Visually impaired individuals can lose friends, who feel uncomfortable around them; lose jobs that they no longer can accomplish; and even lose their normal place in their families. The resulting stress can cause isolation and physical and emotional problems.

As a way of working with these challenges, Susan introduces patients to meditation. Early on, she noticed how this practice helps people reduce their stress. It helps her patients think more clearly and make better decisions. It assists them to communicate better about their many losses. From there, people can start the process of regaining a healthy sense of themselves in order to self-advocate, retrain for new careers, and regain their general health.

Simply put, mindfulness helps them develop the clarity to meet their changing circumstances, which necessitate adaptability. Shining a spotlight on the changing nature of experience is what allows all of us to know it in our bones, so it informs everything we do. Such insight shapes and crafts our being. We then flow better with the shifting rhythm of life, like Susan's patients; we are responsive rather than resistant.

This requires a careful and sustained inquiry into our lived experience of transience. We need to know this reality intimately. When meditating, it means being aware of how every moment is a changing landscape of phenomena. Sounds ceaselessly come and go. Physical sensations are forever pulsing, vibrating, tingling, shifting, and moving — tensing and relaxing, expanding and contracting. Thoughts flicker like static, constantly generating flurries of ideas. Mental images create movies of visual landscapes. The breath is a restless wave moving through our torso. Emotions ebb and flow like tides or storms. Moods forever arise and pass.

Nothing is static in our inner world, which is a dance of ephemeral experience. The closer we attend to this reality, the more we see that no thing stays around for very long. The deeper we penetrate this truth, the more it allows us to not hold on so tightly. We see how experience is like water evaporating into thin air. It's impossible to hold. We learn to release the controlling grip we so often have around our experience, body, friends, work, money, and life. Holding them so tightly, we often squeeze the space or the light out of them. Instead, we can learn to appreciate what we have and not take it for granted.

In time, we learn to savor life's transient preciousness and to let go when that is asked of us. Rather than considering impermanence to be a depressing reflection, we can instead think of it as an urgent call to wake up, to be present and taste the exquisiteness of this fleeting moment. When we really get how brief and uncertain life is, then we stop taking things for granted and pay rapt attention to the beauty and richness of life all around us.

"One less" is a mantra that I developed for myself in relation to this theme of change. Whatever I am doing — whether breathing, watching the full moon rise, the setting sun, spending time with a beloved friend, or visiting with my parents in England — I reflect that it is one less time that I will get to do it in this life. Each breath taken is one less inhale and exhale. Each lunar cycle is one less to witness. Each summer is one less time to feel the warmth of the sun on my skin. Each time with beloved friends and family is one less time to savor their company, and so on. When I do this, I feel the urgency to really take in each moment. To not get complacent thinking I will have a thousand more just like it. Because the truth is, we never know how long we will get to experience this fleeting and beautiful world.

• **PRACTICE** •

Meditating on Impermanence

This meditation can be done anywhere, but it is meant to take place where there is a lot of activity and stimulation — the more the better. Seek out a bench in a city park or train station. Sit in a chair in a busy café or restaurant.

To begin, sit comfortably and lower your gaze; if it is comfortable and safe to do so, you might close your eyes. Become aware of the totality of your experience. Start with being aware of sounds. Listen to all the changing noises, both loud and quiet, distant and near. Attend to people, machines, traffic, birds, and conversations. Notice the constantly changing auditory landscape.

Next, without losing awareness of sounds, become present to all the changing physical sensory impressions in your body. Notice the ever-shifting variety of touch and physical sensation: pressure, movement, tingling, vibration, ceaselessly ebbing and flowing. Feel the breath, that continual reminder of change, which never stays the same for more than a moment.

Next, become aware of all the visual impressions of light, form, color, and texture. If your eyes are shut, notice the subtle dance of light behind the eyelids. If they are open, be aware of the dizzying array of movements, shapes, and colors. Also notice the transitory quality of smells and tastes, so that eventually you become aware of all five senses forever in motion.

Now shift your attention to the domain of your heart and mind. Be aware as emotions come, perhaps triggered by overheard conversations, smells, or memories. Be present to the fleeting nature of your emotions as they pulse like waves in the body. Similarly, notice the rapidly changing canvas of the mind. See how quickly and incessantly thoughts, images, ideas, views, memories, and plans come and go, flickering like a never-ending stroboscope.

Stay present, noticing how nothing stays the same for more than a few moments before something else pulls your attention. For ten to twenty minutes, abide in this clear awareness, remaining still in the center of this hurricane of activity. Notice what happens as you open to the ever-changing nature of life.

If your eyes are closed, open them slowly. See how the inner experience of change is mirrored externally. Nothing stays the same for very long, and even what appears solid and enduring, like a building or a tree, is always changing. Our perception shifts with the time of day, the light, the wind, the people passing, and the birds alighting. Experience varies moment by moment. All things are in flux.

As you emerge from this meditation, see if you can maintain awareness of the transient nature of experience. See if this allows you to relate to things in life differently, with less holding on or resistance. When we fully understand in our bones that everything changes, it allows us to appreciate the pleasures of life, to hold them lightly, knowing they will pass. Similarly, it supports our becoming less reactive to pain, since we know that every experience, no matter how bad, will shift. In this way, we find peace amidst this restless sea of change.

• • •

Chapter 5

Meeting Aging with Kind Awareness

The longer I live, the more beautiful life becomes.
— FRANK LLOYD WRIGHT

For many years I have led wilderness backpacking retreats. Such excursions into nature bring so much joy and wonder. On one particular program, I led a strenuous ten-day backpack in the hot, dry desert in Navajo Country that included three men over seventy and one man, James, who was eighty-four years old. It was beautiful and inspiring to see these elders putting on a heavy backpack and hiking for miles every day in silence through the wild red rock canyons.

If that wasn't arduous enough, after the course ended, James was heading to run in the New York Marathon. His physical capacity brought him great joy, and I was in awe of the way he lived life to the fullest. He kept himself in great shape and served as a role model for aging with grace and passion. This wasn't so much about his physical prowess at such a grand age but how he moved with such embodied awareness and presence. Few people do what it takes to live as healthily and as attuned as he did. He put into action this quote from Betty Friedan: "Aging is not lost youth but a new stage of opportunity and strength."

How do you relate to your own aging process? One thing that is self-evident about our body is that, from birth to death, it's always changing. This is of course obvious, but we are often willfully blind to the truth of change, especially when it comes to ourselves. We don't see what we don't want to see! This means we are often surprised and resistant to aging. But trying to hang on to our youth in an entropic universe causes problems! Everything inevitably deteriorates, yet it is still hard for us to grok this. As Mark Twain put it: "I was young and foolish then; now I am old and foolisher."

Since we live in a culture where youth, looks, and external appearance are paramount, the reality of aging leads to tremendous stress, anxiety, self-hatred, and a host of disruptive behaviors. Our consumer culture preys on our vulnerability and our desire for acceptance, inclusion, and love. The beauty and cosmetic industries exploit that sensitivity to market a plethora of products and diets, all offering a promise of eternal youth. It is a race we can never win. Life is a game where nature always bats last.

How do we develop a wise relationship to aging? This takes a willingness to confront the truth and acknowledge what we see in the mirror. To accept our bodies as they are is wisdom, born out of facing what is true over and over through practice. Since this does not come easily, we need to do so with tenderness for the vulnerability inherent in being human. In this way we cultivate mindful awareness to meet this inescapable truth with a caring understanding.

There are many avenues to live our way into this truth. This extract from a poem by Carmelene Siani speaks beautifully about meeting the aging process with grace and acceptance:

Let me hope that while my body may fail in strength
my spirit will grow in wisdom
Let me see that being independent is not necessarily
an end all and be all
and that embracing interdependence
may be the greatest gift I can give those who love and
    care about me.
Let me look out the window and see not how few
    summers there are left to me
but how beautiful are the summers left to me....
Let me look at my body and see beauty....
Let me be able to lie in my last hour
and feel nothing but gratitude for it all.
Exactly as it is and exactly as it was

When I think of inspiring role models for aging, one person who comes to mind is James Keolker. He was eighty-five years old when he graduated from the mindfulness teacher training program I lead in San Francisco. He is a beautiful example of someone living with awareness and grace as he ages. Since graduating, he has dedicated himself to teaching seniors about mindfulness practice in Napa, California. James recently wrote to me of his work with people in the later stages of life: "One of the hallmarks of working with seniors, a group often marginalized, is their reliance upon the past. However, no singular practice seems as effective in teaching awareness of the present as meditation, breath by breath. They soon realize the past fades, and their fears of the future are quickly . set aside with mindful breathing. The mind simply cannot be anywhere but present when fully concentrating on the breath. And in that the joys of the present moment are revealed."

James and his elder students are living examples of what

researchers have been discovering about how meditation helps fend off some of the corroding effects of aging, particularly in the brain. In a 2014 research study using fMRI scans, findings revealed that long-term meditators showed less atrophy in their gray matter, indicating that meditation appears to slow decline of the brain. Similar findings by Lutz and others have demonstrated that long-term meditators show less deterioration in the prefrontal cortex, the insula, and other key areas in the brain, suggesting that meditation practice could reduce age-associated structural and functional brain changes. This is good news if we want to find ways to stay cognitively sharp and clear into our twilight years. Earlier prevailing wisdom presumed the brain would simply continue to decline with age. These attention training practices reveal this isn't so.

Aging isn't just reserved for the elderly. We are all physically aging. For myself, I remember being surprised the first time I wore reading glasses. I thought my eyesight was fine, and I was proud that I was in my midforties and still did not need spectacles. When I finally realized I was kidding myself and that my eyes could do with some support, I felt like I could see again with the clarity of a child. Flowers, leaves, and wild grasses took on a new crystal clarity that made me fall in love again with the beauty of the earth.

Yet when I looked in the mirror, I got quite a shock. I saw way more wrinkles than I remembered. Not only was my hair significantly grayer than I realized, there was a lot less of it! The thinning on top was quite apparent now that I could see properly. Oh foolish vanities! How easily we trick ourselves and see just what we want to see, believing the story we tell ourselves.

Fortunately, for wisdom's sake, the body never lies. It is reality's gentle reminder that life is finite. Wrinkles are like tree rings; the more lines, the less time we have left in this precious world. Hopefully, we can look at our face and see the lines as grooves of laughter woven into our skin, as creases of wisdom hard-won over the years. Regardless of how the lines got there, they are markers of age, providing a necessary reality check. The key question is how we relate to this truth. Does it lead us into depression and despair? Or does it inspire us to act, to live this life to the fullest, to not take anyone, anything, or any moment for granted? Such awareness can be a catalyst for a full and engaged life.

I have worked with several men in their midfifties who needed the wake-up call of a heart attack to help them realize that aging is real and that flagrant disregard for the body and its limits is harmful. The shock galvanized them to eat better, exercise regularly, and pay attention to their body. It even encouraged some to meditate! Sometimes the clarity that arises with awareness of impermanence is as simple as this. It is so important it could save your one wild and precious life!

When I teach, I encounter many students who have lost loved ones, their husband or their wife, their parents or their children. The shock of that loss woke them to the finite nature of life. They realized how limited time is, which galvanized them to reengage and enliven their remaining relationships and make the most of this fleeting time we have on earth. Similarly, I hear meditation practitioners report how mindfulness practice allowed them to turn to their loved ones, as their health declined, with greater surrender and acceptance. Joanie is one of them.

Joanie spoke to me about her husband, Ron, who was ten years her senior. At one point, he began acting differently — getting lost, not following through, not being responsible the way he usually was. She could no longer count on him, and she sought help from his physician, who diagnosed Ron with Alzheimer's disease. Having to take charge and deal with Ron's Alzheimer's took Joanie out of her comfort zone. She had no experience with it, she couldn't fix it or change it, and she didn't know what was going to happen next. She felt a lot of uncertainty and questioned her ability to handle it.

Joanie used her mindfulness practice to help understand her own reactions and reactivity. She often lost patience with either Ron or herself, and sometimes she didn't interact kindly, snapping at him or criticizing herself. To interrupt this pattern, she tried bringing awareness to it. When feeling tight sensations in her gut, which to her indicated irritation or fear, she tried not to act out those reactions, but she instead took several deep breaths while being aware of the sensations. As she did this, the feelings softened and shifted, and gradually she was able to feel compassion for both her husband and herself and engage with him in a more loving way.

Thanks to her mindfulness practice, Joanie's eight-year journey shifted from a stressful situation to an adventure. It didn't take the pain away from slowly losing her husband to Alzheimer's, but her growing awareness taught her how to find peace with the process, to not make it worse with her reactivity. Over time, she learned to love more deeply and trust life. Ron passed away two years ago and left her the gift of knowing that she has the courage and the tools to skillfully meet whatever life brings with more acceptance and openheartedness.

• PRACTICE •

Embracing Aging with Kind Awareness

I once had a friend who had a twenty-times magnification mirror in her bathroom. I used to tease her that, looking through that lens, of course she would find blemishes and things to worry about on her face. I think anyone would. It makes normal skin pores look like craters! For this meditation, a regular mirror is fine, though using my friend's mirror would certainly make this contemplation more interesting.

Take some time to sit or stand in front of a mirror and study your face. Study all the contours, lines, wrinkles, blemishes, spots, or other signs of aging. Notice what happens when you do this. Without judgment or condemnation, try to let in the reality of what you observe. Without trying to change it, notice any reactivity — whether to this exercise or to what you see in the mirror that you may disapprove of.

Be sure to do this level of scrutiny with kindness and compassion. Can you appreciate your face and body just as it is, noticing all the ways you have changed through the years? Can you access tenderness for yourself and the vulnerability you feel about aging? Notice if you are able to feel affection, warmth, or love for who you are and how you have turned out in this moment. If that is not possible, can you also hold that experience with care?

Over time, mindfulness practice can help us develop equanimity, the ability to radically accept the way things are. To support that, reflect on the phrases "Things are as they are," "Life is as it is," and "The nature of my body is to change and age." By turning your attention in this way, you plant seeds or reflections of balance and steadiness in the face of transience.

Do some version of this reflection each time you look in the mirror. Rather than judging or blaming yourself for how your face or body are aging, acknowledge the truth of this reality and see if you can meet it with a kind, appreciative attention. See if you can remember this is simply the way nature is. Nothing stays the same, especially not our body.

• • •

Chapter 6

Embracing Death's Invitation

The most wondrous thing in the world is that all around us people can be dying and we don't realize it can happen to us.
— MAHABHARATA

Ellen, a recently retired woman from Colorado in her midsixties, attended a nature retreat I led in California. Though you could not tell from the outside, she was living in a tornado of grief. She recounted the devastating losses that had occurred over the preceding two years: both her siblings passed (her sister died in a car accident, her brother died from a heart attack), she lost her father to cancer, and soon after that her only living aunt died.

But her story didn't finish there. More recently her mother had moved in with her due to her debilitating Parkinson's condition. Her mother's physical state quickly deteriorated, and some weeks before the retreat, her mother also passed. Ellen was grief-stricken by the incomprehensible amount of loss. She had lost all the members of her close family in the space of several years. She came to the retreat with tremendous heartache, but despite that, her attitude was inspiring. Undaunted, she was determined to find meaning and perspective in the devastation. She wished to make the most of her remaining years and not take another moment or person for granted.

Coping with the loss of loved ones is one of life's toughest challenges. However, confronting our own mortality is even harder. Death is the ultimate ignobility. It strips away everything we know and have accumulated. It separates us from what we most love. To the ego it is the greatest humiliation, forcing the ego to surrender its attempt at control and give in to the physical laws that govern this world, including yielding to its own dissolution. In many spiritual traditions, meditation is considered a preparation for death. But how could sitting in stillness with one's eyes closed, sensing one's intimate inner world, serve us at the time of dying?

We live in a world that tries to deny the reality of death. In hospitals, death is often considered a medical failure. The dying are hidden away. To see a dead body is a rare event in modern industrial cultures. In recent decades there has been an insatiable quest for youth and peak vitality. Billions are spent annually worldwide trying to counter or hide the effects of aging. While an aspiration for health or long life is natural, denying the reality of death and decay is simply misguided and does nothing to prepare us for its eventuality.

Mindfulness practice offers an altogether different approach, which orients us to meet the truth without trying to hide or whitewash anything. It encourages us to turn toward whatever presents itself, including discomfort and decay. Contemplating death is the purpose of the ancient mindfulness practice called "Maranasati." In this meditation, you explore the uncomfortable inevitability of your demise, reflecting on the certainty of death and the uncertainty of the timing. You also visualize the process of dying itself. Monks and nuns in Asia practice this in charnel grounds as a way to bring mortality close to home, to release any unhealthy attachment to our physical form, and to see through the belief in the body as who we are.

Many people who have never tried this practice assume that it must be depressing and morbid. The reality, however, is almost the opposite. It is true that contemplating death, taking mortality seriously, can be sobering, but the purpose is to inspire us to seize the moment. It helps us avoid sleepwalking through our lives and prevents surprise when death's shadow looms or his scythe strikes out of the blue. This meditation is an invitation to wake up and not live on autopilot, assuming life will go on forever. It reminds us to be fully present and awake for each experience, to live like our hair is on fire, as they say in Zen. What would life be like if we lived with that urgency?

Reflecting on death encourages us to stop taking things for granted, to cease thinking that our relationships and our lives will continue forever. Such reflection is an invitation to be awake for each experience — such as, when we say good-bye, really meaning it because we never know if we will have the pleasure of someone's company again. It reminds us to be fully present for each thing we encounter, each sunrise, each scarlet leaf of autumn, each step our child takes. Carlos Castaneda's shamanic guide told him to live with death standing just behind his shoulder, as a reminder of the precariousness of this life. Can you live like that? It is life's hardest lesson but also its greatest invitation.

In the poem "When Death Comes," Mary Oliver wrote about confronting our mortality with an open, curious awareness. In it, she describes the potential of living with a full embrace of that innate vulnerability, writing: "When it's over, I want to say all my life / I was a bride married to amazement." I think of these inspiring words often. What would it be like, I wonder, to be so struck by the ephemeral beauty of this world that we wished to marry its fleeting magnificence? To be so welcoming that we scooped it up into our arms like a benevolent groom?

In any and every moment, we are given just that invitation. To behold the unrepeatable priceless experiences that present themselves each day. To not take for granted that there will always be tomorrow. The gift of reflecting on death is that it encourages us to live with urgency, rather than regret or postponement, and to be present to the many wonders of this world. Our job is to seize the moment, not knowing how much time we have left. This is clearly illustrated by a story one student, Jennifer, recounted to me:

My mom and I had a troubled relationship. She was powerful. I was powerful. We constantly argued about everything. Even as adults she challenged my decisions. One Mother's Day weekend I called her and asked if she'd like to spend the day together. I don't know what brought me to reach out and offer to spend the day with her. I'd typically want to scream after five minutes with her. Something inside just guided me to make the first step to heal our relationship. She was surprised, and there was silence on the line, until she agreed to join me.

The next day was Mother's Day, and I told her we would pick her up and spend the day with my brother and his kids. When my daughter and I went to pick her up, she asked me, "Why are we hanging with Grandma?" I told her, "We're moving on. I'm the one with an issue here, and it's my job to forgive myself for holding anger toward her." We had a sweet day, and I hugged my mom when I dropped her off at home. Two weeks later I received the news that she had had a brain aneurysm. She died instantly. Without the practice of mindfulness, I wouldn't have moved through my anger toward her. I wouldn't have healed my heart.

• PRACTICE •

Death Contemplation

The goal of this practice is to remind ourselves of what is most precious in this life and to love and treasure these things right now, since one day we will have to let them all go, either all at once or one by one.

On small pieces of paper or on note cards, write down one word that represents something you hold very dear or special to you. For example, on one card you might write "health," on another "nature," on another the name of a loved one, and so on. Once you have named about ten or fifteen things, people, or experiences, take some time reflecting and meditating on each one and their importance to you.

Once you finish, close your eyes and settle your attention on your breath and body as a way to establish present-moment awareness. Then imagine you are very close to the end of your life. Make it as real as possible; imagine these are your last days and hours and that you will never be coming back. Next, slowly open your eyes, pick one card randomly, and put it behind you. This symbolizes how death will take each thing away from you. Close your eyes each time you have selected a card and consider how it feels to know you will be losing that thing forever.

Continue this process with each card, opening your eyes, selecting one card, putting it behind you, closing your eyes, and imagining that this person or experience has been taken away from you. Once you have selected all the cards, sit quietly in meditation. Feel and reflect on what it is like to have all the things that are most precious taken away in this intimate yet impersonal dying process. What arises? Allow a sense of compassion to emerge, both for yourself and for all those, known and unknown, who are close to death at this time.

After you have finished, take some time to reflect or journal about any inspiration or insight that emerges. Does this motivate you to live your life differently in any way? Does it change the way you hold these things that are so valuable to you? What might you do to make the most of this wondrous gift of life that has been given to you? Reflect on any specific intention or action you might take. Is there some person or experience that you wish to connect with after meditating in this way? Embrace the aspiration to be more fully present in your life, since our time is so fleeting and our departure time unknown.

• • •

Chapter 7

Riding the Waves
of Pleasure and Pain

We must have the stubbornness to accept our gladness
in the ruthless furnace of this world.
— JACK GILBERT

This world provides a never-ending range of experiences. Life moves through a succession of peaks and troughs, highs and lows, miracles and disasters. In one place, babies are born to the delight of gleeful parents, while in others infants are starving. Young fawns prance through bluebell woods, while a cougar kills a sleeping deer. Spring flowers blaze across mountain hillsides, while industrial mining lays waste to tropical rain forests in Brazil. Activists devote their lives to protecting the environment, while smugglers traffic young girls for sex. Humpback whales are saved from extinction, while beluga whales are hunted in the Arctic.

Every day we are bombarded with an endless flurry of beauty and horror, of things that both open and shut tight our hearts. This raises important questions about what to pay attention to and how to respond to this roller coaster of experience. Neuroscience tells us our brains have a hardwired negativity bias, so we tend to look at what is wrong, to focus on the negative. This is clearly reflected in the media, which grabs our attention by highlighting the worst news of the day. Do we let that negativity bias dictate what we see and how we view it? Or do we take a different perspective, as offered by Jack Gilbert in his poem "A Brief for the Defense": "We must have / the stubbornness to accept our gladness in the ruthless / furnace of this world. To make injustice the only / measure of our attention is to praise the Devil."

Mindfulness is the capacity to see things as they are. That includes opening to the "full catastrophe," the entire range of beauty and horror that exists. But doing this requires us to stretch to take in such a wide expanse, to appreciate all that is beautiful and wondrous as well as what is tragic.

Every year in the 1990s, I used to travel annually to India to study meditation. As soon as I got off the plane, I questioned why I had come. The polluted air in New Delhi was acrid, and exhaust fumes in Lucknow, the city where I studied, often turned the air into a blue haze. The stench from sewage could be nauseating, and the poverty at times was heart-wrenching. Nothing was hidden away. Funeral processions of families carrying their dead passed openly in the streets. Homeless beggars in Benares sometimes had no arms or legs or displayed crippling leprosy.

Yet on the same street as the lepers, I might see a woman cleaning a public latrine and radiating the most beatific smile, one that melted every brittleness in my heart. Like a momentary scent of heaven, I might catch the fragrance of freshly picked jasmine placed elegantly in a schoolgirl's hair. Little boys would be laughing and giggling with glee in side streets, playing cricket with little more than a stick of wood and a ball of newspaper. Bells ringing from roadside temples and wafting incense suggested that the gods were not so far away. The intensity of India invited a broad lens of attention, one that encompassed the beauty and tragedy of life.

What goes on "out there" in the world is no different from

the ups and downs of our inner landscape. A discerning awareness reveals that when we pay close attention to our mind and body, we see that it, too, is a changing cacophony, oscillating between the poles of pleasure and pain and including everything in between.

For example, take a moment while reading to pay attention to what is happening. Notice the variety of sensations unfolding in your body and mind right now. For myself, as I write this, I notice that my back is unpleasantly tight and achy from sitting too long at my desk, but I can also hear piano music in the background, which is uplifting, soothing, and pleasant. But not everything in my environment elicits a strong reaction, such as the beige color of the walls, which feels very neutral in tone to me. Can you observe a similar variety of experience in this moment?

With awareness, not only do we notice the waves of pleasure and pain, but we can also observe our reactivity to these changing stimuli. Left to our own devices, we tend to react unconsciously, running toward or grasping after what is pleasant and resisting or rejecting what is unpleasant. This creates a constant push/pull, a contentiousness with life that leaves us frequently in a struggle with experience.

To a degree this tug of war with experience is evolutionarily hardwired. All beings and organisms move toward what is safe and pleasurable and away from what is painful and potentially threatening. At times, this is simply self-preservation, like gravitating toward warmth and food and away from pain. Yet we can't avoid all discomfort; we can't experience only pleasure. Trying to achieve this all the time only leads to frustration, since so much of life is out of our control. Even if we do attain some peak satisfaction, it never lasts and is soon replaced by yet another experience.

The question we face, then, is the same one I faced in India: How do we ride the waves of pleasure and pain without being tossed around by our preferences and our reactive nature? Over time, through cultivating mindfulness practice, we can learn to access a more steady presence in the midst of such turbulence. When we observe, over and over, how the knee-jerk habit of chasing fleeting pleasures and running from pain doesn't actually bring peace of mind, that clarity allows us to unhook from that agitation. In this way, we slowly build the muscle of equanimity, the capacity of steadiness and balance no matter what the circumstances.

As an example of this dynamic, I remember teaching a silent meditation retreat in northern India. One day, one of the students, Robert, shared with me the difficulty he was experiencing during the course. He was on a bit of a roller coaster. The first few days were bumpy as he settled into the stillness of the retreat, then one day, as can happen, he became unusually serene. His mind was clear, and his meditations were blissful and spacious. He became so happy that he began to fantasize about how he could maximize this meditation high. Robert mapped out what he would do after the retreat: he would move to Burma, join a monastery, become a monk, and then go meditate in a cave, where he imagined spending the rest of his life meditating in endless rapture.

Of course, all this excited planning destroyed his peaceful meditations. Rather than abiding in meditative stillness, he became restless. His mind became overwhelmed with a torrent of thoughts and plans about his future, and he found it harder to sit and maintain any focus. He lost the desire to meditate and started resisting the tranquility of the retreat. He became uncomfortable, tossed around by the unpleasantness of his busy mind and agitated body. He began to fantasize about getting out of the now-not-so-pleasant retreat and instead chill out some place where he could go surfing. He began judging the other participants and condemning the teachers for misleading him about meditation.

Then one evening during a lecture, one of the teachers described how the mind grasps after pleasure and how this obsession can actually destroy what we find joyful. Robert realized this had been happening to him: he had stopped simply appreciating his serenity and joy. Instead, he'd become consumed with capturing and prolonging the bliss of meditation by fantasizing about becoming a monk. These thoughts — his restless, agitated planning — had eroded the very pleasure he was trying to grasp and caused meditation to feel more and more unpleasant.

This is the hamster wheel of chasing pleasure and fleeing from pain, in which we all get caught at times. Certainly, we can enjoy serenity or bliss when it comes, but we can do so without holding on, since we understand its fleeting nature. Nor do we need to escape or eradicate an unpleasant experience, since we know it too will pass. Yet by simply witnessing the waves of joy and sorrow, the ups and downs, with a clear awareness, we learn to step off the wheel of reactivity. By doing that, we discover freedom and ease right in the midst of wherever we are.

• **PRACTICE** •

Exploring the Waves of Joy and Pain

Practice this meditation in a public place with a lot of activity, such as a city park. Sit with your eyes open, either with your gaze down or looking directly at everything that's happening. Open all of your senses and become aware of the various sights, sounds, smells, and sensations in the environment.

Likewise, be aware of the flow of experience within you. Notice the changing physical sensations, the movement of breath, the ebb and flow of emotions, the flicker of thoughts and images. In general, be aware of the totality of your inner and outer experience with a curious attention.

In addition, notice when an experience is felt as pleasurable, as unpleasant, or as somewhat neutral. All phenomena will have one of these three attributes. As you identify the quality of an experience, become aware of your reaction to it. Do you resist or avoid unwanted smells or noises? Do you reject anxious thoughts? Do you demand to hear only melodic birdsong or grasp after what's beautiful in your surroundings? Do you try to hold on to pleasant feelings? With neutral experiences, does your mind space out or get distracted?

Remember, it is quite natural to react to stimuli. The practice is to simply notice these impulses as fully as possible. If you hear a jarring noise, how do you react? Does your stomach contract or your jaw clench? Do you judge the source of the noise? Does the unpleasant sound overwhelm your enjoyment of other things that are pleasant, or perhaps create so much dissatisfaction that all you experience is negativity?

This meditation trains the mind to recognize reactivity with an open awareness, without becoming consumed by it. With that clearer perspective, we are able to respond more skillfully, whatever the stimulus is. By developing this quality in meditation, we increase our ability to access it when we need it most — in the midst of any strong experience, at work, with others, or elsewhere. To learn to be present with the full range of experience without being tossed about by our impulsive reactions, no matter how pleasurable or painful, is a tremendous support for finding wisdom and well-being in any situation.

• • •

Chapter 8

Understanding the
True Nature of the Body

The Church says: the body is a sin.
Science says: the body is a machine.
Advertising says: The body is a business.
The Body says: I am a fiesta.
— EDUARDO GALEANO

E mbodied attention is a foundational component of mindfulness practice. It serves as a vehicle for establishing awareness
anywhere. Over time we come to live in accord with the maxim:
"Wherever you go, there you are." Wherever we go, there we can
be present. But the point of mindfulness is not just to be aware but
to look deeply into the true nature of experience, including the
body.

"Who am I?" is an elusive query that has plagued philosophers, mystics, and meditation adepts alike, along with neuroscientists, psychologists, and biologists. What is this mysterious thing
called me? Who owns this body that "I" inhabit but over which I
have little control in terms of getting sick or aging? How is it that
I can know myself, can be aware of my mortality, can observe my
body, and yet have so little agency over the process? Who exactly
is running the show? Why is it that I wish to do one thing, but

then watch my body do exactly the opposite, seemingly against my wishes?

These questions rarely yield firm answers, yet this inquisitive attitude keeps us looking. Without inquiring into the mystery of being human, we will never fully know ourselves. Yet the point isn't necessarily to come up with a simplistic answer to this mystery but to keep plumbing its depths, so we can live our way into our understanding. As Rilke once wrote in *Letters to a Young Poet*:

> Try to love the questions themselves as if they were locked rooms, or books written in a very foreign language. Don't search for the answers which could not be given to you now because you would not be able to live them. And the point is to live everything. Live the questions now. Perhaps then, someday far in the future, you will gradually, without even noticing it, live your way into the answer.

Inquiry into the nature of the body, into who we really are, invites us to examine our existential nature. In one sense, we are *Homo sapiens*, having evolved into a particular form with a head, limbs, torso, and five senses. But what animates this body? What dictates how our legs move, and sends electrical impulses so our hands can paint, drive, and put food into our mouth? Are we really the same person despite all the changes to our body, once small enough to emerge from a woman's body and later as big as our parents; once only able to crawl and now able to run marathons? As we become more aware through sensory contact with our body, these questions can take on a pressing importance.

The body is a wonderland to explore. I am in awe of how the body heals. I recently cut my finger while chopping onions (perhaps not as mindful as I should have been!), and afterward I watched a biological miracle play itself out. First, my finger bled, and then without any conscious direction, the wound formed a scab to protect the damage and stop the blood flow. Over time, the scab slowly reduced in size until, miraculously, the rip in my flesh was again healed skin, as if nothing had ever happened. The body is a mystery that seems to function all by itself.

What is so astounding is how this organic process functions without any seeming intervention from "us." Our taste buds replace themselves every ten days, so they stay fresh and receptive, which may be why strawberries taste so good. The body grows a new liver in less than twenty weeks (perhaps a good thing given how much junk food we eat!). The largest organ of the body, the skin, is fully replaced once a month. Even our dense skeletal structure, with its more than two hundred bones, is completely overhauled once every seven years. We get a new stomach every three months! Aside from the cornea, the eyes are one of the few body parts that don't renew themselves. Perhaps this is one reason why our eyes say so much about us, the windows of the soul.

All of this begs the question, who are we? If the body continually replaces itself, part by part, am I really the same person as I was last Christmas, or ten years ago, or when I was a teenager or a baby? And if this process is happening by itself, then who is this "I" who thinks it is in control? We like to think that the self, our thinking mind and personality, is running the show, but if our bodies function on their own — healing and aging regardless of what we think, do, or say — then perhaps we have less ownership than we like to think.

There is an old Sufi story about a crazy wise guru named Mullah Nasruddin. One day he goes into a bank to cash a check. The teller asks him for some identification. After searching frantically through many pockets in his coat and trousers, he is unable to find his wallet. Finally, he smiles, pulls a mirror from his bag, looks at himself, and says wryly to the teller: "Yep. That's me." How often do we do the same thing, looking in the mirror at our face as if to confirm, yep, that's me. But is the body we see really who *we* are?

Mindfulness practice brings an intimate introspection to these questions and reveals that things are not always quite what they appear. This inquiry can overturn our preconceived notions of who we take ourselves to be, inviting us to hold things from a different and sometimes radical perspective.

At times, in deep meditation, the sense of one's body can appear to dissolve and challenge our conventional notion of what a body is. The usual perception of having physical boundaries can fall away, and we can experience ourselves as vast as space with no obstruction. At other times, we may feel the body to be so empty it is like air — transparent, light, and ephemeral. We can also sense the body as mere vibration, pulsing electricity, like waves of photons colliding. Every day, the body completely disappears from consciousness as we enter deep sleep. In fact, for a third of our lives, we live on this earth without any awareness of our body in this state. If all these empirical experiences are real, then what is the true nature of the body? Might it include all of these shape-shifting realities?

The investigation reveals our physical form is not as fixed as we like to think; it is an ever-fluid process. Insightful awareness clarifies that the body is not actually "our" body! We don't own or even control much of our body. What becomes clear is that the body is not ultimately who we are. Yes, we have physical form, a shape, a body that ages. Yet who *we* are is beyond this physical form, beyond definition, category, or any other limited concept. When we misattribute the sense of self to our body, it is clearly a case of mistaken identity. (Later chapters will explore the issue of identity further.)

What we call the body is a construct made up of a matrix of physical processes that have no beginning or end, in the same way that the elements that comprise us do not disappear when we die but simply merge into new forms. It is analogous to a bunch of water molecules bound together as an ice cube. We know the water is just in a temporary, conditioned frozen form. So, too, are the elements that comprise our body.

Our final invitation to explore the nature of the body is at the time of death. From the perspective of awareness, we can see how the body deteriorates, but the clarity of presence can pervade and endure even in death. My first Insight Meditation teacher, Christopher Titmuss, recounted a story from his time as a Buddhist monk studying in southern Thailand. He had developed a friendship with a monk named Por Long Bhut who had developed liver cancer but refused all medicine and painkillers. In his final hours of life, the monk invited Christopher to lay down beside him on his bamboo mat in his hut. "Time has come," he said. Death was close at hand.

Christopher recalled the elder in the final hours whispering faintly about how each sense was fading away one by one. Christopher recounts: "After an hour or so, Por Long Bhut whispered to me in Thai — 'No seeing.' Then he said a few minutes later, 'No hearing.' Por Long Bhut never reacted. He knew deep inner peace before, during, and after the diagnosis of cancer. Por Long Bhut's depth of mindfulness and meditation along with the clarity that he was not the body helped make his transition smooth from life to death. He was a liberated and untroubled human being."

Clearly, the Thai monk felt no agitation about dying, for it was clear to him that he was not the body. This is the liberating power of mindfulness, which frees us from the constraints of the physical body and of our misidentification with it, even at death.

• PRACTICE •

Exploring the Selfless Nature of the Body

Assume a comfortable meditation posture and close your eyes, turning the gaze of attention inward. Open your awareness to hearing and become present to the ebb and flow of sounds. Notice how sounds are known quite effortlessly with mindfulness. Rest in that spacious awareness for a few minutes, noticing how it happens all by itself — a sound arises and there is a simple knowing each time.

Now turn your attention to include awareness of the landscape of the body. Notice as physical sensations appear and disappear; these are also known quite naturally without any need to make an effort. Perhaps you feel the contact of your legs or buttocks with the chair or cushion you are sitting on. Or you may notice the temperature of the air on your skin or the touch of clothing. Attend to the variety of physical experiences for a few minutes, and notice how these sensations come and go by themselves and how easily they are sensed in awareness.

In the same way, sense the breath, moving like a perennial inner tide of inhalations and exhalations. You don't make the breath happen; it moves by itself, ceaselessly flowing, keeping the body alive. Notice any feelings or thoughts about this understanding, how bodily life simply maintains itself organically through all kinds of biological processes. Be aware of the breath for a few minutes in this way.

Then shift the attention to the heart as it beats, the pulse in your veins. Reflect on how the heart, like every other organ, operates according to its own nature, without any prompting from you. In this way, sense directly how each organ of the body operates on its own, and how you are simply a witness to the process. Notice how that observation touches you and affects your relationship to your physical experience. Continue this observation through the day, noticing how the body miraculously functions by itself, selflessly.

• • •

· SECTION 2 ·

FINDING PEACE
IN THE MIND

Chapter 9

Working with
the Thinking Mind

A man is but the product of his thoughts.
What he thinks, he becomes.
— MAHATMA GANDHI

When I first started meditating, I was amazed by the experience of getting to know my own mind. Introspective meditation felt like a revelation. No one had ever talked to me about paying attention to my mental habits, patterns, and thoughts, nor suggested that these might be the primary source of our well-being or stress. Like most people, I was conditioned to think that happiness arose from external sources: that it lay in success, wealth, relationships, and so on. It struck me as confounding that, for all the fifteen years I was getting an education, not one minute had been devoted to paying attention to one's own mind. By the time I came across a quote that said, "Nothing can help you more than your own mind trained," that rang very true.

The mind is an amazing phenomenon. In recent years, neuroscience has barely begun to scratch the surface of what the mind is, let alone develop sophisticated-enough tools with which to study it. Our minds can create beautiful works of art, design cities in the desert, and build satellites that photograph deep space. Great minds can strategize to resolve problems as vast as climate change and develop mathematical formulas to calculate the size of black holes.

As creative as the mind can be, it can also be a dangerous force. Human minds have designed weapons so powerful we could destroy ourselves if they were ever employed. Equally, the mind can turn on itself and create the grounds for self-destruction. We can become tormented by anxious views about the future or riddled with self-doubt and negative self-judgments. The mind can be perceptually brilliant yet also delusional in its observations.

In effect the mind is neutral, yet it is a tremendously powerful tool. What arises within it and how we work with it can make the difference between suffering and peace. With mindfulness practice, we study the mind to uncover dysfunctional thinking and release unhelpful mental patterns. Through observation, we can explore the potential of the mind to create, to envision, and to love. We can also inquire into the nature of reality itself.

One way to help cultivate inner freedom is to turn awareness toward our mental habits and tendencies. Everyone has a mind, yet no one receives an instruction manual! It is like putting a dog into the front seat of a car and expecting it to know how to drive. We are born with a brain whose sophisticated neural circuitry has developed over millions of years. We are prone to innumerable impulses, reactions, and mental biases that have accrued, not just in our lifetime, but over thousands of generations. So much of what we do is just inner programming playing itself out.

Yet surprisingly, we think we are masters of our own destiny. We like to believe we are in control. However, on closer inspection, we see that most mental activity happens by itself. We are subject to constant pushes and pulls; we react instinctively or habitually, but rarely with any sense of agency. Our mind lives in a

Pavlovian world, responding to thoughts, impulses, and impressions as if salivating upon hearing a bell signaling time to eat.

Consider the plethora of thoughts that run through your mind every day. The National Science Foundation posited that we can think upwards of fifty thousand thoughts a day. That is a lot of thoughts — almost one per second! No wonder we feel our mind is cluttered! Not surprisingly, the most common hindrance in meditation is to become lost in those thoughts. And how many of those same thoughts did we think yesterday? Our thoughts are not as interesting or original as we like to believe. They are more like repeats of old TV dramas.

Mindfulness practice brings insight as well as some space from the turmoil of our minds. The first insight people often have is just how many thoughts we think. That is sobering in and of itself. Another insight is that thoughts are just thoughts; they are not as real as we believe them to be. A famous Chinese story describes a Taoist monk who painted a tiger on the wall of his cave. After putting on the finishing touches and painting the eyes, he suddenly became scared, thinking it was a real tiger!

We do the same every day with the creations of our mind. We conjure the memory of a delicious pizza we ate yesterday and suddenly get hungry. We recall a person we are attracted to and suddenly feel aroused. Or we imagine our boss becoming frustrated with us, and our breath shortens and our heart pumps with fear. Our thoughts appear to be real, which plays havoc with our mind, body, and well-being. A phrase attributed to Mark Twain sums this up well: "I have known a great many troubles in my life, most of which never happened." Believing all these mental flickers drags us into a lot of angst.

One key mental habit we uncover with mindfulness is the process of proliferation. This is the way the mind free-associates in a tumbleweed of thoughts. For example, say we notice the smell of fried garlic coming from a nearby kitchen. No sooner does the mind recognize the smells than we find ourselves lost in a flurry of thoughts about lunch. However, it doesn't stop there. The garlic triggers a cascade of memories, perhaps of a delicious pesto pasta dish we recently had, which reminds us of a long-ago visit to Florence, which leads to reminiscing about walking the city streets and exploring its medieval churches and eating in its heavenly trattorias.

Next thing we know, we are planning our next European vacation, perhaps to Venice, and wondering why it has been so many years since we took a real vacation. We start analyzing our work life and our finances and all the recent stress we've been dealing with, and we are reminded of our pledge to take better care of ourselves. Amusingly, that line of thinking leads us to why we took up meditation — in order to let go of the stressful, endless stream of thoughts in our head! This is the folly of proliferation.

The clear lens of mindfulness allows us to see thoughts for what they are: mental images and ideas that flutter briefly across the screen of awareness. A helpful metaphor is to imagine awareness as a vast blue sky and thoughts as clouds that continually float across that expanse of the mind. The clouds, however strong and thick, can never obscure the vastness of the sky. We can learn to abide in this sky-like awareness and not get lost focusing on each individual cloud. Even when large storms come, and we are filled with maddening or even terror-inducing thoughts, they remain only storms that leave the sky unaltered. The grounding quality of awareness has the capacity to hold all experience, no matter how intense or bleak.

By seeing thoughts in this way, we are less likely to be at their mercy. The goal isn't to stop thinking or to achieve a thought-free life. Not only is that impossible, but we obviously need thoughts in order to live in engaged, creative, and effective ways. What is essential is developing a wise relationship with the thinking process. Meditation training teaches us that our thoughts come and go, just as clouds in the sky come and go. In this way, we recognize thoughts without getting lost in endless rumination, nor whip ourselves into a painful frenzy about something that isn't actually happening. This helps us abide much more fully in the present moment, where life actually happens.

A meditation student, Joann, once compared working with thoughts to driving a car with a manual transmission. She wrote to me:

My body is the automobile, my thoughts are the gears, my mindfulness practice is the clutch, and my deeper wisdom is the steering. When the clutch is out, the wheels are engaged and the automobile moves in whatever gear it's in. When the clutch is pushed in, the gears just spin, and the vehicle coasts or stands still. For me, mindfulness is "pushing in the clutch" and allowing the thoughts to just go round and round, giving my deeper wisdom time and space to decide which thought I want to embrace and act upon — which direction I want to go. When it becomes clear the steering wheel is pointed in the best direction, I let the clutch out — slowly, of course.

From the perspective of mindfulness, we learn to discern when thinking brings wisdom, clarity, and understanding versus when thought leads to more painful states of mind and heart. In section 2, we will uncover some of the more subtle, pernicious, and challenging areas of our thinking that undermine our well-being and freedom.

• PRACTICE •

Mindfulness of Thoughts

Find a sitting posture you can maintain with ease for fifteen to twenty minutes. Close your eyes and focus your attention on your breath. The awareness of this practice is twofold: to be mindful of breathing and to be aware of the various thoughts, images, views, ideas, and stories that float through the sky of your mind and ceaselessly pull your attention.

There are many ways to engage with our thoughts. The first is simply to be aware as thoughts arise and to practice what I call the three Rs: recognize, release, and return. We recognize the thought, release our fascination with it, and return awareness to the breath or to the particular object we have selected for our practice. Meditation often focuses on doing this over and over and over, which builds concentration. In this meditation, the goal is to stay focused on the thoughts themselves.

As thoughts appear, label each one to identify what kind of thought it is. First, you can categorize thoughts in relation to past, present, or future. Is the thought a memory or reflection on a past event? Is it a plan for the future or speculation on what might happen? Is it awareness of something occurring right now, perhaps commentary or analysis? Notice if thoughts are more inclined toward the future, the past, or the present.

Then become more specific about exactly what kinds of thoughts arise. This requires a shift from being lost in the content and detail of the thought to recognizing the process or type of thought that is present. For example, if you start planning what kind of breakfast you will make after the meditation, simply become aware that planning or fantasy is happening. In the same way, you can become aware of many types of thinking, like worry, fear, fantasy, speculation, regret, doubt, or desire. Without becoming lost in the specific content, label these types of thoughts, such as "planning" or "remembering," which strengthens awareness of them. The more quickly we recognize types of thoughts, the less likely we are to be pulled into their web. This helps us release them and stay focused in the present or on the task at hand.

A key facet of mindfulness is awareness of both experience and your relationship to experience. In this meditation, as you notice what types of thoughts arise, also notice how you react to them. Labeling thoughts with a negative emotional quality or tone helps indicate this reactivity. Does judgment arise, so that you snap your attention back harshly after being consumed in thoughts? The more you recognize how natural and human it is to be lost in thought, the more easily you will be able to find a sense of ease and humor with this process.

Lastly, observe how much you take your thoughts to be reality. The thought of a ghost is not a ghost. It is simply an image in the mind. The more we believe our thoughts to be real, the more we will be sucked into them. The more you recognize the ephemeral, transient, and insubstantial nature of thoughts, the less hold they will have over you.

Finally, bring awareness to the way you identify thoughts as yours, as if you are initiating them. Most of the time thoughts happen randomly or out of a complex web of causes and conditions. The more you can see thoughts as impersonally as clouds in a sky, the more you can create a more spacious relationship with them.

Once you are finished with this meditation, try to extend this awareness throughout your day. As you observe your thoughts and learn to release being so caught up in them, notice how much more present you are to your immediate experience and the corresponding increase in well-being that flows from that.

• • •

Chapter 10

The Ceaseless Conjuring
of What Isn't

Perception and reality are two different things.
— ANONYMOUS

Contemplative traditions often point out that the world we live in is like a conjurer's trick. Not that the world *is* an illusion, but that it is *like* an illusion. That is an important distinction. The world we live in is real. But what we see, think, and believe does not necessarily reflect what is so. We see life through a range of conditioning, bias, and projections. And what we make of experience is affected and often distorted by influences from our past as well as from the views of family, friends, culture, society, and religion. Therefore, we need to not only be aware of thoughts, but we need to mindfully discern what is true from what is simply a distortion.

My friend Jane once adopted a beautiful golden Labrador puppy from a local animal shelter. The puppy had previously been owned by a man who had gotten quite sick and did not have the ability to take care of her. Sadly, the man not only neglected the dog but took out his anger on the poor defenseless animal, who became traumatized and terrified of men.

Now in a good home and well loved, the dog is relaxed with my friend, and with her female friends and even female strangers. But when the dog sees a man, she cowers and runs for safety. The violence and neglect of the previous male owner conditioned Jane's dog to fear all men, no matter how kind and mild. The dog sees the world through the lens of her harsh history with one man, which is deeply rooted and difficult to mitigate.

As much as we like to think we are independent and autonomous, we are no different from that puppy. We are formed like clay at an early age by the social and cultural milieu we are born into. We are also shaped by our biological hard wiring. For example, as a species, we have been conditioned over millions of years to be wary of snakes, spiders, and centipedes, since many such creatures are poisonous or even deadly. If we see a snake or spider, our anxiety level instantly goes up as the amygdala in our brain triggers our fight-or-flight response. Then, if we recognize that the creature is harmless or no threat, or we see that the coiled thing lying in the bushes is just a piece of rope, we may breathe a sigh of relief.

The challenge is that our perceptions are often wrong, mistaken, or misplaced. In the Indian Pali language, the term *vipalasa* captures this tendency perfectly. It refers to the perceptual distortion we have when we behold something and mistake as permanent things that actually change or perceive things that are actually painful as pleasurable. "Behold" means more, for example, than visual perception; it includes our expectations, assumptions, and perspective. We get caught up in such distortions all the time without realizing it.

Like my friend's puppy, we are often biased with preconceived notions that neither reflect actual reality nor predict what will happen. For example, most children love puppies, and they often harangue their parents to get one. Kids imagine only the cuteness and companionship of the dog. Parents, however, see much more:

years of arduous dog training, a constant source of mess (from shedding hairs to peeing on the carpet), and an ongoing, daily responsibility that includes feeding, dog walking, and expensive vet bills. The dog is the same, but everyone's perceptions are quite different. Which ones are true?

Or consider romance. When we are attracted to someone, what do we see? The mind focuses on what is pleasurable and alluring, while overlooking or ignoring what is disagreeable or potentially problematic. When perceptual bias kicks in with full force, we obsess over and idealize our new love, so that we literally don't see anything wrong with them. Yet as we know too well, when the honeymoon stage is over and infatuation ends, the blinkers to our perception fall away. We start to see the blemishes and faults that we were oblivious to before. Such is the dawning of clear awareness. Sometimes we wake up in a relationship and wonder where our fairy prince or princess went! As one cartoonist put it: "Marriage is a Cinderella fairy tale...just in reverse. You start out at a ball in a beautiful gown and end up spending all day cleaning up after people."

Conversely, aversion, fear, and negativity can distort perception just as strongly. When gripped by reactivity, or any strong emotion, we just don't see straight. When scared, we see only threats, like my friend's puppy. When angry, we fixate on what is wrong, negative, or problematic with ourselves, with others, or the world. When in love, we experience the world as softer, more beautiful, and kind.

When we remain unaware of these distortions, we tend to believe our perceptions are reality. For instance, I had a fear of the dark growing up, and I remember the first time I camped in the Rocky Mountains. At night, I was convinced that every sound was a sinister predator, and I was afraid to leave my tent. One time I dared to step outside, and I laughed upon seeing that the ominous

sounds I mistook for a mountain lion were made by a squirrel rustling in the bushes!

As funny as this can be, this perceptual distortion can lead to
far more serious consequences, such as racism and prejudice. Infants are not born prejudiced. Babies are color blind. While our
evolutionary biology conditions us to be more fearful of what we
consider the "other," racial bias is primarily the product of social-
ization, which distinguishes people based on skin color or ethnic
origin, and then posits one group as inherently superior to all others. Such perceptions of superiority have no basis in fact, but bias
often runs deep and overrides reason or judgment.

With mindfulness, we bring awareness to these veils of perception. We can become aware of our own bias, of the lens we
look through. This can help us recognize when our conditioning
is influencing our perception and is affecting what we believe —
say, that certain people are smarter because of their socioeconomic
class or that darkness represents danger and should be feared.

Perhaps the biggest perceptual distortion is about our sense of
self and identity. We perceive our sense of self as stable, consistent,
and enduring over time. But if we take a closer look at our inner
experience, we behold our sense of self as forever moving, fluctuating, expanding, contracting, and shape-shifting, and this affects
our perception of life around us. For instance, consider how our
fluctuating sense of self-worth makes us view things and the world
differently. When we feel good about ourselves, we view our work
with appreciation and satisfaction. When we feel depressed or in-
secure, we can judge and critique our work more harshly. It is the
same work, but our perceptions cause us to see it differently.

I encounter this when I teach. How I feel on a certain day determines to some degree how I perceive my lecture. If I feel any
flicker of self-doubt, I tend to fixate on what could have been said
better or what was flawed. I have learned to not wholly trust my

evaluation of a particular talk, given the inevitable distortions of perceptual bias. Rather, with awareness, I try to see both the event and my perceptions of the event and to hold it all lightly. This is freeing, giving me room to avoid either inflation or deflation and the perhaps distorted view of my personal vantage point. In the same way, I also hold lightly the views and perceptions of others about the very same talk. I may receive two comments following the lecture, one saying it was fabulous, the best talk they've heard me give, and another saying or implying it was confusing and not helpful. They both heard the same talk, but which perception do we believe? Is either of them real?

Finally, perhaps the most common perceptual distortion is thinking that what is impermanent is permanent. How often do we believe conditions, feelings, or events won't change, only to be surprised and thrown when, naturally, a shift happens? Believing our feelings of romance will last forever, only to be disappointed when they fade? Thinking our flu virus will go on forever when of course it heals in due course? With practice, we can develop a meta-attention to our experience that helps us get closer to the reality of what is happening rather than seeing through the lens of bias and misperception.

• PRACTICE •

Seeing through Perceptual Distortion

It is hard to see our own perceptual distortions. The world seems to be a certain way until we realize that our lens, our perception, is coloring the world. This contemplation explores how your vantage point influences your perspective and thoughts. Begin by standing in front of a mirror. Pay attention to the thoughts about yourself that arise. Do you like or dislike what you see? That preference or bias will determine what you choose to focus on.

Do you notice and fixate on whatever seems problematic? Or do you observe those things you like and appreciate? Do these observations and perceptions, whether negative or positive, seem to reflect the bias of the moment? For example, are you tired and feeling grumpy, and is this mood influencing your attention and judgments? If so, consider how your gaze might change if you were feeling joyful or energized. If you have had a particularly successful day, how might that affect what you behold in front of you? Then ask yourself the question: *Which thought, idea, or view about myself is real?* Indeed, I suggest doing this contemplation on consecutive days and observing how your perceptions, thoughts, views, and judgments differ or change.

Further, continue this reflection throughout your day. While watching the news, sitting on a bus, or participating in a meeting, notice how you view the people around you. Is the lens through which you perceive influenced positively or negatively by something? Is that perception a reflection of your mood, your current state of mind, your energy, how your day has gone thus far, or any other factor from the past or present?

In this way, try to become more aware of the conditioning, perceptions, filters, and biases that are influencing how you are perceiving in any moment. Learning to hold our own views and biases lightly allows us to meet experience more clearly, as we come to see through the distortions that are forever moving through our perceptual landscape.

• • •

Chapter 11

The Restless Comparing Mind

You wouldn't worry so much about what others think of you
if you realized how seldom they do.
— ELEANOR ROOSEVELT

For the last twenty years I have taught meditation retreats with teaching teams comprised of several teachers. I have taught with senior Dharma teachers, world-renowned experts, novices, and peers. It's always a delight to share the teaching platform with friends and colleagues who inspire me and from whom I myself can learn. However, as lovely as that can be, I can sometimes get caught up in comparisons with them, which can be quite painful. The comparing mind, no matter what the occasion, never seems far away, and it's always eager to jump in.

When I first started teaching, this habit was much worse. For instance, if I felt awe for a colleague's eloquence, my comparing mind might use that to put myself down, and I could feel like my teaching may not be up to scratch. Conversely, if another teacher gave an unclear lecture, my ego could use that as grounds for in-flation, thinking it could do a much better job! Each time I encountered a new teaching team, my comparing mind, left unchecked, started contrasting and comparing myself to others. What I didn't fully understand then was that this never-ending anxious drama is all in our heads and really bears little relation to reality. It also leads to a lot of unnecessary anguish.

When I dig deeper, I can see vulnerability underneath the restless comparing mind. Sometimes we fear being seen as less than others and of possibly losing appreciation, respect, and worst of all, love. This fear is rarely conscious, and it rarely is based on what's actually true. Most often these fears relate to old anxieties, especially experiences from childhood that then reverberate throughout our life. Whatever the specific reasons, be they fears of abandonment and rejection or the desire for attention, praise, and love, they are strong drivers for the comparing mind.

Such insecurity lies at the heart of the ego structure. The ego is always on shaky ground, forever nervous about its status. The ego-identity is a self-constructed paradigm, something we create and build up over a lifetime, and its tenuous status has no more reality than what we ascribe to it. Therefore, the ego stays busy trying to prop up its precarious sense of self in relation to others.

There are three ways we are pulled into ceaseless comparison. We either feel superior, inferior, or equal. Yet the restless uncertainty of the ego means we rarely settle in one place for long. We may prefer the feeling of inflation that comes from feeling superior, but this status is vulnerable because at any moment someone else may display more skill, intelligence, or talent, which can elicit a sense of inferiority. Any status is tentative and subject to change, and so our egoic personality is always hard at work, comparing, contrasting, and protecting its identity.

Today, social media further feeds the relentless comparing mind. This creates a tremendous amount of anxiety, particularly for teens, and it's easy to feel that one's social status rises and falls on a whim, depending on how many likes, shares, and re-tweets one gets. The pervasiveness of this medium makes it all the more important to bring awareness to this challenging habit.

Of course, how comparison unfolds depends on how we think of ourselves. If we consider ourselves an expert or the most popular, then the comparing mind will feel threatened by others who have more expertise or get a lot of attention. If we are the office's IT guru, we might feel challenged and undermined if a young new hire, fresh from computer programming school, knows more and outperforms us. This could trigger negative feelings toward the new person and force us to reassess our status. The new hire might threaten our chances of promotion, or the threat might be only to our social standing, but we tend to react as if our survival is at stake.

The same is true in any situation where we have or want the status of being "the best," whether that's being the most supple person in the yoga class, the richest businessperson in the boardroom, the most generous donor, the most humble spiritual devotee, or the most successful politician. The ego generally wants to be top dog, but this effort is fraught with insecurity and uncertainty. It is hard for the ego to suffer the loss of identity that comes from not maintaining one's status. We can see this when renowned political figures desperately try to hold on to fame or power or both, and go to extreme lengths, including a coup d'état, to preserve their status.

Conversely, the ego may have a negative self-identity, one that is perhaps more vulnerable and painful. We can believe we are the worst, the least lovable, unworthy, and incapable. If we carry around a deficient sense of self, the comparing mind tends to put us down while elevating others. As with any identity, we tend to hold on to our status with tenacity. In this situation, the comparing mind might reject positive feedback or appreciation, since that challenges our negative identity. To be "less than" can sometimes feel safe and comfortable, a way to avoid taking responsibility, even though it's an inherently painful position to be in.

I have worked with some of the smartest, most gifted, and compassionate people who carry around a belief that they are stupid, underqualified, or selfish. I have known others where the opposite was true, and their actions did not match their high self-regard. Only self-awareness and an honesty with ourselves can keep us from being imprisoned by false realities.

Even thinking we are equal to others can be a form of conceit, since it still involves an ego-derived comparison to and judgment of others. Being "equal" is the same kind of evaluation; it is a moving target that keeps the ego perpetually ill at ease. Fortunately, with awareness, comparative thoughts can be seen for what they are, just thoughts that bear little relation to the truth. We see clearly they are just unconstructive mental habits that leave us in a state of contraction, anxiety, and insecurity. That clarity then helps us to disengage from constantly measuring ourselves against others and to release the tyranny of the comparing mind.

With a sensitive awareness, we can sense the inherent insecurity that underlies these comparisons. Then, rather than judge ourselves or reject these thoughts out of aversion, we can attune to the vulnerability at the root of the ego-identity structure. As we learn not to buy into such mental games, and feel the deep pain they cause, we come to hold ourselves with compassion. Eventually, our insight into the comparing mind's misperceptions and our compassion for the suffering that ensues for everyone helps us uproot the whole comparison game.

• PRACTICE •

Noticing the Comparing Mind

Everyone can fall prey to the comparing mind. Because that measuring and evaluating can be so painful, it is essential to meet this experience with compassion and forgiveness. That's not to let ourselves off the hook but to simply recognize how powerful this conditioning is. It's important to bring kind attention and a sense of care as you become more aware of this painful process — in the same way we might console a child if they felt hurt by social media–driven comparisons. Mindfulness can help us not only hold comparisons less tightly but also not take the habit so personally.

As you go through your day, pay attention to this habit of comparing. Notice when and how it arises. When you check Facebook or Instagram, do you compare someone else's idyllic pictures of their "blissful" family with your own family? At work, when someone gets accolades, a promotion, or a bonus, do you compare this with whatever you've gotten, and perhaps put yourself down as a result? When you notice comparisons, notice if you feel the pain of this process.

In this practice, simply notice the comparing mind. Whenever you see it happening, just name it: "comparing mind." Often, just the awareness of this tendency is enough to remind us to step back and reconsider our belief or assessment. Recognizing comparisons, and remembering that they are self-created and often don't reflect reality, can make it easier to let such thoughts go.

Also pay attention to your body. Whether the comparison makes you feel inferior or superior (or equal), notice your physical and emotional reaction. For instance, feelings of superiority are usually less pleasant than we may imagine, since they create a sense of separation, or smugness, rather than expansiveness or real joy. Can you sense the inherent instability and uncertainty of that inflated position and the anxiety and contraction that can accompany that status? When you are feeling inferior, notice how painful that state can be.

Bring attention to the vulnerability that underlies so much of the comparing mind. Notice how the comparing habit often arises out of a sense of lack or an insecurity. Can you meet that vulnerability with a compassionate presence rather than judgment?

By observing this roller coaster of comparing, we strengthen our ability to disengage from it. We learn to simply recognize and observe this process with a kind attention, rather than ride the highs and lows of the comparisons themselves. This is like stepping off the roller coaster. Abiding in this knowing presence allows us to feel a sense of space or equanimity even as the tendency to compare continues. Over time, you will find the comparing mind no longer leaves its painful residue. You will see comparisons arise and not take them so seriously, releasing without trouble the self-constructed realities that once caused you so much anguish.

• • •

Chapter 12

Identifying the Judging Mind

The more a man judges, the less he loves.
— HONORÉ DE BALZAC

Self-judgment is a modern epidemic. How often do we swim in self-critical thoughts about others and ourselves? In my previous book, *Make Peace with Your Mind*, I chronicle how frequent and painful the inner critic can be. In this chapter I want to highlight both the ways we judge others and the ways we turn that harsh lens toward ourselves in negative and unhelpful ways, which all too often leave painful scars.

We live in a judgmental culture and in an era of endless social comparison. As I've discussed, social media fuels our habit to judge and compare ourselves by externalized standards. Who doesn't find themselves comparing their life to the heavily curated but "perfect" lives posted on Instagram or Facebook? Such comparisons leave many teenagers and adults in constant angst.

With our brain's hard wiring to a negativity bias, our tendency can be to see all that is wrong with the world, people, and ourselves. This bias selectively looks for what is deficient, problematic, or needs fixing. Yet when we live imprisoned inside that critical mind, our world becomes smaller, negative, and mean. We tend to reject people for not living up to some idealized standard. Such judgment pushes people away, and we can find ourselves isolated and alone in our tower of superiority.

Not surprisingly, we also focus that critical lens on ourselves. That provides lethal ammunition for the inner critic, which can be ruthless in its self-assessment. We can then all too easily fault ourselves for not being good enough or smart enough or for any of the number of ways that we simply don't measure up. Such judgments leave us feeling ashamed, insufficient, and deficient or unworthy. This cycle creates a lot of unnecessary suffering.

Yet this pattern is so ubiquitous we don't even notice it. It has become part of our mental furniture. One of my meditation teachers, Joseph Goldstein, talks about being on a long silent meditation retreat and sitting in the dining room looking around. He noticed his mind rampantly judging almost everyone in the room. Judgments arose about the way people walked (too slow or too fast), and about the quantity of food they took (too much or too little). Then he noticed judgments about people who did not seem mindful enough! As he became aware of what he was doing, he was both surprised and amused. He could see the humor of judging others for not being mindful when he himself was not mindful of his own judging mind! Sometimes the best strategy is to laugh at ourselves and the hubris of our own mind.

Mindfulness can help free us from the painful burden of this powerful mental habit. By bringing the clarity of awareness to the content of our mind, we can track the nature of our thoughts and assess whether they are helpful or harmful, to see if they point to the truth or not. With discernment we can assess whether judging others brings happiness and connection or if such critical thoughts make us feel artificially superior yet disdainful or even misanthropic. Judgments can create a sense of "otherness" that separates and excludes, leaving us alone and far from a sense of well-being.

The poison of the judging mind also erodes our sense of worth and value. If we listen to a voice that only points out our own faults, mistakes, and shortcomings, we will inevitably feel bad or even worthless. Unless we consciously attune to judgments, they can be invisible, slipping under our radar and eluding detection. They become as familiar as wallpaper, so that it feels normal for negativity and self-doubt to decorate our mental space. No wonder that, at times, we feel bad about ourselves.

But we can wake up to the impact of our critical thoughts. With awareness we can notice how such views sap our energy and make us fatigued. Sometimes our brain gets foggy when weighed down by the barrage of self-judgment. At other times we may feel hopeless or unconfident. Tracking the physical, emotional, and energetic impacts of judgment can help alert us to the inner critic's presence.

The good news is that we don't have to take judgmental thoughts personally or even believe them. Many arise unbidden, part of the same habits and tendencies that drive the comparing mind. Our work is also the same: to recognize judgments and meet the pain of the pattern with compassionate attention. With lucidity, we identify painful thoughts, recognize their inaccuracies, and let them go.

In one 2008 study, researchers investigated the impact of mindfulness on negative thoughts and whether the practice improved the ability to let go of negative thinking. They discovered that when people participated in a mindfulness meditation–based clinical intervention, they were able to let go of negative automatic thinking more frequently and more easily.

I have also seen this verified in my own experience innumerable times. As a teacher, I never cease to be amazed by what happens when people shine the light of attention on the inner critic. It is a delight to see just how much space and peace emerges from bringing mindfulness to the judgmental mind. And it provides a sense of empowerment to know that no matter what the current state of our mind and heart, transformation is possible through the simple yet powerful force of awareness. The following practice provides both some theoretical perspectives for working with the inner critic as well as some practical tools for constructively mitigating its impact.

• PRACTICE •
Recognizing the Judging Mind

There are many ways to work with the critical mind. Like the practice "Noticing the Comparing Mind" in chapter 11, the main goal here is simply to observe your mind and to recognize and label judging thoughts as they arise. This can be done anywhere; just sit or walk comfortably in a place where you can safely turn your attention inward.

Our minds are often full of evaluations, observations, and discerning thoughts that are necessary in life. In our work, we need a critical capacity to function effectively, make decisions, strategize, and so on. In this contemplation, however, the intention is to focus on identifying negative judgments, or those often harsh, critical assessments of someone's worth or goodness, whether that person is yourself or someone else. For example, become aware of thoughts that you or others are "not good enough," or that you could or should have done something better.

Once you detect a judgment, label it with a phrase like "judging." This improves your internal radar for critical thoughts. Then notice what impact the judgment has. Does it belittle someone else, or does it make you feel bad, stupid, or any number of painful emotions? In this way, awareness can help you sense the corrosive impact of judging, which in turn can help you disengage from it.

In contrast, for fun, consider counting the number of judgments that arise in a day. This can be an enlightening exercise. When you get to 232 judgments by lunchtime, you will see how ludicrous the judging mind can be.

Beyond labeling and counting, also inquire if a particular judgment is true or not. Universal statements, which include words like *always* and *never*, are usually whisperings of the judging mind. Any thought that includes *could have, should have, would have* reflects the perverted reasoning of the inner critic. Such generalized statements are rarely accurate.

When judgments about the past arise, you can challenge the judging mind's view. Hindsight is 20/20, and what is done is done. Let go of criticisms of past actions based on the unfair vantage point of hindsight. In a similar fashion, question the inner critic's assumptions. Is it true that you are bad, stupid, or unlovable? Is that true about someone else?

We tend to bestow our judging mind with unquestioned power and authority, but this risks an inaccurate self-perception. Instead, listen and question, without believing every word. Take back your right to evaluate the credibility of judgments and your own self-worth. By clarifying your relationship to the judging mind, you can reclaim your power to establish a more accurate self-perception and stable sense of well-being.

One helpful strategy with the inner critic is humor. If you can see the absurdity of judgments, you can disentangle from their hooks. Ultimately, the goal isn't to argue with the inner critic but to have a disinterested relationship with it. Being able to laugh at the craziness of what it says creates space and distance in the same way that comedians poke fun at the absurdity of human behaviors and make us laugh at our own antics. Isn't it amusing that the inner critic is never satisfied no matter what we do? Seeing the funny, nonsensical side of this dynamic can help take the sting out of the inner critic's words, so that we simply roll our eyes at its jabs.

Lastly, you may notice that the inner critic becomes vocal when you feel vulnerable or threatened socially. Our judging mind jumps to help, but not in positive or constructive ways. Notice when judgments arise to defend against the criticisms of others, such as following a performance review at work. Acknowledge that the inner critic's intention is to help us avoid rejection or abandonment, while also recognizing that its punishing and shaming are not effective ways to do that. Instead, when you feel vulnerable, see if you can treat yourself with kindness and care and avoid blaming others. That is a far more effective way to help ourselves when we are struggling, rather than adding fuel to the fire with painful self-criticism and judgments.

As you cultivate seeing and releasing judgment, notice any space or ease that arises, and if it leads to more lightness and joy. When you are less burdened by the inner critic, how does that shift how you view yourself and others? Does it allow you to see yourself and everyone else in a more accurate light? If so, notice this positive impact.

• • •

Chapter 13

The Illusion of Time

We cast away priceless time in dreams, born of imagination,
fed upon illusion, and put to death by reality.
— JUDY GARLAND

One of the strongest habits of the mind is its ceaseless foray into the imaginary world of the future. How much time do we spend ruminating, worrying, and imagining a catastrophe about a future scenario that never actually happens? We can spend hours lost in daydreams and fantasies about plans that never actualize. How many moments do we spend rehearsing a discussion with a loved one or our boss? Then when that conversation happens, it always unfolds differently than the way we had carefully planned.

How often do you wake up in the middle of the night in a cold sweat worrying about some potential disaster, such as the stock market crashing or a family member getting hurt? The mind frequently creates stories about the future that catapult us into a fight-or-flight response, sending adrenaline coursing through our veins as we anticipate a catastrophe. Such mental machinations are wearisome. The poet Hafiz framed it well: "Fear is the cheapest room in the house. I'd like to see you living in better conditions."

The irony is that this dizzying speculation is about a future reality that doesn't exist! Mystics have expounded on the illusion of time for centuries and pointed to its mirage-like nature. Yet humans have carved up time into the concept of past, present, and future, which we take to be very real. But do such classifications really exist outside of our clocks and calendars?

From a phenomenological perspective, the present is the only moment that we know directly, so do past and future exist anywhere but in our heads? Is time just a mental construct? The concept of time is a helpful convention that allows us to prepare for what is to come and review what has occurred. What has happened in the past is not fictitious, and yet it now only exists in our imagination or in history books. Certainly, only humans divide time into seconds, minutes, days, and years. Such divisions often reflect the cycles of nature — each day matches the earth's rotation and each year its orbit of the sun — yet beyond these clocks and concepts, the actual experience of time can still seem mirage-like.

Nevertheless, the brain is hardwired to anticipate future events as a means of survival. Remembering what *has* occurred and anticipating what *might* occur can be an extremely useful skill. We have thrived as a species for millennia partly due to this ability. We can prepare for the hard winters ahead; we can anticipate droughts and plan for food shortages. This beats scavenging what is available in the frozen ground of winter. The brain is amazingly adept at preparing for the inevitable uncertainties of life.

Take, for example, climate change. Our ability to imagine and anticipate — to create models of future sea level changes and rising temperatures for this century — allow us to see the urgency of this impending crisis and to recognize that radical, scalable solutions are needed now for the survival of all species. Understanding the changes and impacts that are possible can help us create solutions to this potential catastrophe. But there is a difference between anticipating future needs — such as by saving for retirement — and predicting the future. We can never actually know what will happen. We need to remember that whatever future scenarios we imagine are at best predictions, a reasonable calculation of possibilities, a set of potential scenarios.

This is one reason this ability is also a source of stress. While anticipating disaster can help us prepare for calamity, we can also fret about all sorts of future scenarios that will never come to pass. Further, anxiety and worry are not in themselves helpful: they can actually thwart constructive action. Such feelings can steal us away from the riches of the present moment. Too often, we can get so stirred up with fear and angst about what we anticipate — whether we are imagining something realistic and unavoidable, like our own mortality, or something fantastical and unlikely to ever happen, like a meteor strike — that we fail to pay attention to what is before us.

If our concepts of the future are clearly constructs in our mind, so too is the past. We sometimes treat the shrine of memory as infallible and wholly accurate, as if memory were nothing but a raw data bank of facts. Nothing could be further from the truth. Our past is also "made up," a particular story we create by choosing and putting together only certain aspects of events and slices of memories.

We do this in the same way we make movies. During a film's production, hundreds of hours of footage are shot, and this is edited and manipulated into a two-hour narrative that evokes, say, the sinking of the *Titanic*. When it comes to our lives, our brain also picks and selects, edits and manipulates, in order to create a narrative of our personal history. We don't remember everything that happened, and what we recollect can be easily distorted by a few salient events. These can cast a light across all of our memories that slants our perspective into a particular story.

For instance, I have a few poignant memories of being psychologically bullied by close friends in high school, and this created a painful impression that cast a shadow over my teenage years. Afterward, and for some time, I looked upon that time with the view that I was living in a harsh, dog-eat-dog world. Moments of being bullied were rare, but they were significant enough that they dominated my mind, which replayed them often and constructed a painful narrative of adolescence. Today I can look back and see that this story, though it felt true then, was incomplete and inaccurate. Sometimes, it takes hearing another perspective — such as from a therapist or from someone else who was involved — to see an alternative vantage point, which can radically change our past narratives.

Much research has been done on the distortion of memory within the world of criminal investigation. An illuminating radio series on National Public Radio called *Serial* explored the world of a young man, Adnan Syed, who had been accused of murdering his girlfriend. He and his closest friends were asked to recollect all of their movements on a particular Monday afternoon, eleven weeks before, during an interview by police detectives. The radio host posed the question to listeners about whether they could remember exactly what they had been doing on the afternoon of a specific day three months ago. How accurate would your memory and recollection be?

We now know that identifications in "perpetrator lineups" can be horribly inaccurate. Innocent people have been sentenced to decades of prison time because of the faulty or biased memories of eyewitnesses to a crime. We assume that people recall accurately, but they often don't, and eyewitness statements are now considered insufficient to uphold a conviction.

The stories we tell ourselves about the past can be sources of great pain or delight. From the perspective of mindfulness, we learn to hold all of our thoughts, ideas, and perceptions lightly.

Thoughts, as the Zen saying goes, are like fingers pointing to the moon, but they are *not* the moon. Yet how easily we mistake our thoughts for reality. In meditation I instruct students to see that the thought of their foot is not their foot; it is just an idea, a mental representation. A thought about the future or the past in the same way is not actually real. It is only a fleeting mental image or memory. The extent that we mistake them for reality determines to some degree how much power they will have to affect us.

With practice we can learn to hold all thoughts of past and future with a spacious awareness. Our memories can inform us in helpful ways. They can be moments to cherish, like seeing our children take their first steps or recalling beautiful sunsets. And they can be the source of heartache, such as actions we regret or traumatic events from the past.

Lastly, all our measurements of time can fool us into thinking time is an object, something we can carve up or lose. We can live with an ever-increasing fear that time is running out or worry that there will never be enough of it. Ironically, we are in an age in which time is the most precious commodity, more valuable than money. The speed of life, of business and communication, has clearly increased, in large part due to our digitally connected world. With our smartphones and communication devices, we expect others and ourselves to be connected and responsive anytime, anywhere.

Alternately, slowing down, being present, and bringing awareness to our moment-to-moment experience allow us to see that all our rushing will never gain us "more time." We have to taste, directly, immediately, that time is both expansive and available. Our experience of time is directly determined by our perception and conception of it.

Through awareness and contemplative meditation, we discover how we live in a seamless, timeless present. Our direct experience of reality is that the past, present, and future all happen in this eternal now. Think about this: Where does the future happen? Through thoughts in our mind that arise in this moment. And where is the past? It is gone, except for memories and influences flitting through our mind and heart in the present. All is happening right here, right now.

When we see that, we understand that all we can do is be present for and take care of this moment. This is all there is and ever was. When we get this, we slip out of the prison of time scarcity and panic about the future. Life is simply a series of experiences unfolding in this ever-present moment. To know this is to be released from the trap and burden of the concept of time.

• **PRACTICE** •

Mindfulness of Time — Exploring Past and Future

Establish yourself in a comfortable meditation posture. Close your eyes and bring attention to your immediate experience. Observe how the five senses are only happening in the present. Notice how sights, sounds, smells, tastes, and touch happen only in *this* moment. See how the gift of sensory stimuli — like the sound of birds, the movement of breath, the smell of coffee, the shafts of sunlight coming through a window, the tastes in your mouth — invite you into the present over and over. The sound of traffic outside is not happening in the past or future. We can recall a previous experience of hiking in the mountains or imagine a future one, but even those thoughts are happening in our mind in this moment.

Remain aware of your unfolding experience of breath, body, sounds, and sensations. Notice how easily the mind's attention drifts from the sensory present into the conceptual mind, which imagines and prepares for the future. If your thoughts drift to planning, observe how real that future experience feels. Watch how easily you become absorbed in a world that feels as real as your body breathing. Can you see that the future scenario is just a thought? Mindfulness practice helps you wake up from this dream over and over again.

Similarly, notice if you start reminiscing. Observe how that experience feels real, as if you are actually reliving it. We get as lost in our memories as we do in our fantasy; they both seem equally real and compelling. Mindfulness helps us see and release such meanderings, so we return to the aliveness and preciousness of the present. With this awareness, observe how two-dimensional these past and future journeys are compared to the richness of the here and now.

As you end the meditation, stay cognizant throughout your day of when you become lost in a future landscape or mired in memories. Notice how they take you away from this unique moment. The more you unhook from these habits in your day, the less often you will choose to be lost in these imaginary worlds, both in meditation and in your life.

• • •

Chapter 14

Shining the Light
on Views and Beliefs

Do not seek after the truth,
simply cease to cherish opinions.
— THIRD ZEN PATRIARCH

The seventeenth-century Zen master Bankei once wrote, "Don't side with yourself." When I first heard this teaching, I was immediately struck by its originality and insightfulness. I pondered how many times I have been lost in endless arguments in my head defending my position, siding with my perspective. We become similarly consumed as we plan conversations, adamantly stating our viewpoint or holding court.

Our views tend to hold a lot of power over us. If you doubt that, consider what happens when someone challenges them: all hell can break loose. A view can form in the space of a few moments that can influence us for a lifetime. Watching one's fortune slip away during a stock market crash can instill the view that Wall Street is a terrible place to invest. If you get bitten as a child by a German shepherd — as I was — it can implant the belief that some dogs, but especially German shepherds, are not to be trusted. Our views, whether we adopt them consciously or unconsciously, are like the course we set for our ship, often affecting the direction of our life.

So many of our cherished beliefs are adopted unconsciously, implanted at an early age by family, culture, and church. How much energy do we pour into defending or advocating such beliefs? People can lose loved ones, friends, and jobs in fights over religion, ethics, and politics, and the more attached we are to our views, the more aggressively we tend to defend them. It is not uncommon for families to ban certain topics at the dinner table, as entrenched views easily cause arguments and worse. So it requires discernment to uncover those unconscious views that guide us. Often, they are hidden and only come out in our interactions with others.

For my friends Ginny and Joan the bell of love rang at first glance. They shared so much in common: interests, political perspectives, musical tastes, and their work as child psychologists. They both longed to have children, and quite soon after they got married, they happily gave birth to twins, two healthy, lively boys. That's when both the joys and troubles started.

Unbeknownst to them, they each held strong, divergent views about parenting, which reflected differences in their own parents and upbringings. Ginny's parents were "old school." They were kind but very strict, believing kids shouldn't be mollycoddled but instead taught to toughen up. For instance, crying infants, they believed, should learn to comfort themselves. Joan's parents, on the other hand, were very doting; their babies never left their arms. Ginny and Joan quickly got into disagreements and then bitter arguments about how to respond to their infants' distress. They continued to justify their beliefs about parenting and the rightness of their positions until they were clearly at loggerheads. Eventually, they went to therapy to find resolution, and this work helped them unpack their views and see their attachments to them. They realized they were both acting out of old family beliefs that had existed for generations and that lived unconsciously within them.

When I first began studying Buddhist teachings in my late teens and early twenties, I went from being an anarchist, punk, antiestablishment rebel to a proselytizer about that religion. In a short span of time, the teachings of mindfulness transformed my life, and I wanted everyone else to reap the benefits. I preached passionately to my loved ones. What I didn't understand then was that you can't just unleash unmetabolized views onto others and expect them to be interested! And you certainly can't convert anyone by doing that.

Of course, the prevalence and power of views are not a modern phenomenon. For centuries, people believed the world was flat and dared not sail to the end of the world for fear of falling off! The Roman Catholic Church was convinced all the planets and stars revolved around the earth, not the sun. Astronomers like Galileo were persecuted for heresy for daring to say otherwise. Indeed, these are the types of views that are hardest to recognize: those that are shared by an entire society.

We only need to look at wars throughout the ages to see the painful legacy of this. In the last century, clashes over political belief systems, whether in the name of communism or capitalism, have killed millions, while in the distant past, wars over religious beliefs were even more common, like the centuries-old battles between Christianity and Islam. The human psyche seems hardwired to seek meaning and understanding, as well as, sadly, to defend one's worldview to the very end. The bitter irony of people killing and persecuting heretics in the name of God never ceases to amaze. It reveals the immense power that views have, both personally and in society.

Through paying attention to the views that flow through our own psyche, we can become aware of our own belief systems, particularly those we didn't choose but have adopted unconsciously. We can then assess whether our views are actually true, in alignment with reality, and support our well-being, or if they are harmful. For instance, if we identify with the belief that we are not good enough, we can understand that belief as the voice of the inner critic or a message perhaps absorbed in childhood, not an actual fact. Often such views can live within us for decades unnoticed, blending in like white noise. When left undetected, they can wreak painful havoc in our life. With awareness, we can see clearly the damage they cause and learn to release them, or at least to cease believing them.

We can do the same with our beliefs about others. Do our views of others reflect bias, prejudice, or fear? This can be easiest to see when nations are in conflict. When other countries have different beliefs or viewpoints, citizens are often encouraged — by politicians, protagonists, and media propaganda — to fear or demonize them, to see "them" as not just different than "us" but even evil. This conditioning might target other customs, cultural perspectives, or religious beliefs. At its worst, such conditioning hardens our hearts and closes us off to whole categories of people as the "other," thus justifying war, discrimination, and, at its worst, genocide. This occurred in Rwanda with horrific consequences, where up to eight hundred thousand people were killed in one hundred days, partly instigated by propaganda fueling rifts between Hutu and Tutsi tribes.

With mindfulness, we attend not just to beliefs but to our relationship with them. For example, the more attached we are to our views, the more vociferously we hold on to and defend them. Entrenched attachment to views is what, in its extreme form, can lead to violence and hatred, as clearly evidenced in countless acts of racism and homophobia worldwide. But self-awareness can help us see our mind and its thoughts clearly for what they are: a thought is just a thought; a view is just a view. A thought's power is in the authority we bestow upon it and how much we believe it to be true. What we do with that information can be the difference between harm and harmony.

One of the most entrenched, unconscious beliefs is the notion of permanence. How often do we suffer when things change? We tend to fall into the trap of believing that life will continue as it is, and when things are good, we desperately want that to be true. But life constantly undermines our cherished belief of continuity. We often rail against change, yet the more we fight against transience, the more constricted we become and the more we suffer, since life will always keep pulling the rug out from under our illusion of stasis.

Perhaps the most pivotal view we cherish concerns our sense of self. We tend to believe we are separate, independent individuals. One example is the notion of the rugged individual in North American culture. However, nothing could be further from the truth. Who and what we are is embedded in a matrix of interconnection, constantly under the influence of interpersonal, environmental, social, and political forces. Mindful investigation reveals the falsehood of separateness by showing us how interdependent we are and how much the world influences us in every moment. Ironically, our very beliefs demonstrate that. We can come to discern that our views and opinions are rarely our own but are instead the result of multiple influences.

In conclusion, mindfulness, or the clear knowing of what is, helps us see through the veils of our beliefs, views, and ideas. These views are powerful, and they influence our perception, thoughts, and actions. Being aware of our beliefs is essential if we are to understand the forces that move us, that can influence whether we cause suffering or cultivate the conditions for peace and happiness, both for ourselves and for others.

• PRACTICE •

Mindfulness of Views

In this practice, write for a few minutes in a journal about all the views that feel important to you. Write about whatever comes to mind, stream-of-consciousness style. Then take a few more minutes to write about all the views you have of yourself. Lastly, jot down your views about meditation and about your ability or capacity in mindfulness practice.

Now read through what you have written. Do you agree with everything you wrote? Does every statement seem accurate and true? Inquire into the origins of some of your long-held, cherished beliefs. Observe what happens when you agree with a view versus when you feel as if a belief is neither objective nor accurate.

Another way to explore views is to engage in a friendly debate with a friend. Choose someone you trust who has an opposing view on a particular subject. As you engage in conversation, notice when and how you become entrenched in a particular position. Pay attention to how attached you feel, or to your need to be right. What happens when your friend challenges your view or questions it? Do you identify with your point of view so strongly that as your friend disagrees with your view, it feels as if they are attacking you personally? The more attached we are to our views, the more entrenched we become in our position and the more aggressively we defend it and become reactive when we are challenged.

To loosen up any clinging to your own views and opinions, try putting yourself in the position of the opposing point of view. Ideally, we want to be fluid, to be able to see all sides and perspectives. That helps us see the reasons for the other person's views so we can interact from a place of understanding and compassion, not judgment. It might also lead to a compromise that solves the problem of apparent disagreement.

• • •

Chapter 15

Knowing Dissatisfaction and Its Causes

I can't get no satisfaction.
— MICK JAGGER

I remember going on holiday with a friend to a luxury resort in Southern California. We had booked a deluxe cabin on the bluff overlooking the ocean. It was a spectacular setting with a stunning vista of ocean and sky. The cottage was well appointed in a Cape Cod–type beach style. I thought it was a dreamy place to vacation. My friend, however, had a very different standard than I, and she was not altogether impressed. She was used to high-quality hotels, and no sooner had we walked into our suite than she ran her fingers along the wooden blinds in the window and noticed a thin layer of dust, which in her opinion should have been cleaned prior to our arrival. This set a tone of disappointment for her, though I would have never noticed or cared.

This is just a small example of how we can find dissatisfaction in any experience. This quality is referred to in the Pali language as *dukkha*, a characteristic that runs through every human experience. This complex word has multiple meanings, but essentially it refers to the unsatisfactory nature of all things, the perennial disenchant-ment or disappointment we can feel about any experience. It is also translated as "stress," or the frustration of nothing ever quite "do-ing it" for us. As a result, we perpetually seek pleasure without ever quite quenching that need. No matter how good something seems to be, we often have a niggling sense of dissatisfaction.

Consider this for yourself. How often are you excited for an event — attending a concert, joining a family outing, playing a sports game, watching a movie, or simply relaxing in the garden — and when that experience comes, something interferes with that pleasure: some persistent back pain, your neighbor's lawn mower, performance anxiety, people whispering during the film or con-cert, or simply being too tired to fully enjoy what is happening? Few moments live up to our anticipation, which can leave us dis-satisfied, no matter how pleasant things are otherwise. This expe-rience of *dukkha* is like an ill-fitting wheel that creates a slight rub of discord with every turn. This feeling is subtle but enough to impart discontent.

Rather than ignore or turn away from this dissatisfaction, with mindfulness, we can inquire directly into the unsatisfactory nature of things. How does this help? The more we are aware of this qual-ity of experience, the less reactive and surprised we are likely to be when things are not quite what we'd hoped. With awareness, we can notice how experience often falls short and even peak moments fail to last. This enables us to appreciate each moment for what it is, with all of its imperfect and fleeting beauty. This interrupts the frustrating tendency to want or demand more from experiences than they are able to deliver.

The world is full of pleasurable things, but there is always some kind of subtle rub that accompanies them. The laws of en-tropy and impermanence mean that everything changes, all highs are sure to fade. All pleasures suffer from habituation, in which their impact inevitably diminishes. No matter how delicious fresh-picked strawberries are, by the fifth or tenth piece of fruit, the taste will fail to deliver the same punch as the first. That rule runs through all sensory experience. I happen to be a chocolate lover, but there is only so much I can eat before it all starts tasting the same and ceases to interest me.

The real question is, how do we respond to such disappointment? Often we complain or feel dissed, and we hunger for more. Sometimes, we don't even wait for the pleasurable activity to end: as we eat ice cream or enjoy a sunset, we sense its demise and start chasing the next pleasure. However sublime a conversation or a concert is, if it goes on for hours, our interest generally wanes and we start to muse on what's next. Relationships are not spared. They often begin with a passionate honeymoon phase, but as we all know, the honeymoon high rarely sustains itself. Given this reality, how do we step off the wheel of relentlessly reaching for more?

By discerning how no experience can provide lasting satisfaction, we stop expecting that some experience might. We unhook from the painful tendency to grasp for the next shiny thing, and we learn to meet each experience as it is, without clinging or holding on. We simply enjoy each moment while it is here, and for what it is, not looking for or demanding more. This can bring a huge sense of relief.

However, just because we cultivate mindfulness, we don't suddenly stop seeking pleasant experiences. But we can understand that such pleasures are transient by nature, and wisdom can help keep us from seeking happiness in the wrong places or demanding lasting fulfillment from things that can't provide it. We abide in a middle way between indulgence and rejection. We appreciate when beauty and pleasure arrive and remain untroubled and not disappointed when such moments pass.

The Buddha, in his insight, spoke to the deeper layers of dissatisfaction in the human condition: being alive means we must inevitably confront the hard realities of aging, sickness, and death. In addition, he said, life involves a triumvirate of challenges: (1) not getting what you want; (2) losing what you have; and (3) being separated from what you love. These painful situations run through the veins of life, and however blessed our life may be, we will have to face such difficulties.

The point isn't to avoid being deprived of what we want nor to prevent losing what we love, since these things happen to everyone. The question is how do we relate to these vexing challenges when they occur? As Professor Randy Pausch spoke about in his book *The Last Lecture*: "We cannot change the cards we are dealt, just how we play the hand." This is what determines our well-being more than the particular circumstances or challenges we face.

For example, Aishin, a mindfulness student in her thirties from the San Francisco Bay Area, attended my nature meditation teacher training. She is a living example to me of how one learns to skillfully and eloquently play a challenging hand. In her teens she came down with a very painful joint condition, Ehlers-Danlos syndrome, that made every physical movement a challenge. It literally hurt to move, walk, sit, and even lie down. Upon waking, pain wracked her body, and it didn't let up until she fell asleep. She came to meditation desperate for some relief, but it did not deliver in the way she hoped. Meditation did not make the joint cramps go away. However, she learned important skills that helped her navigate the adversity.

Drawing on her mindfulness practice, Aishin began to shift her harsh attitude and judgment toward the pain. She saw how contracting against the pain just created more tension. Instead, she learned to meet her searing sensations with a kinder attention, which allowed some ease in relation to the discomfort. In addition, she realized she was not beholden to always attend to the pain. The freedom of awareness, she discovered, allowed her to direct attention in ways that created a sense of ease or space. This is an essential skill when pain is your constant companion. Making peace with the condition of her body enabled her to find peace in her heart, despite the burden.

Not only does life teach us that we can't always get what we want, but life can also give us what we don't want. Most of the time these are temporary problems, but not always. No one wants their child to bring home head lice from school or catch a cold; no one wants to hit traffic on the way to work. More seriously, nobody wishes to contract a degenerative illness or lose their youthful vigor or vitality. No one desires to lose their job, their house to a fire, or their savings to an economic downturn. No one wants to live in constant pain or to die, and life can often seem random and cruel when it challenges us with these things. Yet such adversity is simply part of the human predicament.

What can we do? We can, and sometimes do, collapse in self-pity, rage against God, or blame ourselves. However, we can also learn to adapt and embrace such conditions with kind presence and self-compassion. Not only can mindfulness help us meet and accept our difficulties, but it helps us have compassion for ourselves when acceptance is hard, when we fail or struggle to find a skillful response. We can't take misfortune away, which comes with the territory of being human. Loss is part of the harsh fabric of life. But through practice we can learn to navigate this terrain, to meet challenges as they arrive, to not take them personally, and to avoid judging ourselves for doing something wrong. As we mature, we can learn to meet loss and change with tenderness and surrender and find an ease with it all that we didn't think was possible.

• **PRACTICE** •

Understanding Dissatisfaction

Contemplating what is unsatisfying is not a popular pastime. However, doing so can be remarkably fruitful. As you begin any activity, like taking a walk, eating dinner, or exercising, bring awareness to whatever is pleasurable about the experience. Then notice how your experience of it changes. Become curious about the entire process — about the complexity of whatever you enjoy, and how any delightful experience has a beginning, middle, and end.

For example, when you eat, fully enjoy what is delicious about your meal, and then consider how you feel when your plate is empty. Are you satisfied or disappointed? Do you long for more? If we follow that longing, we could make ourselves sick by overeating. The body reminds us to stay in balance, even though our mind often overrides that sensation, such as when we eat too many chocolates! By bringing awareness to the fleeting aspect of simple pleasures, we can discover how we relate to all experience. That pleasure is temporary is no reason not to enjoy it. However, why let enjoyment, simply because it's temporary, lead to dissatisfaction, stress, and suffering?

Just as pleasure has its unsatisfactory side, so too does every other human experience. Bring this same awareness to any moment of gratification. Be curious about your own reactions when life is flourishing. Can you simply enjoy it, or do you anticipate its ending and so become anxious or restless and undermine your own positive experience? Be aware even in times of contentment how easy it is to feel an itch of doubt or discontent. Can you recognize that dissatisfaction within even the greatest of experiences, with the awareness that it is a natural part of human experience? As we explore our experience in this way, we come to hold things and experience more lightly, neither demanding that they continue nor fretting when the highs begin to change and fade.

• • •

Chapter 16

Learning the Wisdom
of Letting Go

To let go does not mean to get rid of. To let go means to let be.
When we let be with compassion, things come and go on their own.
— JACK KORNFIELD

Letting go, the process of not holding on, is an important facet of mindfulness practice and a key determinant in our well-being. It is the potential for how we can relate to each moment's experience without contention or trying to grab or control it. As soon as we grasp something, it's as if we strangle it. That is particularly true if we cling to another person or to something that will inevitably fade. A cause of so much of our anguish is this tendency to grasp after, hold on to, or reject experience. This leads to an endless struggle with what is and leaves us perennially ill at ease.

However, this habit is deep-rooted. My friend Leslie told me a story recently that points to how grasping starts when we are very young. Learning to let go can also start at an early age as well. Leslie wrote to me about her three-year-old son:

> Kiko's morning meltdown today was because he made up his mind that he wanted syrupy waffles. My "no" and

offering of oatmeal with honey and a few rainbow sprinkles led to a good fifteen-minute cry. He was so stuck on the idea of syrup that he couldn't relax enough to hear me explain that he could have a waffle after he ate his oatmeal. He'd calm down for a few seconds and look at the oatmeal just long enough to tell me how it was too bumpy or not bumpy enough. Eventually, he found a book he wanted me to read to him at the table and calmed down enough to actually enjoy the sprinkles on his oats. While his three-year-old tendency to freak out over whatever it is he wants in that moment can be challenging, thankfully it's matched by his ability to just let it go as soon as something else shiny catches his attention.

Fortunately, we are not simply victims to this process. We can shift our response depending upon how we view each experience. Marcus Aurelius, the Roman philosopher and emperor, put it this way: "If you are distressed by anything external [or internal], the pain is not due to the thing itself, but to your estimate of it; and this you have the power to revoke at any moment." This is as true now as it was two thousand years ago.

What is remarkable about human beings is their ability to express this principle no matter how wretched the circumstances. In *Man's Search for Meaning*, Viktor Frankl wrote about his experiences in the Nazi concentration camps. He observed how even in the most despicable of conditions, people still had the power to decide how they related to what was happening. He wrote: "Everything can be taken from a man but one thing: the last of the human freedoms — to choose one's attitude in any given set of circumstances, to choose one's own way." Having choice over one's attitude or relationship to experience is the potential of what mindfulness practice offers. It is the doorway to liberty.

I recall talking to a spiritual teacher in India who had been held as a prisoner of war in a brutal internment camp in Japan during World War II. He said one of his daily tasks was to be lowered into a septic tank full of human feces, shoulder-high, and to empty the tank out with a bucket. The stench, heat, and revulsion almost overwhelmed him. Yet deep in his psyche, he found the space of awareness that could hold and even transcend the toxic horror of that situation. He described how hard it was to find inner resources to face that challenge day after day. Yet the pressure of the situation birthed a realization that awareness contained within it the power to hold any experience. Despite how wretched those circumstances were, he was able to access a presence that was unperturbed and free, neither caught in reaction nor grasping for something other, even amid that noxious environment. That is letting go on a profound level!

Thankfully, we don't have to experience such extremes to discover this. We explore this in our meditation practice and in our life on a daily basis. Ajahn Chah, a renowned Thai meditation master, once said: "If you want a little peace, let go a little. If you want a lot of peace, let go a lot. If you want complete peace, then let go completely." That instruction is quite simple. However, like many things regarding mindfulness practice, it is hard to accomplish that level of release.

I often smile wryly when I hear the sometimes glib, co-opted New Age advice to "just let go" in response to some hardship or struggle. For example, someone may be advised to "just let go" of their fear, struggle, grief, or loss, whether they are gripped in white-knuckle panic during a turbulent flight or mourning the death of a loved one. Well-meaning people say, "If you would only let go, you could be free from pain."

The obvious response to this is: "If I could let go, I would." It is when we can't let go of a feeling, thought, or reactive state that the real work begins. Of course, many reactions and thoughts can be released. We can at times recognize the futility of speculative worry and put aside those thoughts. We can see our frustration at rush-hour traffic and put it down by listening to the radio or taking some deeper breaths. But at other times, "just letting go" is not possible in the moment. For example, when we are gripped by grief, heartbreak, and loss, "letting go" of our emotions is not only implausible but often not healthy. What is required is to feel fully those painful feelings and allow them to unfold and release over time.

In this case, *letting go happens through the process of letting be.* The grieving process takes time and is a necessary part of healing. We can't rush the tears, nor can we skip them. With grief and other powerful emotions, "just letting go" and trying to move on too quickly can be a type of avoidance, denial, or "spiritual bypass." Wise mindfulness is the ability to meet ourselves as we are, with patient, tender awareness, and allow the sadness, tears, and all. It is only by surrendering to grief and heartbreak that we eventually come to resolution with loss. Through that process, we can find peace by not fighting, by not resisting or thinking our experience should be different or our emotions should be over.

Laurie shared with me her story of learning to let go during her dog's death:

Through my practice I was able to support my beloved poodle, Peanut, through her transition without my own grief and attachment interfering. The dread of imagining my life without her initially thwarted my ability to feel the deep sadness in the moment, as well as the intense love and growing tenderness that I felt for Peanut, who became more dear to me in her final days than I ever could have imagined. Instead of avoiding the painful reality of her loss, I opened myself to the experience. I began to notice how fleeting each emotion was. Amidst the tremendous feelings of loss were moments of bliss with just being with her in her final moments. Peanut's death and dying was one of the most beautiful and painful experiences of my life, one that was held in equanimity through my awareness of each precious moment.

The practice of letting be also applies to being with physical discomfort. I have, like many people, been afflicted over the years with chronic lower back pain. Sometimes it is worse than others. But it has also been a great teacher. Pain acts like a mirror. When I wince and contract around the spasms, it is as if my body condenses into a knot of hardness. This contraction seems like a natural reaction, but it just intensifies the sensations. The suffering worsens when I resist, judge, and fight, or if I collapse into self-pity or feel like a victim.

When I can meet back spasms with spacious awareness, I don't resist or avoid feeling the pain, twinge, cramp, or piercing sensations. I notice it is unpleasant, and I acknowledge that I really don't want it or like it. Acknowledging both the experience and my grumblings about it helps access a sense of ease, even though the difficulty remains. As I've said before, it's not what happens that defines us, but how we relate to it.

Mindfulness helps us both illuminate our reactivity and recognize just how painful that activated state is. This provides the impetus to release the grip of whatever we are consumed by. We all get reactive, but we don't always realize how unhappy it makes us. For instance, I have a friend in LA who loves to drive but hates "bad" drivers. As we drive, if he gets stuck behind a slow driver, he frequently has a tantrum, exclaiming about how terrible their driving is and describing everything they are doing wrong. My friend erupts in such hostility you would think the person had delivered a personal insult. These tirades are amusing from a distance, but they are consuming and painful when we are caught up in them. My friend is not alone in this. I know others who get similarly riled up watching a football game or when someone takes their parking place or expresses a different political opinion.

We can all get upset and reactive, whether about the smallest of things or over deeply important matters. It all depends on the strength of our attachment in the moment. However, it is important to remember that simply letting go, or nongrasping, does not mean passivity. We can care deeply about the world and act to change what needs improving, such as working to relieve the suffering of others and helping to end injustice, poverty, and racism. We can respond to problems in life that cause pain, not with blinkered, knee-jerk reactivity, but with passionate engagement and a compassionate desire to help. It is the space of letting go that frees us up to respond more effectively to such things.

• PRACTICE •

The Practice of Letting Go

In meditation, the habit of grasping and holding on can be as pervasive as in life, though more insidious. Begin your meditation by turning awareness to your body. As you establish a healthy posture, be aware if there is a twinge of grasping, of wanting your posture to be more comfortable than it is. Notice if there is a trace of the fixing mind state that is rarely content no matter how perfect your posture is. See if you can simply be with your physical experience, whatever it is like.

In the same way, bring attention to breathing. Breathe naturally, allowing the breath to find its own rhythm, to breathe itself.

Then notice any subtle or not-so-subtle attempts to control, change, or manipulate the breath to your liking. Are you trying, for example, to have a different, longer, deeper, calmer breath? Notice any grasping, such as wanting or demanding that the breath be a certain way.

Attending to the breath is a barometer for how we control or grasp even the smallest thing. Does what you observe in how you try to control or subtly change your breath relate, or not, to any similar impulse to control your thoughts, your spouse, your work, your children, or your environment? Notice without judgment the deep-rooted habit of grasping in yourself. Nonjudgmental awareness allows us to disengage and create some space in which to release the pattern. When you notice the grip around your breath, you can shift your attention elsewhere, to sounds or other parts of the body, which can allow any subtle urge to control to naturally release.

Next, observe any grasping or reactivity in relation to your emotions. In meditation and in life, we often try to hold on to pleasurable states and reject uncomfortable ones. Is this true right now? Do you clutch after bliss, peace, calm, or joy, and are you pushing away or rejecting fear, loss, or other more challenging emotions? Both are reactive movements toward or away from experience. Either impulse can create inner tension, or conflict with what is actually happening, and leave us restless and discontent.

As you notice this, can you release the reactivity and orient to meet and feel whatever emotion is present? If that is not possible, then bring awareness to the reactive state itself. No matter what the contraction or fixation is, like fear or longing, turn to it with mindfulness, which allows a more complete embracing and understanding of it. The more we can hold such states in awareness, the less likely we are to act out from them.

Next, notice any grasping or reactivity to your thinking.

While meditating, do you resist, judge, or contract around your busy mind and its commentaries and memories? What about your thoughts themselves? Do they express grasping in the form of fantasies, rehashing an argument or desire for any number of things or experiences? Awareness can be like the sun, evaporating clouds of thought upon contact. Rather than engage or reject the flurry of thoughts, shine the light of awareness upon them, which allows the ability to release mental fixations.

Lastly, track your relationship to the environment, including to temperature, smells, and sounds. Noises you hear during meditation are an excellent place to practice letting go. Notice any reactivity to sounds: Do you grasp after silence or resist unwanted noise? If there is a contraction against certain noises, bring awareness to the aversion itself. The more we can bring mindfulness to reactivity, the less we are caught in it, which expands our capacity to be with a fuller range of experience.

We may dislike many sounds, like traffic, truck engines, people shouting, and dissonant music. Cultivating the space of nongrasping allows us to hear these sounds without becoming riled. They are just sounds, fleeting, often unpleasant, but all workable. Thus we learn to move through the world with greater peace. Notice this for yourself directly as you meditate. Notice how mindfulness gives us the ability to hold all experience with a nonreactive attention.

• • •

Chapter 17

Freedom from Attachment

Great trouble comes from not knowing what is enough.
Great conflict arises from wanting too much. When we know
when enough is enough, there will always be enough.
— LAO-TZU

I have heard that when monkey hunters set traps, they drill small holes in coconuts and put a banana or peanuts inside. When a monkey reaches their hand in and grabs the food, they get caught because they can't remove their clenched fist from the coconut and they won't release the food. We are no different. We get attached to so many things in life, often to our detriment, that it seems like it must be in our DNA.

Living in a consumer culture doesn't help. Years ago, a magazine ad for a Ford pickup even commodified consumerism as a spiritual pursuit. In the ad, a man sits in front of his truck surrounded by all the toys and gear any young adventurer might want: a surfboard, scuba equipment, a TV, a computer, skis, golf clubs, climbing gear, a guitar, a dog, and on and on. Below, the caption says: "Spence put a new twist on an old philosophy. To be one *with* everything, he says, you've got to have one *of* everything. That's why he also has the new Ford Ranger. So he can seek wisdom on a mountain top. Take off in hot pursuit of enlightenment. And connect with Mother Earth. By looking no further than into the planet's coolest four-door compact pickup. He says it gives him easy access to inner peace. Which makes him one happy soul." When we are bombarded with advertising like this, no wonder we get attached to stuff!

Mindfulness can help illuminate our attachments, not just to our stuff, but also to our preferences, views, beliefs, self-image, and a host of other things. In all cases, the strength of our attachment influences the extent of the pain we feel when we can't have or we lose what we want. Yet we rarely realize how tightly we hold something until it is challenged. Then we feel the full force of this reaction, as a mama bear protects her cubs.

Sometimes we don't see our fixations until someone takes away the very thing we cling to. We may not feel attached to coffee until we can't have it for a week while on a cleanse. We might feel relaxed about money until the stock market crashes and financial insecurity sparks panic. We may not realize until retirement just how dependent we are on our professional identity. We take youth for granted until our hair thins and laugh lines etch deeper into our face. On a silent meditation retreat, we may feel a desperate need to check our phone and be entertained. We grasp in so many ways. The key is to recognize all the myriad ways we get attached, for it is this awareness that allows us to disengage from the vice-like grip of attachment and find peace.

For myself, I have a certain preference for peace and quiet at home. I am reminded of the strength of this predilection whenever construction workers are jackhammering nearby, gardeners turn on their noisy leaf blowers, or my neighbor's TV is turned up loud. My own reactivity can erupt quickly to this noise, and it's humbling to see how fast I can go from reading or quietly writing to frustration, contraction, and blaming. Then, reminded of the strength of my attachment, as evidenced by the clutching in my belly or my judgmental thoughts, I can reestablish awareness, which allows me to hear the sounds and be present to the noise without the inner disruption of reactivity.

Of course, no one likes to be disturbed by loud noise. And everyone has preferences. Likes and dislikes are a natural part of the human experience. This is even a biological imperative: to survive, we prefer safe environments, nourishing food, and companionship. There is also nothing wrong with preferring peace and quiet or a particular flavor of ice cream, car, or sports team. It's fine to prefer certain political systems, social mores, and religious ideals.

Opinions and predilections are not problems in themselves. Our level of attachment to what we prefer, however, can wreak havoc in our lives. If we demand, expect, or insist that an experience, other people, or the political or social world conform to what we want, we will suffer. The equation is simple: the larger the attachment, the greater the pain. We create so much unnecessary distress this way because life is inherently out of our control. It does not bend to our will or our desires.

My English friend Phillip is quite attached to sunshine. Many people are. But because he lives in northern England, bright days are relatively few and fleeting! The real problem, however, is that Phillip actively resents every cloudy or rainy day. He tends to become contracted and grumpy when the inevitable rain and stormy skies blanket the landscape, and so he spends much of his time in a bad mood. Sunshine may make him happy, but his attachment to sunny days, far more than the actual rain, is what fuels his unhappiness.

The Third Zen Patriarch, a famous Chinese Chan meditation master of the fifth century, wrote: "The Great Way is not difficult for those not attached to their preferences. To set up what you like against what you dislike is the disease of the mind. Make the smallest distinction, however, and heaven and earth are infinitely set apart." Jesus of Nazareth pointed to something similar when he said that it is easier for a camel to go through the eye of a needle than for a rich man to enter the Kingdom of Heaven. That is, our attachments to wealth and possessions are what stand in the way of spiritual peace. The Great Way, the peace we all seek, is already here, but only if we let go of attachments to our preferences, if we release the tight fist that grasps after what we want and recoils when what we desire eludes us.

Consider for yourself: What is it you are attached to that causes dis-ease? What for you sets heaven and earth apart? How do you demand that life be a certain way? Do you insist on solitude, a slim body, a certain political party to be in office, your partner to be more communicative, or the need to own a new car every year? We all have preferences. They are not problems in themselves. The key is to make them conscious, to realize we have a choice and so not be driven or enslaved by our attachments.

Sometimes I laugh at myself about all the small ways my mind gets hooked by attachment. I once became particularly fond of a blue Patagonia shirt that I wore every time I backpacked. I must have worn it for ten years, and I associated it with every hiking trip. Then one day it got caught in a bramble patch and an arm ripped off. I was shocked, and I immediately resented the thorns for tearing apart the shirt that had become my wilderness companion! Then I had to laugh at my own pettiness. We cannot rid ourselves of preferences, and I'm not suggesting we try. However, we can come to release the grip of our attachments to them, so we can find the space and ease to dance with life, rather than demand that it conform to our desires or have tantrums when it doesn't.

Another common place I see my own attachment is when I watch my favorite boyhood soccer team on TV. I love soccer and am very attached to the success of my team, Newcastle United.

However, this is a bit of a setup for misery, since my team is notoriously hopeless, often lying close to the bottom of the Premier League they play in. Yet I continue to watch in the vain hope of a great victory or a thrashing defeat of an archrival team. Of course, my attachment to my soccer team creates as much or more anxiety, stress, and tension as joy. During a game, I sense my body become tense, my breath shorten, and my heart and mind tighten. When I do, I try to release my attachment to the result, which allows me to relax some and actually enjoy the very sport I am watching to bring me pleasure! I remind myself that it's just a game and will be over in ninety minutes, which also helps me to lighten up.

Indeed, a useful support for living free from attachment is to realize the transience of everything. As the Taoist philosopher Lao-tzu wrote: "If you realize that all things change, there is nothing you will try to hold on to." The wisdom of awareness is our greatest ally here. It helps us see how nothing lasts, how we are unable to hold on to anything because experience is always slipping through our fingers like sand. This knowing allows us to hold everything lightly. Rather than feel entitled to what we want, and feel animosity toward what we don't want, we foster the conditions to grow the heart of acceptance and ease for whatever happens.

• PRACTICE •
Abiding in Nonattachment

Find a comfortable posture. If you are sitting on a chair, have both feet on the floor and keep your spine upright yet relaxed. Place your hands on your legs and either close your eyes or keep your gaze lowered.

First attend to any sounds. As you listen, notice if you have any reaction to or preference regarding the soundscape. Notice which sounds you prefer, like birdsong or rain, and which you don't, such as sirens, traffic, or mechanical noise coming from a heater or AC system. Be present to whether you are attached to particular sounds and whether that attachment triggers any reactions. If you feel contracted against a certain sound or grasp after quiet, notice what that is like. Feel the rub of discomfort that arises when attachments create a certain desire for or resistance to experience.

Notice how the spaciousness of awareness can support you to release the demand that sounds or experience be a particular way. Is it possible to let go and simply be with whatever sounds are present? If it helps, remember that all sounds are fleeting. No matter how pleasant or unwanted, sounds will not last long. Observe how much more peace is available when you simply let sounds be, letting them wash through you like wind blows between the limbs of a tree.

Now become aware of your body. Scan your physical experience. Notice the places that feel pleasant and those that feel tight, tense, fatigued, or in pain. Then observe any attachment that arises, whether preferring what is relaxed and pleasant or wanting to avoid or be rid of what is challenging, achy, sharp, or restless.

Observe how you may want your body to feel a particular way and what happens when it does not. Do you reject the experience, hate it, contract around it, or long for a different experience? If so, notice how that makes you feel. Rejecting ourselves or our experience can be alienating and painful and can even create more physical discomfort. If it helps, remember that all is transient, and notice if this knowledge allows you to find ease within the ebb and flow of your physical experience.

Next, bring awareness to your mind and heart. In the quiet of meditation, notice any attachment related to your emotions and mental states. Do you want to feel and think in a particular way? Do you want your mind to be quiet and your heart to be happy?

Observe how grasping or contracting can arise with these prefer-ences. When we demand that we be a certain way, it creates a lot of unnecessary internal conflict. If it helps, remember that what we think and feel changes ceaselessly, and we rarely remain in one state for very long.

When you end the meditation, maintain your attention on how attachment functions as you go about your day. Notice how eas-ily you can get attached to wanting events to go a particular way, such as a conversation, a work meeting, or a sports event. When that happens, without judgment, notice the tension or contraction this can create. Life is full of unexpected events, many of them unwanted and challenging. Paying attention to the force of attach-ment creates the possibility of disengaging from it. This can help you navigate life's innumerable vagaries and find some ease within the uncontrollable nature of life.

• • •

Chapter 18

The Changing Nature of Self

Yesterday I was clever, so I wanted to change the world.
Today I am wise, so I am changing myself.
— RUMI

When we are born, we enter this world without a sense of self, free from any identity. We are simply an undifferentiated flow of experience. However, by the time we are less than a year old, the mind has begun to construct a sense of self, one built from a conglomeration of physical, emotional, mental, and relational processes. As we age, that notion of "self" becomes more solid, definite, and real, so much so that we genuinely believe that our image or identity is who we are.

Yet this idea of self is not as substantive or enduring as we like to think. It is a constructed notion, based on a matrix of ideas, memories, perceptions, and reflections from people and the world around us. As we investigate the "self" with awareness, we see that it is as elusive as it is unreal. It is like a mirage or rainbow that appears solid and substantive, but under close examination, it fails to have any enduring existence.

The felt sense of our self is a defining aspect of our personal existence. We know ourselves by a sense or feeling of "me-ness." Hard to describe and define, this identity is a familiar sea of feelings, thoughts, perceptions, bodily experiences, and memories. Sometimes we call this our personality, but if we look closely, we notice how this, too, is just a concoction of fleeting experiences that change day by day, hour by hour.

We tend to think of our sense of self and our identity as fixed and enduring over time. But are they really? On wilderness retreats, I invite students to contemplate their own sense of self while in nature, and I often offer my own experience as an example of how the self is constantly in motion, flighty, changeable, and elusive.

One morning during the retreat, after a cold night camping on uneven ground, I wake up having slept badly. I may feel a bit irritable and tired, and I notice "grumpy Mark" is present. He tends to look at the world somewhat negatively. From the perspective of that "self," the day's activities will look like hard work. Then I will have a strong cup of black tea, my morning ritual, which helps wake me up and brightens my mind. Between the caffeine and splashing my face with cold water, I will feel brighter, more positive. In the short period of time it takes to drink some tea, "grumpy Mark" vacates and I feel excited about spending the day outdoors. I start to look around at the natural beauty all around me and feel rejuvenated, inspired, and happy.

This buoyant sense of self may not last long. I might remember a disagreement I had with a teaching colleague the night before who critiqued my course structure and teaching style, and now reactivity surfaces: I become angry over being judged; I feel a little hurt inside. A righteous personality quickly emerges, one filled with indignation, and this self gets swept up in a flurry of planning how to rebut my colleague. Usually, after a few minutes, I recognize this reactivity and laugh at myself: "the mindfulness teacher" planning revenge! A wiser self now takes the place of the vengeful one, and I adopt a different view of my colleague: he is, in fact, an old friend whom I know appreciates me and has only my best interests at heart.

Seeking further relief from that confining straightjacket of anger, I decide to hike to a nearby meadow, a beautiful landscape of emerald grasses. Soft dawn light illuminates the ponderosa trees that flank the meadow. I breathe in the fresh mountain air and feel a moment of heartfelt gratitude for being in this magical place, far from the bustle of my urban life. I'm transported into an expansive sense of self that feels love and appreciation for nature and its beauty. In that expansion, I feel the rigidness of the angry one fully dissolve.

I then sit at the foot of an old Douglas fir tree and meditate. As I abide in that contemplative state, my mind quiets, my heart opens, and I have a sense of merging with the landscape. In that quietude, "Mark" as a sense of self becomes hazy. There is no more self-talk, no more feeling separate, just a flow of experience. There is a visceral sense of being one with the living forest. This is all witnessed effortlessly in awareness. The familiar sense of self fully dissolves, leaving just a quiet, awake presence.

Then I am jarred out of this tranquil, serene place by the sound of the retreat bell, summoning everyone to the meditation circle by the campfire. I am jolted out of this sense of connection, where all sense of me, my life, my little separate part of the universe, has disappeared, with no self to be seen. Rapidly, "teacher Mark" emerges, the self who is concerned about getting to the meditation on time and busy planning what kind of practice to lead that morning. This sense of self feels more dense and opaque in comparison to the state where all self-referencing disappears.

And so it goes throughout the day. When we observe ourselves closely, we find that our sense of self expands, contracts, disappears, and transforms, not unlike someone playing an accordion, stretching open and closed through the melody of the song. The key with mindfulness is to observe this dance of the self, to not take any one position as real or as ultimately who we are. Our sense of self changes and flows in the same way thoughts come and go ceaselessly. We see how this experience of a fixed, enduring self is illusory, in that nothing stays around for more than a few moments. Our job is to abide in awareness, notice this ebb and flow, and not be bound by any particular position or vantage point. This releases us from being defined or confined by any particular view or identity.

The wisdom that arises from mindfulness makes space for the sense of self to be and not to be. Not believing any one of these fleeting identities to be who we really are, we release being concerned about any of it. In fact, we sit back and watch the whole show like an amused grandmother, quietly watching over the antics of her grandchildren. This is the profound peace we are so busy searching for. It does not come from creating and perfecting our personality. Freedom comes when we see through the machinations of "self" and cease to be bothered by or believe in any of it.

• PRACTICE •

Exploring the Changing Nature of Self

Take a day to pretend you are a journalist, scientist, or biologist, and your chosen subject is your own sense of self. This experiment requires suspending all previous notions and preconceptions of self and who you think you are.

From the moment you wake up to the time you go to bed, observe your sense of self. Notice how you experience it. Is it observable as an image, a thought, a memory, a felt sense experience, something physical, or a particular identity? Does it feel positive, negative, or neutral? In your body, do you sense it as contracted or expansive or both? Does the sense of self have a particular location in the body?

Can you sense the changing inner landscape of self? Notice how it rarely stays the same for very long. Can you observe the shape-shifting nature of identity. In the same way you may reflect how even today your sense of self has morphed from perhaps being expansive to contracted, from confident to shaky. As you observe the fleeting nature of self, notice how that makes you feel toward the "personality" that may have defined you, and you may have cherished, for a long time. Does it feel freeing, scary, confusing, or liberating to see your sense of self as malleable, insubstantive, or elusive?

What happens when you contemplate who you are and discover it cannot be defined by any of these momentary experiences? Reality makes space for these various appearances of self to be and also not to be. Your practice is to abide in awareness and observe as all these momentary experiences of self and not self come and go. Notice how this practice allows you to not be bound or confined by any of them, and in this way you can find a sense of space and freedom in relationship to this dance of self.

• • •

Chapter 19

Releasing Mistaken Identity

When I discover who I am, I'll be free.
— RALPH ELLISON

The issue of identity brings up the important question "Who am I?" This is perhaps life's most perplexing riddle, one of the hardest nuts to crack. It surfaces more questions than answers. Who is this personality that I profess to be? Am I the same person as the one who was born, or am I different? If my body is me, then why do I seem to have so little control over it? The same is true of the mind. Can I really call all these thoughts mine? What happens to "me" when I die? Where do "I" go during sleep? And what of dementia and Alzheimer's patients, who seem to lose all sense of identity and memory and even forget their personal history?

These questions have long troubled mystics, philosophers, and psychologists. Through mindfulness practice, we can explore these unchartered realms, bringing an attentiveness to examine the complex and subtle dimensions of self. As I discuss in the previous chapter, the notion of a fixed, separate self does not hold water under close scrutiny. In this chapter, I want to explore how we build a sense of identity around key areas of our personal experience, starting with identification with the body.

Most people would ordinarily say about themselves: I am my body and my body is me. There is generally not a lot of doubt or questioning about that. We relate to our physical experience as primary, as essentially defining who we are. We look in the mirror in the morning while washing our face and say, "Yep, that's me." We post photos on Instagram and Facebook as proof that this is who "we" are, how "we" look, and what "we" are doing. We can spend an inordinate amount of time, energy, and worry trying to improve our body, to make it look presentable or beautiful, often treating it as a reflection of our true self.

By bringing mindfulness to our somatic experience, we can behold the body in a different way. When we close our eyes, the body feels a lot less solid and substantial than it appears when we look in the mirror. Attuning to our immediate sensory experience, we discover that the body is made of innumerable fleeting, sensory impressions. The fixed notion of a head, legs, arms, and torso is replaced with a flow of sensations: pulsing, pressure, tingling, vibration, heaviness, lightness, contraction, warmth, coolness, itchiness, density, and so on. Or we may sense how the body feels spacious, vast, or like a flow of energy or light dancing within our interior landscape. Take a moment now to close your eyes and explore this in your experience.

In the intriguing book *On Having No Head*, the psychologist Douglas Harding describes how people can never see their own head directly. They can only intimate that it is there through touch, memory, and as a reflection in a mirror. Though we have a very fixed notion of our head, we can only know it through inner sensory experience, by sensing the muscles move on our face and so on. This is not unlike what happens when we meditate. As we cultivate mindfulness, we see that what we call "my body" is simply a concept that describes an incredibly complex and mysterious range of experience, the external shape or form being simply one dimension of it. Further, we experience how many of the body's movements, sensations, and so on happen involuntarily, somewhat independent of us.

This leads to another existential question: If my body is me, then shouldn't I control it? Of course, we do and can control our body's movements. We can mostly move our limbs the way we want, direct our gaze, chew food, and so on. But much of what occurs in the body happens all by itself. For example, we don't instruct our heart to beat — which it does on average 108,000 times per day — or our lungs to breathe, which they do about 23,000 times a day.

Astoundingly, over half our body weight is made up of microorganisms, parasites, and other bugs that live in and on us. The ratio of "other organisms" to our own body mass is 1.3:1. But don't worry, they are not foreign invaders! They are essential to our survival and gut health. Our body and in particular our digestive tract contains a microbiome of trillions of cells. Yet we have little cognitive control over any of them. So if the proportion of what I call "me" (the nonforeign cells) is less than half of my overall body mass, whose body is this, anyway?

Perhaps the most potent reminder of the selfless nature of the body is when we age and get sick. When we become ill, we realize how little control we have over our physical experience. We can take our vitamin pills, aspirin, and other medicine, but the body is subject to physical laws, many of which are beyond our control. This is particularly true with aging. No matter how much we wish to stay young, and no matter what we do to maintain our vitality, our body degenerates, losing energy and suppleness, and it naturally declines over time. In this way, the body teaches us to surrender to these natural laws, reminding us that the body is not "ours."

Death is perhaps the ultimate teaching that who we are is not this body. We inhabit a physical form and wear body clothes for a while, but eventually we die and shed our physicality. That becomes so clear when we witness the death of a loved one. We may have cherished and nurtured their physical form when they were alive, but when they die, their body becomes a cold, inanimate lump of flesh and bone. It becomes obvious that who they are is not contained within that decaying matter. Their spirit, presence, or consciousness appears to leave behind the materiality of the body that housed them but which in essence was never who they really were.

I remember vividly when a friend of mine, Vanessa, died some years ago. She was a vital person, very active in the community, a philanthropist and mother. I have strong memories of her hiking, walking her dog, gardening, and generally living life to the full. Then she contracted breast cancer, which metastasized, and her life went through a radical change. Her vitality left her, and the chemotherapy sucked out her life force. After she died, going to see her as she was laid to rest was still quite a shock. Gone was the vitality, the color in her cheeks, the suppleness of her body. Absent was the sparkle in her eyes. What I saw was a lifeless corpse. It was clear to me that who Vanessa was in her essence was no longer residing in that physical body. Perhaps, in some ways, this allows us to let go more easily of the physical form of those we love.

In addition to identifying with the body, we often mistake our mind and its thoughts as who we are. In *Apocalypse*, D. H. Lawrence hypothesized poetically almost a century ago: "We will come to know that the mind is no more than the glittering of the sun reflected like shining lines on the surface of the water." Neuroscientists have been trying to discover what the mind is for the past few decades, while mystics have been exploring this elusive part of human experience for millennia. Though they come at it from different perspectives, both would agree that it is hard to pin down, let alone define. Trying to understand or measure what consciousness is has proven to be elusive to science. It appears to be too subtle to even measure with existing scientific tools. The direct experience of meditators perhaps offers some clarity on this subtle experience.

We often pride ourselves on our thoughts, views, and ideas, considering them perhaps what is most unique and personal about us. For many, the mind and its perceptions are what people most associate with as "me." But when we observe our mental processes, we see how they, too, are not wholly in our control. We are capable of intentional thought, yet tens of thousands of unbidden thoughts pour through our mind each day. They are triggered by a host of causes and conditions, including conversations, memories, life experiences, schooling, political and religious associations, and countless other influences. The mind flows with thoughts like a bubbling spring.

We like to think, as in *The Wizard of Oz*, that we are the person behind the curtain running the show. Yes, we can reason and pursue a particular line of thought, but can we really take ownership of the entire process? Are we responsible for the millions of thoughts that flood through our brain each year? How many do we will into being? As our heart beats, so our thoughts think themselves. Speaking to this topic, the psychologist Mark Epstein titled one of his books *Thoughts without a Thinker*. That title encapsulates this reality of thinking quite accurately; there is no "thinker" behind the thoughts, just thoughts thinking themselves.

The thinking process often amazes me when I write. I may have a particular topic in mind when I start writing, but what flows out of my pen onto the paper seems as if it comes *through* me, not from me. One of the delights of writing is to see how new ways to express ideas emerge as if from nowhere. Did "I" create those new turns of phrase or particular forms of expression, or did they just flow out of the confluence of my brain and all of the innumerable influences that I have been exposed to?

This raises a further existential question: Do we even have agency around our intentions and choices? When I scratch an itch, did I decide to move, and if so, who is deciding? When I swerve to avoid a lizard that runs in front of my bike, that action begins before I consciously register the situation, in the same way the eyes blink automatically when an object suddenly comes toward them. Instinct guides certain reactions, but even seemingly "directed" action is often conditioned by innumerable processes that often don't come into conscious awareness. If I am sitting on a plane and my head turns to look out at the window at the dusty desert land- scape below, did I choose to do that or was the movement triggered by a passing thought or memory or physical impulse that I was un- aware of? It seems like "we" direct the show, but when we attend closely, we see how much happens by itself, the body breathing and the mind thinking without a "self" giving instructions.

From this perspective, the concept of the self is just another thought. *Time* magazine once reviewed the neuroscientific liter- ature from decades of studies about the self. In all those studies, researchers have been unable to locate a specific place in the brain where a self exists. Our sense of agency seems to lack any central command center. The so-called self is perhaps no more than an interconnected web of electrical and chemical impulses moving in the vast matrix of the brain, constellated perhaps within the default mode network.

In the 1990s, I studied with the Advaita Vedanta teacher Poonja-ji in India. He used to ask his students to notice how the "I" thought arises in the mind. For example, we may have a sub- lime experience in meditation, in which we experience peace and the mind feels silent and vast. Then after the fact, an "I" thought usually arises and "claims" the experience: "Look what happened to 'me' in meditation today," we say to ourselves. "*I* had a cool, blissful experience." The mind can then build a story that enhances a spiritual identity that we are usually eager to tell others about. In reality, that experience occurred void of any sense of I or me. What allowed that moment of spaciousness in the first place was in part due to the mind not being preoccupied with itself nor being lost in thoughts and narratives about "self."

Mindfulness allows us to examine the process by which we create our own mistaken identity. We can observe how the mind conceptualizes experience into ideas like "me," "mine," and "self." We can notice the process of how we try to reduce the unfathomable matrix of what it means to be human into the concept of an "I," an individual self with a name like Bill or Jane. We can watch how we concoct concepts and take them to be reality. When we are unconscious of doing that, we create a lot of confusion because we keep building a house of cards on shifting sands. Trying to create solidity in something that is essentially groundless is stressful!

Of course, naming and differentiating things can be a useful convention. However, what is key is to not be defined by such labels or to think these concepts are substitutes for actual experience. For instance, if I am in a parking garage, it is helpful to know which car is "mine," since I need it to drive home. Yet the car is only "mine" because of human concepts and agreements — I paid money to buy it, a conceptual transaction verified with my registration and title. And the car itself is just a collection of metal, rubber, and other parts, which when assembled in a certain way we label "car." In the same way, modern society agrees on the concept of buying and owning land, but "possessing" land is a human fiction. When America's first European colonists arrived, they brought this concept with them, but Native Americans were perplexed about this strange idea that a person could actually lay claim to, let alone own, land.

The identifying labels we use to define ourselves are the same. We give ourselves individual names, and these are helpful in everyday life. But we are not our names in the same way our pets are not their names. We named our family dog Patrick, but this label is merely a convenience, as are the words *dog* and *pet*. The problem is that we often mistake the name, the concept, the label, and the idea for the reality.

I spend a lot of time in nature, which makes this distinction between our concepts and reality very apparent. I love redwood trees. I admire their tall majesty, their thick rusty barks, and how light pours through their branches in the afternoon. I walk past a particular redwood tree regularly on my hikes, and my lived experience of this tree defies and overwhelms what I think I know about redwoods as a species. No amount of words, no idea or concept, can ever bring me close to the vitality of a living tree. The concept is like a finger pointing to the moon. The name refers to the thing, but it does not come close to the actual living, breathing aliveness, complexity, and uniqueness of a redwood.

The same is true for each person. We can spend an inordinate amount of time cultivating, crafting, and perfecting our personality, the type of person we want to be, and then broadcasting this personality to others, such as through social media. This is often an idealized portrait, a certain image we prefer, but how close is it to the ever-changing reality of who and how we really are? Indeed, social media only fosters and reinforces our ongoing cult and myth of personality.

But is this personality that we project to the world ultimately real? Further, does it really serve us to claim an identity that we must defend and bolster when it's attacked or rejected? A discerning awareness helps us see that our "personality" is a collection of ideas, self-images, memories, views, and thoughts. We are conditioned, shaped, and influenced by our childhood, culture, religion, media, and a whole host of other seen and unseen forces. And like everything, personality is changeable. Sometimes we fight to maintain our identity and how it is perceived as if our lives depended on it, but this is an inherently unsettling process because there is never any solid ground on which to rest.

With mindfulness, we can observe this process and track how we construct our own sense of self. When you wake up in the morning, notice if you start to worry about how an important meeting at work will go and whether you will be perceived well. As you dress, muse on the image you want to portray. If you trip over the sidewalk, notice how you immediately feel self-conscious, as if all eyes are on you and judging you for your mistake. Notice how you feel after receiving an unfavorable performance review from your boss or when you get home and your kids give you loving and appreciative hugs. Observe the ways that your sense of self, and of self-worth, are undermined and bolstered at various times. Because external circumstances are forever out of our control, our personality always undergoes turbulence like a plane riding through a storm.

Rather than judge this process and these reactions, hold this tenuous, uncertain experience with a compassionate attention. In essential ways, we remain like teenagers still trying to develop their sense of identity and feeling terror over every perceived social slight and rejection. We are fragile social creatures. And the more we are attached to an identity, to a persona, the more we will feel anxiety and stress. A kind, caring response is vital for dealing with the vulnerability of this fragile sense of self — especially for all the ways we believe it is who we are and struggle to present a positive version to the world. Not only is this self-compassion important but we can also extend this kindness to others when we see them holding on to a self-image or identity as if their lives depended on it. Wes Nisker, a colleague and meditation teacher, gave this solution to the problem of our identity or personality:

> One suggestion is to regard your personality as a pet. It follows you around anyway, so give it a name and make friends with it. Keep it on a leash when you need to, and let it run free when you feel that is appropriate. Train it as well as you can, and then accept its idiosyncrasies, but always remember that your pet is not you. Your pet has its own life, and just happens to be in an intimate relationship with you, whoever you may be, hiding there behind your personality.

• PRACTICE •

Examining the Nature of Self

In the previous meditation, we explored the changing, transient, insubstantial nature of self. This meditation looks at how we identify with various aspects of our experience so that we can free ourselves from this misidentification, which is a limiting, painful habit that misleads and constricts us.

Sit comfortably, close your eyes, and rest your attention on your breath. Observe how the breath breathes itself. Perhaps you identify the breath as yours, since to a degree you can influence it. Notice how this "I" thought arises and claims the breath as your own, as if you can possess it. As you inhale and exhale, inquire if this is true or if breath is like the breeze on your face or the sound of a bird — felt but not owned by you.

Similarly, turn your attention to sensations in your body, like pressure, pain, tingling, aching, and pleasure. Notice as "I" thoughts arise and claim the experiences, thinking "my" body, "my" knee, and so on. From the perspective of mindfulness, these are not "your" sensations. They are simply phenomena coming and going in the field of awareness. Consider: Does this process of identification of labeling things as "I" or "my" feel real or true? When you can see that physical processes just happen according to causes and conditions, and don't necessarily belong to you, how does that shift your perception?

Now turn your attention to your thoughts. Observe thoughts as they come and go; see how they have a life of their own. Thoughts think themselves, triggered by a host of conditions, including memory, perception, and sense experience. Can you really claim that all the thoughts pouring through your head belong to you or are "yours"? See how thoughts are like clouds moving across the sky of awareness. Does that allow you to reduce the sense of ownership or identification with them?

Next, attend to the ebb and flow of emotions, which are often triggered by thoughts, conversations, memories, and sensations. Notice the process of identification, where you may observe a sense of ownership of these feelings, as you did with thoughts. See that they occur selflessly, in their own way, in their own time. While you can influence them, you can't control or own them. Observing your emotional experience with awareness allows a greater sense of space and perspective, and it helps you avoid becoming so caught up in or defined by or painfully identified with your ever-changing moods.

Notice how it feels to observe your inner experience through the spacious lens of mindfulness, where you can learn to release identifying with your individual body, thoughts, and emotions. What happens to your sense of "self" when you do this? The more we see the selfless nature of all experience, the more it allows us to feel an expanding connection to all life. Limiting our sense of "self" to this body and mind means believing and feeling we are separate, distinct, and even isolated from everything else. Meanwhile, releasing our identification with this narrow sense of self can open a connection within the vaster web of life. Rather than feeding the fear and anxiety of separation, this experience fosters a sense of ease and peace. Notice if this is true for you as you practice seeing through the "selfing" process in meditation and in life.

• • •

Chapter 20

The Causal Nature
of Everything

The thought manifests as the word. The word manifests as the deed.
The deed develops into habit. Habit hardens into character.

— ANONYMOUS

Joanna attended her first meditation retreat at a center in the forests of New England. Although excited about this inner adventure, she had trepidations. Her mind tended to fixate on the negative. The first day started off well. She enjoyed the peace and quiet of the center, the lovely grounds, and the generally mellow atmosphere. Her body felt healthy and her mind was open. Day two was a different experience. It was as if she woke up on the wrong side of the bed. In a particular walking meditation, she felt irritable and began to judge her fellow participants. All she could see were their faults.

Then Joanna started to question her decision to attend the retreat in the first place. *What is all this mindfulness stuff, anyway?* she thought. *Who cares about being aware?* In the next walking meditation, she felt even more restless, irritated, and doubtful. She questioned everything and judged the teachers for creating such a difficult retreat. Then, as people can do, instead of meditating, she began to scheme how to leave without being noticed!

The next practice was a standing meditation, and the instructors directed the students to pay close attention to their feet. As Joanna did, a light bulb went off. She realized that her painful plantar fasciitis had flared up in her left foot and was quite uncomfortable. She first contracted the condition while playing competitive tennis, and it resurfaced at random times. This was one of them. The longer she stood in meditation, the more the pain gnawed away at her. She saw how, unnoticed, that low-grade physical discomfort had triggered her negative and irritable state of mind.

Deciding to rest her foot, Joanna sat down and stayed off her feet for the rest of the day. She put orthotics in her shoes, which eased the soreness, and as the pain subsided, her irritability and plans to escape faded. She realized how physical discomfort had caused all kinds of reactive emotions and thoughts, and if left unchecked, they would have bounced her out of the retreat. Instead, she got a direct glimpse into how causal processes drive so much of our experience, usually outside the realm of awareness.

However, we don't need to go on retreat to notice this. In any moment, we can observe how our moods, feelings, and thoughts are constantly being conditioned by inner and outer experience. For example, like many people, I frequently wake up in the morning tired and groggy. If I'm not aware of my state, it easily leads to feeling resistant about my day. However, as soon as I have a strong cup of tea and do a little stretching, my mind brightens, my mood lifts, and I'm much more ready to embrace the day.

This is the simple law of causality. Everything arises based on causes and conditions. Biology and physics point to this as a central principle in the universe. With mindful awareness, we can track this causal process internally and learn how to create conditions that allow us to thrive and work skillfully with the many things that cause us stress. This is the "good news" of practice, as it means we are not stuck with our lot in life nor with our conditioning or history. We have the potential to change and transform the raw material of our life and circumstances.

Without self-awareness, it is easy to feel that our thoughts, feelings, and impulses just happen by themselves. We can then feel victim to our inner life, tossed around by emotions, and assailed by reactions that come seemingly out of nowhere. However, when we pay closer attention to our inner process, we see that everything arises due to causes. This can seem obvious in the physical world: when the sun rises, heat follows; when the sun sets, heat wanes. Yet we often overlook this process internally. By paying careful attention, we have the opportunity to intervene in this casual chain reaction, so we are no longer victim to the causes and conditions that can negatively influence our life.

How does that look in actuality? Joanna's retreat experience is one example of how the mind is influenced by our physical body, which includes injuries that cause not only pain but corresponding mental anguish. The same is true of the food we eat and the medicine we take. When hormones change or fluctuate, such as during adolescence or menopause, this causes radical shifts in energy, mood, and thinking. It is humbling to consider how easily we are affected by minute doses of chemicals in our bloodstream and brain. Understanding this causal nature helps attune us to the conditions that influence us. It also helps us take these circumstances less personally and respond to them more effectively.

Another example is our social conditioning, in which we internalize beliefs and ideas from others. Consider racism. If a child grows up in a household where another race or ethnicity is viewed with fear and suspicion and judged to be inherently lazy, violent, or "less-than-human," then the seeds of that distorted perception and bias are planted in the child's mind. If those views are reinforced by other people, society, and the wider culture, such beliefs will be further entrenched, even if the child's direct experience contradicts those views. Conditioning sowed at an early age is hard to dislodge, and so, without awareness of such bias, the painful wheels of intergenerational prejudice keep turning.

We are all subject to conditioning, and mindfulness helps bring our own into plain sight. For example, I was raised in a "working-class" culture in northern England, and I grew up with the sense that refined or highbrow culture, like opera and fine art, was "beyond my station." Wealth and privilege were for the upper classes, and someone in my place was supposed to get a manual or trade job upon leaving school and not be "too big for their boots." That conditioning has been hard to overcome. I can still feel out of place when I go to an art opening at the Royal Academy of Art in London or to the opera. I still feel a quiet concern that, if I am discovered, someone will know I don't belong. I don't really believe that, but I can still feel the imprint of my social conditioning.

The inner critic is another example. Students routinely tell me stories about being told as children, "You are lazy and will never amount to anything," or "You will never be as smart as your brother," or "You are not pretty enough to marry." Regardless of the origin, such harsh judgments and mean statements can be internalized as our "inner critic," who repeats them endlessly from then on. These judgments can become enshrined as beliefs that we really *are* unworthy or unlovable. In turn, those ideas can cause us to act in unhealthy ways, such as seeking love or validation in all the wrong places. Conditioning can also influence us in positive ways; when parents bestow unconditional love on children, it lays the groundwork for feeling held and can support a beautiful sense of belonging. However, negative conditioning, left unchecked, can give rise to unworthiness, self-hatred, self-harm, and worse.

As self-awareness grows, we see how we are constantly influenced by causality. We begin to see how habits, behaviors, and relationship dynamics can be shaped from the past, from the conditioning of our family, particularly how we were parented. Our moods are affected by our self-talk and what people have said to us. We are influenced by the kinds of news media we watch. Our perception is affected by where we place our attention and what we focus on. Our well-being is affected by our friendships and the quality of our relationships. Given that we live in an interdependent web, connected to all life, not a moment goes by when innumerable conditions are not affecting us.

A more recent noteworthy phenomenon is the effect of technology on our brain, attention, and well-being. Researchers in Canada have found that, over the past twenty years, the average human attention span has reduced from twelve to eight seconds, a 33 percent drop. That is, while working on a computer, for instance, we only stay concentrated for eight short seconds before getting distracted. Goldfish, it is reported, have an attention span of nine seconds! I can't help thinking that all our multitasking and hyper-distracted screen time is a significant cause for the decline.

Think of the attention that arises as we read a book — it is a calm, focused, centering attention. How different is that from looking at a computer screen, when there might be multiple windows open, music playing in the background, a sports game in one corner, and text conversations happening while you are trying to write a report. If one does that for a few years, the attention becomes conditioned to be scattered, restless, impatient, and distracted. No wonder it is hard for us to focus anymore!

Yet once we understand the nature of causality, we can work backward from the consequences of such behavior. For instance, when you notice attention withering due to multitasking on a computer, you can condition yourself in ways that foster sustained attention. While writing a document on your laptop, you might eliminate all distractions, such as closing other windows, turning off music, and hiding text and email notifications. You might put your phone into gray scale so its bright colors do not grab your attention. As you wisely create the conditions for focused attention, this restores a greater sense of calm, ease, and satisfaction.

Such rewards create a positive feedback loop supporting us to make healthier choices. Those wise choices reinforce how pleasurable it is to set up the causes for optimal and fruitful behavior in our lives, whether we are writing, working on our computers, relating with others, or attending a meditation retreat.

• **PRACTICE** •

Reflecting on Causality

We all desire certain experiences and aspire for specific outcomes regarding our finances, health, family, and work. To achieve those outcomes, we have to lay a foundation of supportive conditions in order for that aspiration to bear fruit. For example, to be more concentrated in meditation, we must understand and foster the causes that support our focus.

In this reflective practice, write down one aspiration or intention for your life. This can be anything that is important to you. Then reflect on and make a list of the causes and conditions necessary for that to arise.

Take the case of wishing to improve your concentration. Some of the causes and conditions that will support that are the following:

1. Sitting for longer periods of time in meditation
2. Receiving one-on-one guidance about your practice
3. Studying different techniques for focused attention

4. Finding environments that are quiet and conducive for meditation
5. Attending a concentration meditation course
6. Having a strong intention to release mental distractions, thoughts, plans, and concerns during meditation

The list may also include what needs to be released or stopped in order to support the particular aspiration. As with any goal, we must be clear about the obstacles that we need to work with. In this way, you come to be more cognizant of the causes and conditions that are necessary to support your aspirations.

• • •

Chapter 21

Exploring the Nature
of Awareness

Be the knowing, not the conditions that are known.
— AJAHN SUMEDHO

One of the perennial mysteries of human experience is the phenomenon of consciousness. Neuroscience is still trying to understand what the mind or consciousness really is, but the predominant scientific view is that awareness is a product of the brain, perhaps arising out of its complex matrix of billions of neurons. This materialistic premise says that without organic life, no sentience would exist. From the scientific perspective, since there has been little verifiable evidence that consciousness exists separate from the body, to posit otherwise is simply speculation.

In contrast, mystical traditions for millennia have postulated that mind or consciousness is not confined by physical matter, nor is it located in the brain or body. Some perspectives propose that consciousness itself animates and gives birth to the human body, the mind, and even life itself. One only has to be present at the death of someone to intuit this perspective. When a person dies, it is clear that the "consciousness" or "presence" — or whatever we choose to call this awareness — that previously animated the body has ceased, and only a lifeless corpse remains.

How do we reconcile the differing perspectives of science and mystics? Mindfulness practice is a phenomenological methodology. That means we look to our own empirical experience to verify what we know to be true. Rather than look to science or religious philosophy to understand the nature of awareness, we instead turn our attention to our own awareness to learn.

What exactly is awareness? This is a challenging question. Its very nature eludes being confined by definitions. However, we can come to know it by inference, by what it does, what it reveals, and how it functions. By observing how awareness works, we can shift our lens from looking for a thing to understanding awareness as a process.

Awareness is what allows human beings to know and observe. It is what observes our moment-to-moment experience. This observation is neutral, without preference, and it includes the five senses — sight, hearing, smell, taste, touch — along with thinking. Awareness is ever-present, regardless of our personal circumstances, moods, or energy. And it requires no effort to be aware; it simply happens by itself. If you don't believe me, then try to switch this knowing quality off!

My favorite meditation with students is what I call "unmindfulness" meditation. The instruction is to try to not be aware, not be mindful, not pay attention, not notice anything. Experiment with this idea right now. Close your eyes and see if it is possible to not be aware for one minute. As you will discover, this is impossible. Awareness is always "on," always present to something. Even in deep sleep, we can be aware of our dreams, and afterward, we can have some sense that we slept well or not. This practice is instructive for mindfulness meditation, in that it reveals how effortlessly we can be present to experience.

After students try this meditation, I pose a question: "If awareness is always present, then what is it aware of? What does it attend to?" Most often, what occupies this valuable resource is our thoughts, usually to the detriment of our other senses and everything else. However, in recent years, in this era of what is sometimes referred to as the "attention economy," companies vie for the precious commodity of our attention. Subsequently, awareness is now oriented in ever-increasing measure to the screens on our phones and computers.

We utilize this same awareness in the practice of mindfulness. Without it, there is no cultivation of attention. Mindfulness is the conscious knowing of what we are present to. Take, for example, the sound of a bird singing in our garden. We may not be conscious of the birdsong if our attention is absorbed in something else. Although sound vibrates in our ears, we may not even recognize that a bird is singing. However, when we are mindful, we not only hear the song but consciously recognize that we are listening to a songbird.

Another common example is driving. We must keep our eyes open while driving, or we risk crashing our car. But most of the time, we don't pay much attention to what we are seeing. Our minds are elsewhere, and if someone asks us what we saw on our journey, we may have difficulty remembering. (We often can't even recall which route we took to our destination!) We are present at a basic level to function and drive, but without mindful attention, our memories become a blur of impressions — nameless cars, buildings, trees, colors, shapes, and people. Mindfulness is the conscious knowing of experience as it happens, along with knowing that we are aware. That is what enables recollection, another function or outcome of mindfulness.

None of this, however, necessarily explains what awareness is. A text called *The Flight of the Garuda* by Shabkar Tsogdruk

Rangdrol, a renowned eighteenth-century Tibetan teacher and poet, tackles this difficulty directly. In this text, Shabkar asks his students to inquire deeply into the nature of awareness by posing many questions: Does awareness have a shape, a color, or a size? Does it have a location? Does it have a gender or an age? Does it have any history? Does it come and go? He then asks his students to look directly at their immediate experience of awareness to discover empirically the nature of awareness.

In mindfulness meditation, we can turn the lens of our attention to become present to awareness itself. And what we discover is mysterious. As Shabkar teaches, there is no "thing" to find. Nothing with a location, shape, color, or form. Yet awareness is unmistakably present. In the Tibetan Dzogchen tradition, they say it is "empty." Awareness is empty of any "thingness," empty of any separate, substantive existence. Yet at the same time, it is understood to be luminous, brightly shining like a light, and cognizant, clearly knowing.

Experiencing this directly can be transformative. One of my meditation students, Stinus, who is from Denmark, shared with me a story of when this happened to him on a mindfulness retreat I was leading. He wrote:

> We were thirty minutes into our group meditation, and my mind was calm. Now and then a thought came. They seemed distant, almost like an echo. It felt like awareness was watching them from afar. Minutes passed in this expansive space, simply observing. Now and then our teacher would ring a bell and instruct us to notice who or what was hearing the sound. Toward the end of the sitting, the teacher said: "Now turn awareness toward itself." And then it happened. Awareness watching itself. A formless, nondualistic, nonchanging presence that I cannot describe.

If I had to try, the best word would be *sacred* or *divine*. I noticed that I was silently crying. I felt humbled and in awe. The experience left me with a knowing of what is behind the physical world. When this body dies, it will only be my body that will disappear and not the formless. This was perhaps the most liberating thing I have ever done.

Awareness is neither a thing nor not a thing. It is clearly present and is what illuminates our experience. It is what allows us to know ourselves, one another, and the world. Awareness helps reveal the laws that govern our experience, for example, understanding that to cling to the transient is to suffer. Such insights, which arise from the clarity of mindfulness, are indispensable for awakening and freeing us from suffering. Yet awareness is also what allows us to function in a simple day-to-day way, to walk down a busy street, to drive our car, and to behold the vistas on a hike.

On a meditation retreat, I once received a beautiful teaching from Ajahn Sumedho, a senior monk from the Thai Forest meditation tradition. He said: "Be the knowing, *not* the conditions that are known." He was pointing to an essential aspect of mindfulness practice where we train to abide in awareness and not get caught up in all the various things that we attend to. Like all practices, this is easier said than done. Yet through mindfulness practice we can learn to reside in this knowing presence, this awareness that knows experience, without being tossed around by the circumstances of life.

As our practice of mindfulness grows, we strengthen and deepen this capacity of awareness. In the beginning of practice, moments of present-moment attention seem fleeting. Over time we come to establish ourselves in awareness, and that knowing quality of mind becomes our fundamental orientation. In doing so, it is moments of un-mindfulness that become the infrequent visitor. Instead we come to abide in this ever-present awareness, which is the conduit for living with clarity, wisdom, and peace.

This spacious awareness allows us to access a sense of freedom and peace amid the turbulence of change and adversity. It becomes a refuge when facing uncertainty and stress. And it is something we can trust like a true friend. Over time we come to see its value and treat it as a precious gift, not wishing to do anything that dulls or diminishes its illumination. Yet it remains one of the great mysteries of life, as transparent as air, as vast as the sky, and piercingly present in all moments.

• PRACTICE •
Mindfulness of Awareness Itself

Begin this meditation by sitting in a comfortable, relaxed, but alert posture. Close your eyes and attune to the presence of sounds. Open awareness to expand to the farthest sound, and invite a quality of openness and receptivity in your attention. As you attend to sounds, notice how, when each noise occurs, it is known quite effortlessly by awareness. A sound appears and is known. Then ask yourself: "Known by what?"

This inquiry invites a direct observation of awareness itself. What is it that knows, and how does the knowing happen? Avoiding a flurry of thinking and speculation, observe how hearing, and the knowing of it, happens all by itself, quite effortlessly. That still may fail to answer the question about what awareness is! So it is important to maintain this inquisitive observation.

Similarly, notice how all experience is known in this way. Sensations of pain, pressure, or itchiness occur and pull the attention. Awareness automatically becomes cognizant of such experiences, often without any conscious directing of attention from us. When our eyes are closed, sensations appear in the seeming darkness of our interior landscape. They appear like touch points of sensation. In this way, the nuance of breath sensations are also known in awareness. When we see how effortlessly this happens, it begs the question of why it is so hard to maintain concentration in meditation, since awareness of experience occurs so naturally.

Observe this same process of how awareness becomes present to thoughts, emotions, moods, ideas, and any other phenomena. They all seem to appear on the screen of awareness, as it were, cognized in the same way we feel the breeze on our face or taste mango on our tongue. When you sense how awareness knows experience so effortlessly, how does this impact your understanding of meditation?

Now turn your attention to awareness itself. Follow Shabkar's instructions and ask: Does awareness have a shape? A size? A color? A location? Does this knowing presence have a gender? An ethnicity? Is it the same age as you, or is it timeless? Does it come and go, or is it ever-present? Is it confined or unobstructed? Is it limited or boundless? Don't look to your mind or the past for answers. Turn to your direct experience in this moment and look directly at awareness itself. The answers may not come readily, so treat this as an ongoing reflection on the nature of this wondrous aspect of human nature.

Perhaps the most important question is whether you believe awareness is yours. Does it belong to you? Is it part of you? Is it under your control? How does your sense of awareness relate to the consciousness that resides within every other human being and other conscious life-forms? With these questions, don't seek any definitive answer. Simply let the reflection percolate in your meditation. As you end the meditation, stay curious about how awareness reveals experience throughout your day. Return to this reflection frequently in and out of meditation. Such inquiry will help illuminate your understanding of both awareness itself and your mindfulness practice.

This investigation into awareness raises profound questions, ones that have fascinated humankind for centuries. Thus far, our understanding of awareness remains elusive, and perhaps that will always be the case. Personally, I like that such things remain in the realm of mystery because that encourages us to inquire with earnestness into this important facet of reality, which is a key aspect of who and what we truly are.

• • •

· SECTION 3 ·

FINDING PEACE
IN THE HEART

Chapter 22

Opening to Vulnerability
with a Kind Heart

Do not say that kindness and awareness are separate.
One cannot arise without the other. Awareness is the foundation
of kindness. Kindness is the expression of awareness.

— ANONYMOUS

A dear friend of mine was once living in Ibiza, Spain, with her beloved longtime partner. They were approaching their retirement years and almost finished building their dream home, where they longed to spend the rest of their days together. Then out of the blue my friend sensed something was not right with her body. After several rounds of tests, she was diagnosed with advanced ovarian cancer. She had to leave their island paradise to get immediate surgery in Madrid, followed by a year of intensive chemotherapy and radiation. Then, while taking a stroll in the city, her partner was tragically killed by a drunk driver.

Within a year, my friend's life was ripped apart. She was still fighting her cancer and receiving chemotherapy, and she had lost her husband and soul mate. Their dream of retiring and living a pleasant life in Ibiza had been snatched away. She did not know where to turn. She was in pain and disoriented and now had to face her difficulties alone. Even though she had an active spiritual practice, she needed tremendous courage to meet all of that heart-ache and loss with a kind heart. It took her a long time to pick up the pieces of her life again.

To be human is to be innately vulnerable. There are thousands of illnesses in the world today, but we only have effective treat-ments for some of them. We are also subject to a host of environ-mental dangers, such as famine, drought, earthquakes, hurricanes, forest fires, and more. In the United States alone, more than sixteen million children go hungry each year. We also face societal chal-lenges like unstable economies, civil unrest, warfare, and poverty, which affect billions of people worldwide. Every day, people lack or have limited access to basic necessities like healthy food, sani-tation, and clean water. And people suffer from a range of social pain, from domestic violence to racism, incest, and homophobia, just to name a few.

We are also vulnerable to mental and mood disorders, addic-tion, and the cognitive decline that comes with aging. If that weren't enough, we inflict more pain on ourselves through self-judgment and self-hatred. Up to 10 percent of the U.S. population is on some kind of mental health medication, but this fails to solve the di-lemma. Suicide rates, an expression of many people's inner strug-gles, are also increasing; suicide is now the tenth leading cause of death in the United States.

However, perhaps the most vulnerable place for human beings is our heart. We are social creatures. We have strong needs to be loved and cared for. As infants, healthy bonds of attachment to caregivers are essential for our survival. As adults, healthy social connections and friendships are important for our mental health. Such meaningful contact is even more vital for our well-being as we grow older. Yet how easily can others harm us emotionally. We can quickly be hurt, rejected, ridiculed, shamed, or shunned. Further, our social connections are ultimately transient; they are all subject to the winds of change and loss.

How do we find peace in our heart given all these challenges and the inherent vulnerability of the human condition? When we meet painful experience, it is crucial that we do so with kind attention and self-compassion. This is the potential of mindfulness practice when imbued with kindness. It supports us as we meet each person, each vulnerable moment, including ourselves, with a sensitive presence. Nothing will help us on this journey more than the combination of love and awareness.

This is the key question: Can we bring a kind presence to the ways we feel vulnerable — physically, emotionally, and socially? Mindfulness invites us to be radically honest with how we meet experience. How kindly do you meet your deficiency, loneliness, or free-floating anxiety? What do you do when parenting feels overwhelming or you are struggling with insecurity? When these things happen, how do you relate to that pain? What would it be like to give yourself caring attention rather than to blame yourself or to compare yourself to others?

The more we can bring tenderness to our own struggles, the more likely we can do that when we confront pain in others and in the world. In that spirit, mindful awareness can encourage a kindhearted embrace of whatever we meet: whether it is a fledgling bird fallen out of the nest or a homeless veteran shivering on cold winter streets. Whether a friend is confessing to troubles in their marriage or a child is getting teased and bullied at school. As the quote in the epigraph says, "Kindness is the expression of awareness." When kind awareness is fully integrated in our day-to-day life, we can say our practice of mindfulness has truly matured. This maturation is what allows us to meet the inevitable vicissitudes of life with openness and love. Then we can go anywhere, meet any hard or painful experience, and hold it with a caring presence.

This is not so far away as we might imagine. Examples of tenderhearted presence are everywhere we look. I think of the countless nurses who bathe and feed sick patients. Or the people from church missions and homeless shelters who help vulnerable people living on the streets. Or the schoolteachers who bring kindness to the challenges their students are facing. We can see it in our own lives when we are with someone who is struggling, whose life has been shattered by pain, who is struggling in a relationship or feeling the grief of loss, and we help them, in ways large and small, to tenderly pick up the pieces and gather strength and faith.

We can also learn to meet ourselves with a similar kind presence. I remember my own dark night of the soul when I developed chronic fatigue. I was so weak sometimes that I could barely get out of bed to eat or bathe. It was hard for me to be present with a body so depleted and a mind so weary and depressed. It was obvious, though, in the light of awareness, that whenever I resisted, struggled, or hated the illness or blamed and judged myself for being so weak, I felt infinitely worse.

The fatigue became my Zen master. It was a hard but beautiful lesson in surrender. The fruition of my years of practice gave me the ability to listen intimately and sensitively to the needs, wishes, and most of all limitations of my body. This kind presence became the healing path forward. When I was able to access that fusion of awareness and love, then everything was bearable. I met my own vulnerability with self-compassion and tenderness, and this became the foundation for genuine self-healing and a full recovery. The seeds this experience sowed have helped me meet the pain of others with that same kind presence, which has been invaluable in my work, whether that be in therapy, coaching, or teaching.

• **PRACTICE** •

Attuning to Vulnerability

Find a comfortable posture where you can sit in meditation for fifteen to twenty minutes. Take some minutes to settle your awareness into the sensations of sitting and breathing. Allow yourself to fully arrive in your body.

Now turn your attention to all the ways you may feel physically vulnerable as a human being. Perhaps you feel acutely aware of aging, as the body becomes less strong, more prone to injury, and less energetic. Reflect on your everyday aches and pains, on your vulnerability to colds, injury, and fatigue. Contemplate how this body, however young, healthy, or beautiful, will decline over time and ultimately be no more. What arises when you reflect in this way? Can you bring tenderness and kind attention to this reality? If they are not available, notice what else is present.

Now turn to the vulnerability of the heart. Think of the difficult emotions you experience, like fear, loss, grief, anxiety, and shame. Reflect on any psychological challenges you encounter, such as depression, self-doubt, loneliness, or confusion. How burdensome do these feel? Are you able to hold all that arises with an openhearted presence, or is there reaction or judgment?

Similarly, open to the vulnerability of having a mind that is so rarely in our control. Consider to what degree you are afflicted by a racing mind, catastrophic thinking, and self-judgment. How are you affected or troubled by states of mind, moods, and other mental qualities? Can you bring a caring awareness to this reality? Lastly, contemplate your feelings of social vulnerability, such as the need to be seen, connected, loved, accepted, and approved of. Contemplate the quality of attention you meet these emotions with.

When you reflect on these things, try to bring a kind awareness to all of these states, feelings, and qualities. What is it like to acknowledge the vulnerability of the human condition, which is often out of our hands? Is it possible to bring tenderness and care to your experience? If these qualities are not available, notice what does arise in relation to these difficult experiences.

Now turn that same attention to the experience of loved ones, friends, and colleagues. They, too, are vulnerable to aging, sickness, loss, heartache, rejection, and stress. They, too, have limited control over all the things that affect their well-being. Appreciate the commonality of this human experience. We are all in this together. We are all subject to similar physical, emotional, and mental challenges, no matter how blessed our circumstances. Does reflecting in this way open the heart to tenderness?

As you continue through your day, try to maintain this kind presence as you meet the vulnerabilities of people and life everywhere. The world needs this quality so much, and we all have the capability to develop it.

• • •

Chapter 23

Learning to Manage
Triggering Emotions

At the end of the day we're all reactive personalities.
We just don't know it until we meet the right catalyst.
— MICHELLE PAINCHAUD

Jo was serving a long sentence at San Quentin correctional facility in California. His inability to control his anger had landed him in jail, and though he believed his rage helped him survive the jungle of prison life, he also knew it was the source of his troubles. Eventually, after many years of good behavior, he was admitted into a prison gardening program, which he'd always wanted to do as a way to escape the boredom of cell life and get precious moments of fresh air outside. It was also a chance to put his hands into real soil and create a tiny piece of beauty inside the barren landscape.

One day while out in the exercise yard, working on one of the vegetable beds, he put his thermal coffee mug down on a ledge near where he was weeding. Then he got caught up in conversation with other guys in the yard, forgot about his hot coffee, and went back to digging. While gardening, he caught sight of someone stealing his cup. Stealing from fellow inmates violates an unwritten code of conduct, and Jo was furious. However, his mindfulness practice allowed him to witness his body's familiar response to rage: his racing heart, shallow breathing, and clenched teeth. His fingers tightened around the shovel.

As he neared the opportunistic thief, he felt the impulse to lift his shovel and strike the guy in revenge. However, just before he acted out, his awareness surfaced, and he paused, took a breath, and put space between his feeling of anger and his actions. Jo realized he was caught up in rage. In that split second of mindfulness, he understood that if he followed through, there would be huge consequences, not just for the man who would be injured but also for himself. He would be kicked out of his beloved garden program and thrown into solitary confinement. His parole board hearing would probably be pushed back years. He put the shovel down, and that wise restraint possibly saved him years of extra time inside, and it may have saved his life.

We all get triggered. Like many things in life, it's unavoidable. What makes the difference is how we respond to it, or what we do with it. I remember a radio report of a Texas accountant who shot his computer with his handgun because he was so frustrated with his work. Easy access to guns has sadly led to many worse things than computers being destroyed, but that powerful impulse can arise in anyone. The most common situation is road rage: someone's reckless driving triggers a moment of terror, and that terror instantly turns into rage or righteous indignation and the desire to retaliate, perhaps by engaging in the same dangerous behavior!

The limbic system is the emotional heart of the brain. The amygdala within that structure is our inner sentinel, always on the lookout for danger and possible threats. The amygdala is designed to catapult us into an alert, fight-flight-or-freeze state, and without that circuitry, we would not have survived as a species.

For millennia it helped us guard ourselves against faster and more powerful predators.

However, that survival circuitry does not distinguish between physical and emotional threats. It gets triggered if a bus is about to knock us over or if someone insults us during a casual conversation. Threats to our self-image and social status are treated the same as if we had accidentally run into a grizzly bear: we become instantly ready to fight for our lives or run for the hills at the smallest of slights. As a result, we are bombarded with potential triggers all the time. It can be as simple as someone not holding a door for us or the perceived negative tone of an email. It can happen when a loved one speaks insensitively or curtly. A few careless words can easily spark a flash of anger and a desire to verbally retaliate.

This is why we need the vigilance that mindfulness practice provides, to skillfully manage our reactions in the way Jo did. In a situation of real physical danger, we are grateful for the amygdala and its fight-or-flight mechanism, but in most situations, this is an overreaction, and it would be inappropriate and counterproductive to act on it.

Part of the problem is that when we are triggered, the prefrontal cortex, the center of decision-making, becomes occluded. When rage spikes, the brain prioritizes blood flow away from thinking centers and toward our muscles in preparation to fight or flee. The commonsense adage of not acting in the heat of anger is a good one because we literally can't think clearly.

The key, then, is learning to find some space between the trigger and our subsequent reaction. The motivational speaker Stephen Covey has pointed to this key principle: "Between stimulus and response there is a space. In that space lies our ability to choose our response. In our response lies our growth and happiness." How many times in our lives have we wished we had acted with that sage wisdom? How much pain and heartache would we have saved if we had been able to find that space between the stimulus and our reactive response? The good news is that this space is within reach, as Jo experienced. Mindfulness can help us find and grow that gap, that moment of pause.

The key is developing self-awareness, particularly of the body, so that we learn to recognize and track the various signals that indicate we are getting triggered. For example, during an argument, we may feel the heat or tension rising in our body. We may sense the tightness in our belly or throat. We can track our rising frustration or irritation and feel our heart tightening. We might notice a torrent of angry thoughts and recognize that we are becoming defensive, that we feel cornered. All of these responses, if left unchecked, can easily build like a volcano and trigger a full-scale eruption.

Tracking such signals in the body, heart, and mind can give us that split-second moment when we can intercept our response before we act on it. Some simple physical practices can also help during such moments. One is to take five deep, slow breaths, which is a simple and immediate way to calm down the reactive nervous system. We can also ground our emotions by focusing on our body, such as by sensing our feet touching the ground or our legs resting on the chair. We might also get up if we are sitting, walk around, and use movement to settle the heightened energy that may be flowing.

This kind of tracking and centering can prevent us from becoming lost in a flurry of anger or fear. This awareness helps create some inner space and gives our prefrontal cortex time to reengage. Once we have enough clarity to interpret the flood of signals coming from the amygdala, from our triggered nervous system, we can plan a more reasoned response, one that avoids unnecessary pain and heartache.

In that space, we have options: Maybe this is not the best time or place for this conversation. Maybe it simply needs to be revisited, once everyone is in a calmer place. Maybe we realize we don't have all the right information, are misinterpreting the other person, or are caught up in our own assumptions or projections. Whatever the situation, mindfulness helps us avoid acting out our fight-or-flight response.

We are perhaps most frequently triggered in intimate relationships, where conversations about everyday issues can easily explode into heated arguments over larger matters, leaving both parties hurt, misheard, and upset. I remember one particular day when my partner said she needed to discuss something that was upsetting her about our living situation. As we sat down on the gray living room couch on a sunny afternoon, I felt some apprehension about what was coming. I was immediately defensive, expecting criticism, and as the sun poured through the living room window, she explained her frustration with all the ways I wasn't pulling my weight around the house.

As she talked, I became triggered. I felt wrongly accused and unfairly judged. As she recounted my behavior over recent months, I was convinced she was wrong and that her perspective was inaccurate. I felt my heart close, my throat tighten, and my breath get shorter as a whole whirlwind of arguments proving my innocence started to race in my head.

However, I was mindful about being triggered; I had recently taught a class on emotional self-regulation. I had the wherewithal to simply listen, to wait to respond until my partner was done talking. I knew I needed to calm myself as I felt the defensiveness rise. So I took some deep breaths, felt my feet on the floor, and noticed the reactions in my body. After doing this for some time, I was able to listen more attentively to her point of view, and I realized, ironically, that she was right! Her perception was completely valid. I was in fact not seeing or attending to the issues she was raising, and I admitted it. Had I not tracked my reactivity and instead become defensive, the whole thing would have exploded into an unnecessary and painful argument.

Mindful awareness can help us when we need it most, freeing us from so much reactivity and unnecessary pain. But it requires practice to pay attention intimately to our experience in the heat of the moment and stay steady in the fire of that experience.

· **PRACTICE** ·

Working with Triggers

In this meditation you will recall a time when you were triggered or got reactive to a person or in a particular situation. Then you will reimagine the episode by moving through four steps in what is known as the STOP process, an acronym that stands for "stop, take a breath, observe, and proceed." Using the STOP practice during this meditation will allow you to access it more readily in everyday life.

Find a comfortable posture, and first settle your awareness into the sensations of sitting and breathing. Then recall a recent time when you were triggered. Try to remember all the details of what happened, who said what, how you felt, and what was hard or troubling for you in this situation. Notice what caused your frustration, fear, or other strong reaction. Allow yourself to feel the strength of the emotions as if the event were happening now.

The moment you feel yourself becoming triggered, the first and perhaps most important step is to stop. Take a moment to recognize that you are triggered. This pause helps interrupt the reactive spinning mode and allows you time to assess what is happening.

The second step is to breathe deeply. This is a support for the pause. So take three to five deep breaths with long exhales. Notice how slow breathing immediately calms the nervous system and brings clarity to the mind.

The third step is to observe your inner experience. Bring awareness to all your physical reactions, like shortness of breath, tightness in your heart, and tension in the throat, chest, belly, or face. Bring awareness to your emotions. Name them if possible, and sense where you experience them in your body. Are you feeling anger, fear, or jealousy? Can you feel how even the strongest emotions inevitably change, ebb, and flow?

In addition, observe your thoughts. Name the types that occur, like blame, judgment, defensiveness, and self-righteousness. Notice how observing your thoughts creates space around them, so you are not so lost in them. As this happens, try to identify what triggered or provoked you. Consider if your reaction related to what was going on in that moment or perhaps related to another incident with this person or situation. Was the strength of your reaction due to circumstances or conditions beyond that moment, perhaps from your past?

Once you feel calmer and more clear, then the last step is to proceed, which means to act or respond in an appropriate way, one that ideally creates a positive solution for both parties. Once you have stopped, taken a few deep breaths, and observed your reaction intimately, you will have hopefully interrupted the triggered reaction. You will then be better prepared to reflect on the next steps and respond effectively in ways that help everyone.

As you meditate on these four steps, imagine how your previous encounter might have unfolded if you had followed them. What lessons can you learn, and what might be a helpful way to move forward? This might mean communicating clearly or allowing time for the dust to settle before doing anything else. If your reaction was overblown, this might identify a particular personal issue to address, perhaps with help from others. Whatever the decision, it is important to find a way to move forward that both lessens the pain of the experience and sows seeds that make it less likely to happen in the future.

• • •

Chapter 24

Cultivating Self-Compassion

Feeling compassion for ourselves in no way releases us from responsibility for our actions. Rather, it releases us from the self-hatred that prevents us from responding to our life with clarity and balance.
— TARA BRACH

Early in my spiritual journey I read Meister Eckhart's writings on the "dark night of the soul." In my youthful naïveté, this sounded romantic, the archetypal wrestling with existential dilemmas and being plunged into darkness where light seems elusive. I hadn't learned that many things in life cannot be understood until we truly live through them. No amount of reading or talking will nurture the wisdom that comes from such a journey. The descent into those long bleak nights is truly the cauldron in which the fires of transformation occur.

I dove into the world of meditation when I was nineteen, and this passion consumed me for decades. I devoted years to silent retreat practice. I was committed to awakening, and intensive meditation was the vehicle. After many years of focused study, I decided to ordain as a monk in Burma to deepen that pursuit. Immediately prior to that, I attended a three-month silent meditation retreat in New England, one of many I had attended during that period. Looking back, I have to admit I was rather full of myself. I had an inflated spiritual ego, and I thought that all this meditation practice made me special. Little did I know that life had other ideas for me.

On that retreat, waves of early trauma surfaced, and I was battered with levels of emotional pain I had never encountered before. It felt as if I were being annihilated. I was consumed by profound grief, confusion, and despair. I lost all direction. Meditation seemed impossible, as it only intensified the trauma and regressed states I was grappling with. The months of the retreat were very bleak, followed by even darker months of depression and chronic fatigue. I had always thought the "dark night of the soul" was a single night. What folly! This persisted for interminable months. What was I to do?

Fortunately, I had been training in meditation for many years. Even though I literally felt flattened by the pain, that practice helped me meet it with awareness and compassion. This was not coming from my spiritual ego, since that had been pummeled to the floor. This warmheartedness emerged as the fruit of the years of my meditation practice, which allowed the beautiful gifts of presence and kindness to hold me and my pain. This response took me by surprise, and more importantly, it allowed me to surrender as each painful wave continued to crash onto shore.

When there is no resistance, I discovered, one can feel immense pain without suffering. It is reactivity that creates distress. Mindfulness is a liberating force that can allow us to open to the challenging waves that can smash into the shores of our life. When that awareness is infused with love and turned toward our pain, it becomes a potent source of self-compassion. This loving awareness allows us to hold any painful experience, enabling us to soften into and welcome it. It still isn't easy or pleasant, but it is the key that allows us to work with trauma and other challenging eruptions. It supports us to move through such episodes and be transformed by them.

Kristin Neff, a psychologist and leading researcher on self-compassion, talks about three key components necessary to foster self-compassion: (1) common humanity: recognizing that pain and failure are unavoidable aspects of the human experience; (2) mindfulness: having the ability to observe rather than avoid painful thoughts and feelings; and (3) self-kindness: being kind and understanding to oneself in instances of suffering or perceived inadequacy versus self-judgment. Awareness infused with care helps each of these key components to open on this journey.

For myself, the descent I went through opened me up to the immense pain that human beings can go through. This experience continues to be a humbling gift that has cultivated greater compassion for the wounds we all carry. It has given me courage to turn toward any difficult place, whether in myself or others. Once someone goes through such "dark nights," it creates a fearlessness to go into hard terrain. This has been invaluable in my work as a therapist and teacher, giving me capacity to work with those who walk in the same barren, raw, and sometimes terrifying territory.

The third component for self-compassion, releasing self-judgment, is key in learning to open to pain. I have a strong inner critic, and working with it led me to write my book *Make Peace with Your Mind*, about freeing oneself from self-judgment. In any painful inner journey, nothing is less helpful than critical thoughts that close down one's process. When I shifted from condemning myself for my "fall from grace" to softening with kindness and acceptance, I could work with my experience in a much more skillful and open way.

If you have experienced your own dark nights, look back with the perspective of time and reflect on the gifts they have bestowed. Maybe they opened you to a greater alignment with yourself, moved your heart to feel your common humanity, or strengthened your capacity to endure hardship. Perhaps they woke you from being asleep to yourself and the wounds you carry. Navigating such hard experiences can support us as we take greater risks, giving us courage to face our deepest fears and to make the most of this one wild and precious life.

Whatever your experience, everyone at some point grapples with loss, heartache, and confusion. What is necessary then is to reflect on what will help you meet your own struggles with compassionate presence, to see pain as a gift or an opportunity and not an enemy, to give yourself love and understanding, not rejection and judgment. Only when we can soften into pain, with tender arms of loving awareness, can we really heal and grow.

On a recent trip to England for the Christmas holidays, I had an unusually frank talk with my father. We were in a lively English pub, full of holiday cheer, and after chatting about various things, he began sharing how much pain he still carried inside. My father had a wretched early childhood. He was born out of wedlock in 1939. Unable to be raised by his mother, he was fostered by a multitude of families until he was seven. He said he lived with so many foster parents that he forgot the names of his caregivers.

All this happened during the six years of World War II, when England was focused on surviving the war against Germany, and there was little attention or time to spare for a little fostered child. As children do, my father internalized his miserable predicament by assuming something must be fundamentally wrong with him. He developed scars of unworthiness and shame. This left him hungry for love that he hoped would mitigate the hole of deficiency that lived in his heart. Being so young, he had not learned the skills and coping mechanisms needed to deal with such pain.

The tragic pain from those early years remained with him all his life. He had found many ways to hide it, to ignore it, to drink it away. But like a shadow, it was always close to hand. Now, in his later years, the pain was tugging even more on his heart. He felt a desire for resolution and healing, and he felt remorse for the ways he had acted out from the pain. Yet he was unsure how to resolve the painful emptiness inside.

During our conversation in the pub, my father took the risk to reveal this vulnerable hurting place to me. It was a beautiful moment of intimacy, and I had tears in my eyes as he talked of the pain he had held in for so long. I reflected to him from my own struggles that the only way forward is through pain. I reminded him that he had to turn toward that scared, lonely, rejected boy inside and give him the same love that he was clearly able to give to his family, children, and friends. To heal, I suggested he hold his wounded heart with compassion, feel the tender pain, and meet it with kindness and forgiveness.

I also offered him resources to begin that work. One suggestion was to do an eight-week Mindful Self-Compassion training, developed by Kristin Neff and Christopher Germer. Coincidentally, and unbeknown to us, that exact class was being offered by a trained Mindful Self-Compassion teacher the following week in a nearby village in southern England.

Courageously, my father leaped at the chance and began a profound self-healing journey. Afterward, he spoke to me of the powerful practices of mindfulness and compassion he learned from the course. He felt less alone, and he felt empathy for his fellow participants, who were also going through their own difficulties. He understood that healing a lifetime of pain, rejection, and unworthiness would take time, understanding, and patience, but he had taken the important first steps on that journey. His heart was beautifully tender and open in a way that it had never been. This is the gift of our wounds, in which healing them opens us like nothing else can.

Developing Self-Compassion

Holding our pain with compassion, rather than judgment, is a landmark when it comes to finding peace in our life. It is a calming salve for our emotional wounds. When we can access this attitude of self-care in times of distress, the experience of pain can shift from being unbearable to being tolerable and workable. This meditation will help you learn to meet your pain with compassion and care.

Find a place to meditate where you can be undisturbed. Sit in a chair, with an upright yet relaxed and comfortable posture. For a few minutes, close your eyes and feel your breath in your heart center, in the middle of your chest.

Now call to mind any stress, pain, hardship, or suffering you currently feel. It may be physical, emotional, mental, or spiritual distress. It could be a stressful life circumstance or relationship difficulty. Take some time to explore the particular challenges and suffering involved in these experiences. With kind, caring attention, feel the pain or the struggle. If judgments or other thoughts arise, acknowledge them and try to let them go.

While holding the pain with this kind, caring presence, say these phrases slowly and meaningfully to yourself, as if you were consoling a dear, distressed friend:

May I be free of pain and suffering.
May I hold my suffering and myself with kindness and ease.

Repeat these phrases slowly and as genuinely as you can, taking time to connect with the meaning of each phrase each time you say it. Don't seek any particular feeling; simply offer these kind, caring wishes to yourself. You may add your own phrases or use ones that speak more directly to your pain and the wish for relief.

If this practice accentuates the pain too much, then let go of focusing on the pain, take some slower, deeper breaths, and open your eyes until you feel centered again and not lost in the pain. Then resume saying the phrases while kindly holding your suffering. When you feel ready to end this meditation, slowly open your eyes and gently move and stretch.

After practicing this meditation a few times, you can offer these phrases to yourself at any time, whenever you feel pain or distress. You can also offer them to others whenever you encounter their suffering.

• • •

Chapter 25

Developing the Kind Heart

Stay out of the court of self-judgment,
for there is no presumption of innocence.
— ROBERT BRAULT

One modern epidemic that plagues most people I know is the scourge of the judging mind. This is the constant negative self-talk that relentlessly reminds us we are not smart enough, not good enough, not enough in so many ways. This habit of negatively critiquing everything we do and say erodes our well-being and thwarts our ability to accept and love ourselves just as we are. This voice condemns our all-so-human foibles and fosters chronic low self-esteem and unworthiness.

Many people I work with don't even notice the presence of the inner critic. They are so accustomed to that negative voice in their heads that it is part of their mental furniture. This means it gets a lot of airtime. Worse still, we tend to believe everything it has to say. We think it is the voice of truth, and we allow it to dictate what we do and what we believe. It alters how we view ourselves and our accomplishments, so that we focus mostly on our shortcomings and dismiss all the ways we are good, kind, human beings.

When we allow the inner critic to measure our worth, we don't need to wait for St. Peter to pass judgment at the pearly gates of heaven. The inner critic banishes us to a hellish place right now. Listening to that judging narrative day after day, year after year, our sense of our own value plummets, until we feel worthless, without any goodness or merit. We question why anyone would like us or love us, and we doubt our own skills and smarts. We may develop the "impostor syndrome," which is the fear that if people really knew who we were, they would fire us from our jobs or avoid any relationship with us. All this can lead to chronic depression, self-hatred, anxiety, and in the worse-case scenario, suicidal thoughts.

If all this is true, why would any sane person give the judging mind any attention whatsoever? Why would we listen to such an unkind, harsh, critical, and inaccurate self-perception, one that only makes us miserable?

One answer is that we are conditioned to believe this voice. For example, I met Jodie in England on a meditation course. She is a smart, accomplished doctor, working with children in poverty-stricken neighborhoods in London. She cares deeply about the families and children she works with, people who live on the margins of life and suffer hardship and malnutrition. On the surface she comes across as a naturally good person doing compassionate work in the world. However, that isn't the story she tells about herself on the inside.

Jodie was born out of wedlock. As teenagers, her parents, both Roman Catholic, had a brief affair in the 1960s and never intended to marry. Both had plans to go to college and pursue careers in medicine. The pregnancy changed everything. Her mother abandoned college, and her father took a restaurant job so they could rent an apartment and raise their daughter.

However, this was not done with joy or openness. Jodie's

parents eventually married, but they felt bitter resentment for the way having a daughter impacted their lives and restricted their dreams. Unexpected, unwanted pregnancies are not uncommon, and in Jodie's case, her parents never got over their negative feelings, and they did not mince words. They regularly and painfully reminded their daughter that she had ruined their lives, their careers, and their hopes of travel and what could have been a happy marriage.

Sadly, Jodie, like countless others in her situation, internalized the experience of being unwanted and turned it into a deeply held view that she must be unworthy of love. To make sense of marital conflict, children commonly believe their parents' pain and unhappiness is their fault. This results in deep feelings of guilt and shame and a free-floating sense of wrongness. Planting such seeds in a child is like planting a virus that spreads and seeps into every part of their being.

When children are regularly blamed and criticized by their parents, this becomes internalized as the inner critic. As she grew up, Jodie's inner critic repeated her parents' cruel words, time and time again. This is a misguided attempt at self-preservation. The inner critic tries to minimize the threat of rejection from caregivers. It attempts to ensure their love by shaming us into conforming to their needs. For Jodie, her inner critic scolded her anytime she risked her parents' disapproval, in the hope of trying to find morsels of kindness in a barren field.

Today, fifty years later, those words and their scars are still playing themselves out for Jodie. Despite a life of service, helping those who have been neglected and downtrodden, she still hears those tunes of unworthiness in her head. For years she lived alone, feeling unlovable and avoiding romantic relationships. She still distracts herself with food and overwork to try to drown out the negative voices. Fortunately for Jodie, she found meditation and has begun to address her feelings of shame, to cultivate a genuinely kind self-regard, and to gain an objective perspective on her goodness.

Mindfulness practice is an invaluable tool for working effectively with the inner critic, as it gives us the capacity to know our experience just as it is. Without that clarity, we will be unable to know our own minds and identify what is helpful and what is harmful.

When we bring that laser quality of awareness to our judging mind, we see how unconstructive and painful those thoughts really are. Awareness identifies when judgments occur and gives us the choice to release them or shift our attention to something more constructive. We can also track the impact judgments have on our heart and our well-being. Once we see the harm they cause, we are more likely to release such patterns. However, being aware of this process is not enough. A compassionate response to the pain is also required.

In my own journey working with a harsh and punishing inner critic, one thing that helped me find space from it was feeling the hurt those judging thoughts caused. Feeling the bruising of my heart each time a negative thought landed helped me realize how painful it was to talk to myself like that. This fostered a sense of self-care, a warm tenderness to both ease the pain and thwart the impact of such words. That flowering of self-compassion, the shift from self-harm to kindness, eventually allows us to shift away from supporting and engaging with the cruelty of self-judgment to relating to ourselves as we would to a loved one, with care.

The desire to free ourselves from the inner critic is the same self-protective force we draw on to protect a child who is being harmed. That compassion can be fierce, refusing to listen to or tolerate the inner critic's harshness. Such healthy defensiveness allows some inner space or distance from the wounds caused by judgments. Once that space is established, we can inquire into whether such critical comments are useful, accurate, or true. When we examine them in the clear light of awareness and see their folly, they begin to lose their grip and we can let them go more easily.

From that more spacious place we can cultivate a more positive and appreciative attitude toward ourselves. We can take note of our strengths, good qualities, and other positive attributes. This helps balance the ledger that has been skewed by the negative lens of the inner critic.

Over time these expressions of kindness establish a sense of worth and authentic value as a human being. They provide a genuine bulwark against the years of negativity from self-judgment. Such a warmhearted embrace of ourselves is what allowed Jodie to slowly find a way back into her own heart. You can do the same.

• **PRACTICE** •

Shifting from Judgment to Kindness

Transforming judgments is key if we are to truly find peace. To do this, we must become aware of how we meet these painful thoughts and how they affect our heart and body. We can shift away from listening to these harsh critiques to sensing the pain and negativity of such words. The next time you are self-critical, hearing self-judgments, register how this is experienced in your heart. Reflect on these questions:

- How does it feel to talk to yourself this way?
- Do you feel the residue of those judgments in your body?
- How does your heart feel in response to such criticism?
- What is the emotional repercussion of the judgments?
- How do they impact how you perceive yourself?

When you notice the impact of judging thoughts, feel into the tenderness for the pain self-criticism causes. Transformation comes when we are vulnerable enough to open the heart and feel the impact of the inner critic. Also notice the pain that is driving these critical thoughts. Judgments of the inner critic are often a misguided attempt to help or protect, but they do so in a hurtful and often destructive way.

From this soft but strong place, sense the voice that lovingly but firmly says no to these judgments. Find the compassionate strength that cares for you and for the parts of your psyche that feel young, vulnerable, or overwhelmed. When you do, you are less likely to feel like a victim. Instead you can begin the slow but important work of self-protection, which is an expression of love for yourself.

Finally, an important antidote to the critic and a powerful force for developing self-compassion is the practice of loving-kindness. A simple way to develop this practice is to wish oneself well. So each time you hear your critic's judgments you can replace them with a phrase of loving-kindness for yourself, a phrase that expresses your deeper aspirations. Such phrases could be: May I be happy. May I be peaceful. May I be free from self-judgment. May I love and accept myself just as I am.

You can also do this as a formal meditation, in the same way you offered yourself phrases of self-compassion in the previous chapter's meditation. You can offer yourself these wishes of kindness, repeating them slowly and meaningfully to yourself. As simple as this practice is, when cultivated over time, such expressions of self-kindness can have a profound impact on our well-being and be a truly effective counterpoint to the negative messages coming from the critic.

• • •

Chapter 26

Embracing Loss

Grief is like the ocean; it comes in waves ebbing and flowing.
Sometimes the water is calm, and sometimes it is overwhelming.
All we can do is learn to swim.
— VICKI HARRISON

Freeing the heart entails learning to navigate the storms of life and the shipwrecks that can follow with skill, clarity, and kindness. Mindfulness and kindness are essential tools that build the life raft that brings you to shore. One of the core challenges we face, particularly as we age, is the tender arena of loss. It is impossible to go through life without losing things, people, and experiences that are precious to us. How we handle this loss determines how much we suffer. The Palestinian American poet Naomi Shihab Nye speaks of the inseparability of loss and heartfulness in her beautiful poem "Kindness."

Before you know what kindness really is
you must lose things,
feel the future dissolve in a moment
like salt in a weakened broth....
Before you know kindness as the deepest thing inside,

you must know sorrow as the other deepest thing.
You must wake up with sorrow.
You must speak to it till your voice
catches the thread of all sorrows
And you see the size of the cloth.

Sarah, a Canadian psychologist and single mother, attended a course I taught in the Rocky Mountains. She was motivated to come because a tornado of loss had ripped through her life, leaving her exhausted and washed up on the shore of despair. A year before, her only son, a competitive athlete and an avid heli-skier, had been left paralyzed from the neck down by a tragic skiing accident. Sarah felt as if her world had been stolen from her, which in some ways it had. She had to quit her job and move back in with her parents in Ontario so she could attend to her son full-time and care for his needs.

The silent nature retreat was an ideal place to simply let the river of tears flow. The blessing of a silent retreat provides a space to breathe, to feel whatever your heart is feeling. It allowed Sarah to bring awareness to the natural disorientation and disbelief that comes with upheaval. However, Sarah, like many people dealing with loss, wasn't really allowing the process to flow.

She was filled with self-judgments. She didn't think she was doing enough as a caregiver, and she didn't understand why she felt so confused and lost. She thought she should be over her grief by now and moving on with her life, or at least moving on from her pain, and she was frustrated to still be coping with residual denial, anger, and disbelief, which are common stages of the grief process. In addition, Sarah felt guilty for resenting her son's risky skiing behavior, which led to his accident. It was a classic case of increasing the suffering of tremendous loss by engaging in self-criticism and blame.

Sarah's reaction was not unique. Many times we increase the burden of an already painful situation because of our own assumptions or judgments about how the process should go or how we should be handling it. These views not only shut us down but further close our heart and interfere with the organic unfolding of the grief process. Such reactions are normal, yet they obstruct our ability to heal. Sarah's judgments — especially that she should be over her grief and moving on with her life — were definitely hampering her ability to grieve. Only by allowing the tears to flow can we eventually surface from that well of sorrow and pick up the threads of our newly emerging life.

So how did attending a meditation retreat help Sarah in such a difficult situation? Mindfulness can help us develop the capacity to radically meet the conditions of our life with clarity, nonreactivity, and warmhearted presence. It does not take away the pain of loss, but it helps us hold our suffering and avoid making it worse through resistance, blame, or judgment.

During Sarah's retreat, she learned to hold and surrender into her loss, grief, and disorientation with a kind presence. She gave herself the gift of not needing to figure anything out, and instead let the waves of pain wash over her. This allowed the suffering to shift into a natural tender sadness over time. From this softened and surrendered place, a caring responsiveness arose for the pain she and her son had been through and for the overwhelming hardship of the situation. She realized she couldn't leapfrog to this place but instead had to walk through the tender path of grieving.

By leaning into and opening to loss, we allow those cold winds to blow through us. As hard as those storms may be, fighting them compounds the torment. Ironically, as we surrender to their flow, this can often, as the Sufi poet Rumi suggests, "clear us out for some new delight." As we move through the waves of heartache and are softened by their blows, such melting can open up new horizons; influenced by loss, we discover new possibilities we had never thought possible. Conversely, if we don't open, we may stay entombed in a suspended state, as if frozen in ice. The tears of kind presence allow this precious melting to happen and for new life to emerge.

Michelle, a longtime meditation student, shared with me this beautiful description of how this process unfolds:

> When I was forty-one years old, my twenty-one-year-old son died in an accident while he was away at college. That was twenty-two years ago, and I cannot say or write those words without an enormous wave of grief and sadness. But I don't drown. I can let that wave wash over me. I can live my life with interest and even joy along with the great sadness. I have learned to do that, I believe, largely with the help of my meditation practice, turning toward, not away from, the tenderness of grief.

Anticipation of potential loss is another facet of this terrain that we have to learn to work with. The dread of losing the people we love can cause unnecessary suffering and keep us frozen, so we don't fully embrace the present moment. This happened with Maddie, a woman in her early forties from Oakland, California. Maddie had already known a fair amount of loss. She had lost a baby in childbirth, and when she was eight years old, she had lost her father in a car accident. However, she had a strong bond with her husband, whom she had married young and who was her rock through losing their son.

Maddie would often lie awake in the middle of the night in fear of what might become of her life partner. His family had a history of heart disease. She worried about all the stress he went through at his law firm. If he reported feeling pains in his chest, she would panic. Her worst nightmare was the thought of losing him. She decided to work with me to help relieve her anxiety and insomnia, and she expected me to help her be less attached, to let go. I instead shifted her in a different direction.

In a guided meditation, I asked Maddie to allow her anxiety and worry about her husband to surface, so she would feel the fullness of those emotions in her body. Mindfulness helps us acknowledge our experience and find a spacious capacity to hold even challenging emotions. This is the first step in working skillfully with anything, rather than avoiding it or being caught up in a stressful contention. Once she was able to find some steadiness simply being with those feelings, I then, to her surprise, directed her to feel the ocean of love that lay underneath the surface ripples of fear.

In meditation, Maddie found it easy to access the deep love she felt for her partner. The fear of losing that wealth of love was the cause of her duress. I invited her to really bathe in that love that flowed from her heart. As that quality pervaded her mind and body, she noticed her anxiety abating until she was able to rest in the sweetness of their connection and the power of her own kind heart. I then asked her to inquire about the source of that love. Certainly she received love from her partner, but the origin of her loving experience was coming from the depth of her own being.

Often the thought of losing someone we love feeds the fear that we will lose the essence of love itself. The more we realize that love is the nature of our own heart, the more we realize we cannot be separated from it. Such realization does not take away the sadness that comes when we lose loved ones, but we see that loss neither diminishes our capacity to love nor prevents access to that beautiful quality of openhearted connection.

As Maddie bathed in the depth of her love for her husband, she realized this was the doorway to diffusing her fear of losing him.

The next, equally important step was turning that love toward herself, toward her own feelings of fear and panic. Once we access the kindness in our own hearts, we can focus that caring attention on the scared parts of ourselves. In Maddie's case, the young child who lost a parent still lived within her, and that same anxiety was feeding her fears about losing her husband.

Maddie realized, as we all can, that healing comes when we tenderly embrace the scared, anxious parts that lie within us. Our nervous system settles, our breathing slows, our thoughts stop racing, and we find some ease in the present moment. It is a way we practice not abandoning ourselves. When we can hold ourselves with a loving mindful presence, we have the capacity to endure anything.

• PRACTICE •

Softening into Loss

Find a comfortable meditation posture and close your eyes. Settle your attention on your breath, breathing naturally and gently. Then shift your focus to feel or sense your heart area in the center of your chest. Feel the breath there. Then take some moments to reflect on someone or something you have lost. This could be a loved one or even a pet. It could be an experience, such as the loss of a good friendship. Take time to feel into both your love of that person or experience and the loss connected to that.

Finding peace in the midst of loss centers on whether we can hold ourselves with loving presence as we navigate the tender pain. As you feel the pangs of loss and grief, allow yourself to open to the rawness of that experience. Can you feel it in your heart or elsewhere in the body? Do thoughts, images, and memories arise with it? Without getting caught up in memories or carried away by thoughts, keep experiencing any waves of feeling that arise.

If possible, hold yourself with the kind attention you would offer a dear friend who is going through a difficult time. Particularly if the loss feels strong, try placing a hand over your heart as a gesture of self-love and soothing. Take some slower breaths and maintain a warm, friendly attitude toward yourself and your tender feelings. If you need to reduce the intensity of feeling, know that you can shift your attention away at any time, focusing on something more neutral like sounds or looking around the room you are in. You may also whisper to yourself that this too will pass. Remind yourself that the essence of your heart is love and that you always have the power to access this kindheartedness, as it is your nature.

At the end of this practice, shift your attention to something neutral in your experience, like the breath. Sense your connection to the earth through the contact of your body with the floor or the chair. Take a few minutes to allow your focus to shift until you feel ready to end the meditation. At the same time, know that feelings of tenderness or sadness may linger after the reflection is done. That is natural, so continue to hold whatever arises with tenderness and kindness.

• • •

Chapter 27

Living with a Steady Heart

When attachment does not occur when someone gives flowers,
and no abhorrence occurs when someone throws stones,
that is considered equanimity.

— DADA BHAGAWAN

When I first started to practice meditation, I brought along old misinterpretations of my early Catholic faith. I had learned from my churchgoing days the view of "'being in the world but not of it." That is a beautiful and elusive teaching. Hearing the Buddha's teaching on renunciation sounded surprisingly familiar. I mistakenly took it as license to unconsciously reject things in myself I thought the church considered unholy. This led me to reject the wilder, passionate, unruly parts of my being. Unfortunately, that meant I also cut off the playful and creative parts of myself, which included abruptly ending my phase as a spirited punk rocker, someone who made his own gaudy clothes, dyed his mohawk white, wore crazy earrings, and squatted in empty houses. That vivacious, wild side got sadly buried.

I let go of a lot in order to become what I thought was a "good Buddhist," which repeated my youthful attempts to win approval by being a "good Christian." I shut down parts of myself to fulfill some false notion of being calm and collected, of what I imagined detachment and equanimity to be. But what I really engaged in was repression and what some call a "spiritual bypass." This led to long years where my vitality went underground. It wasn't until I went to Burning Man in the deserts of Nevada that I rediscovered that more creative, playful, and wild part of myself.

People often equate equanimity with being uncaring or coolness, as if it means becoming like a cold statue, like the ones we may see in temples and monasteries. Far from being aloof, equanimity refers to a connected presence that allows us to meet any experience with grounded balance. It's the steadiness of heart that helps us not get lost in reactivity. Given the ceaseless demands and challenges of life, who wouldn't want that quality?

Mindfulness meditation is like a training ground in which we get to practice how to meet an extensive range of experience in our body, heart, and mind. We sit still and bear witness to whatever happens, with the intention to be present with curiosity and openness. That is not as easy as it sounds, given the intensity of physical pain that can happen, or the waves of grief that flow, or the anxious, frenetic thoughts that can assault us.

Typically, when we don't like what is happening in life, we try to avoid it, ignore it, or do something else, like switching TV channels. This habit can leave us with an impatient mind, unwilling to tolerate even the mildest unpleasantness. As my friend and colleague Howard Cohn amusingly asks students during his lectures: "What is it we practice in daily life? Follow every thought, chase every desire, get rid of everything you don't like, avoid pain, and try to control experiences and people around you!" Not only is this exhausting, it is impossible. It fails to equip us to respond appropriately to life. It does not prepare us for things we have no control over, like our variable health, the rapidly changing economy, the instability of relationships, and the uncertainty of our work.

Mindfulness offers a different orientation, one that develops a steady heart to face life's inevitable ups and downs. This balanced attention helps us respond to what are known as the "eight worldly winds." These are the polarities of experience that are inherent in life: pleasure and pain, gain and loss, success and failure, and praise and blame. These storms are forever blowing and create uncertainty at every step. They make it hard to find stable ground, since they represent the unpredictable, changing fortunes of experience, and not a day goes by when we don't experience one or more. In Zen, the perennial highs and lows of experience are called the "ten thousand joys and sorrows." They remind me of a poem by the Russian poet Anna Akhmatova:

Everything is plundered, betrayed, sold.
Death's great black wing scrapes the air,
Misery gnaws to the bone.
Then why do we not despair?
By day, from the surrounding woods,
Cherries blow summer into town;
At night the deep transparent skies
Glitter with new galaxies.

Life is this fluctuating sea of change. It is rarely just one thing or the other. It is seldom just wretched or exquisite but often both and everything in between, even in the space of one day or a single moment.

We can see this polarity everywhere we look. There is beauty and horror in the lives of children, whether they come from the wealthiest families or the poorest. People can be magnificently kind and coldly cruel to one another. The economy surges and crashes on a dime. Love blooms only to be followed by betrayal. As one species is saved from extinction, another is lost. One minute we are praised for our accomplishments, and in the next we are torn down for our mistakes.

How do we manage this constant array of swings and round-abouts, of highs and lows? We can do so through equanimity, the principle of meeting all experience with balance. In mindfulness practice we learn to turn toward the truth of what is with clarity and acceptance, similar to the way rocks on the shoreline stand steady, unmoving, against the relentless onslaught of the waves. That quality of steadfastness is informed by the wisdom that knows that, however intense experience can be, it is transient and can change in any moment.

Research seems to support this notion. In one 2007 study, researchers found that people who had even minimal experience with mindfulness practice were more capable of dealing with pain than people with no training. The study suggested that mindfulness practitioners were more aware of pain's fleeting nature and more able to release any distress that came with it.

Similarly, by embracing both joy and sorrow, we grow our capacity to be with either. Being able to enjoy pleasure knowing full well that it will fade is what also allows us to meet pain, for we know that it too will change, morph, and release. Equanimity does not mean we turn away, become numb, or are indifferent. It means we delight in the joys of spring daffodils and the first steps of our children, and we also have some capacity to embrace the pain of losing a loved one and the decline of our health as we age. Equanimity doesn't necessarily make painful things easy, but it's the understanding that to resist or contract around pain simply makes matters worse.

In the same way, this balanced presence holds lightly all the praise that comes our way, not letting it go to our head or inspire us to build a new identity around it. For we know too well that just as praise comes, critique or blame may be close on its heels. The more we build our pedestal on the shaky foundation of praise, the farther we will fall when it inevitably fades. Similarly, our pride can bloom with the fame that comes with success, only to have our name later smeared by some accusation.

Equanimity looks upon this whole show of life with the gaze of a grandmother watching her grandchildren play. She sees how they squeal with delight, fight with vengeance, and cry with loss all in the space of an hour, yet with the wisdom of age and perspective, she gazes upon them all fondly. She has strong feelings, and she takes appropriate action to help solve problems, correct mistakes, and discipline misbehavior. But under all of those feelings and responses, she sees the big picture: the nature of this world is unceasing change, ups and downs, and her grandchildren need love and guidance to help meet this reality.

This is equanimity, the balance that guides amidst the turbulence of life. What erodes our ability to abide in such a state? Most commonly, it is our resistance to or rejection of what is, when we are attached to a view that something is unfair or wrong or "should not" be happening. Or we are caught in blaming and judging someone or something for the problem. Many things in life can seem unfair or cruel, such as childhood cancer or a car accident killing a loved one. However, nature or the universe is neither fair nor just. It simply moves in accordance with natural laws. Sometimes the most innocent are harmed, the most generous lose everything, and the most loving lose the very people they cherish.

Equanimity asks us to meet such hardships with acceptance and discernment, since complaints and resistance can be counterproductive. This does not mean our response should be passive. Nor does it mean we tolerate anything that is harmful to self or others or the planet. Of course, the appropriate response to tragedy and intense pain includes helping and caring in all the ways we can — whether the misfortune is ours or someone else's, and whether what happens is fair or not. Indeed, focusing on "unfairness" can lead to a sense of victimization or hopelessness, which can make us less able to respond.

Further, equanimity doesn't mean that we like what has happened, that we want it to have happened, or that we ever want to experience it again. It simply asks that we turn our attention toward, and unconditionally allow, the truth of our experience. From that clarity, we can then respond wisely and appropriately.

Lastly, we can also bring equanimity to our own resistance and judgment, which at times are unavoidable. When equanimity is not our first response to pain, we can practice and learn to be tolerant and accepting of our own limitations. We can acknowledge our reaction, bring warm attention to what is hard and unwanted, and let this compassionate attitude ease the suffering that arises from our reactivity.

By riding with life's ups and downs, we learn to act with fluidity in the same way water flows downstream. As water encounters obstacles, it adapts, yields, and shifts in an ever-responsive movement. The poet Wendell Berry wisely wrote: "It is the impeded stream that sings." Without the obstacles, creeks would not make the delightful sounds we so enjoy. The same is perhaps true with life. It is so often the hard places that encourage us to grow and find the strengths, tenacity, and gifts we may have believed we never had.

• PRACTICE •

Cultivating a Steady Heart

This meditation explores developing equanimity. To do so, we practice meeting what is with balance, steadiness, and acceptance. This doesn't mean we like or want what we meet or that our response is passive. But equanimity asks that we first open to whatever exists.

To begin, sit comfortably, take some deep breaths, and settle your attention on your posture and physical experience. Invite a quality of relaxation and ease. Then call to mind something hard in your life that you resist. Anything is fine: conflict with a partner or coworker, aches in your body, political or societal dramas, or even bad weather. Call this issue to mind and explore this experience. What do you notice in your mind, heart, and body? Let yourself feel both the experience that is difficult and your reaction to it.

Now become present to your own awareness. Observe how that presence is like a space that makes room for an experience to unfold. When we can abide in awareness, rather than get caught up in the experience itself and our reaction to it, it allows breathing room to accommodate whatever is happening. This is like a child's inflatable castle. Inside the walls of the castle, experience happens. Kids can scream and be as wild as they like, and it is all accommodated.

Then notice your thoughts or views about the difficult experience. Pay attention to judgments (*I shouldn't have let this happen*) and a sense of injustice (*What's happening is unfair*). Such beliefs compound the difficulty and only add fuel to the fire of reactivity. Hold these thoughts in awareness and try to let them go, then return your attention to the actual experience.

See if you can let your attention be fully present without these views interfering. Simply witness the experience rather than resist or avoid it, and notice if this makes it easier to be with. You may never like it, but you may find more capacity to hold it. And if there is resistance, know that you can bring the same spacious awareness to that experience also. Imagine your mind is like the sky and has the capacity to hold any cloud-like experience.

Then remember that every experience is fleeting and transient and will eventually change, no matter how painful or challenging. Reflecting on impermanence is an important support for developing a steady heart. This helps develop tolerance. Thinking that pain will last forever makes it much harder to accept, but understanding that nothing lasts helps us be less reactive and more patient with difficulty.

The final key is to bring kindness to the difficulty. Try to bring a warm, friendly attitude to this experience. Notice how that can melt some of the rigidity or contraction that arises with reacting to what is hard to bear.

As you bring this practice to a close, make a commitment to apply these principles to any reactivity or challenging situation that occurs during your day. Notice how this approach can increase your capacity to stay steady in the midst of any experience.

• • •

Chapter 28

Delighting in the Joy of Others

If you can't find joy in the path you are on and what you are working toward now, how do you expect to find joy once you get there?
— ANONYMOUS

I remember visiting a friend whose baby was on the cusp of that miraculous transition from crawling and rolling around on the floor to taking her first wobbly, tentative steps. It was hard to know who to be happier for: Davina, the eleven-month-old blond-haired toddler, or her parents, who were beaming with pride and joy. There was a lot of laughter as we watched Davina be helped up on her legs by her proud dad, stumble a couple of steps toward the outstretched arms of her radiant mother, and then fall back on her bottom to a fit of giggles and laughter. It was a momentous day in her little world, as this was the first time she had successfully taken more than one blessed step.

In that moment I was very aware of how joy is infectious. It reminded me of the sympathetic joy meditation in which one rejoices in the happiness of others. This beautiful quality significantly increases our opportunities for experiencing delight. By appreciating the happiness of others, we do tend to improve our chances of joy

220 • From Suffering to Peace

by about seven billion to one! I don't gamble, but I do know those are good odds. Sympathetic joy means the heart is like kindling, ready for sparks of happiness wherever gladness and success are found.

The other upside to this lovely quality is that it cuts through feelings of jealousy. Envy is a painful domain of the heart, so anything that helps undermine it is a welcome guest. The contraction we feel when others are doing well or enjoying good fortune is a common way the ego self keeps us in poverty. Not celebrating the happiness and achievements of others robs us of our own well-being.

Often, the root of jealousy is fear and anxiety about the lack or scarcity of our own circumstances. For example, I remember nearing the end of my four-year, meditation teacher–training program with Jack Kornfield. It was 2006, and finding sufficient teaching opportunities was not easy, so all of us were anxiously contemplating our next steps.

Then one of my dearest friends in the program announced that she had been offered a full-time position with a six-figure salary leading a meditation research center in a prestigious university. This was an amazing position and fantastic news for her. My friend had been trying to pull herself out of ongoing money struggles, and this job would allow her to flourish and become economically stable. Further, not only would she be teaching mindfulness, but her new role had the potential to have a significant impact in the nascent mindfulness movement.

I had to admit: while I was certainly happy for her, I was in equal measures jealous! Hearing the news triggered a sense of envy. I also desired to be on a more secure financial footing. I similarly aspired to have work with a high impact. In truth, I didn't really want this particular job, which required relocating to Minnesota, a place that didn't interest me, but my friend's success triggered a sense of scarcity and insecurity about money and my own work.

The logic behind this egoist reaction is that if someone gets what we want, then there will be less or nothing for us. This distorted belief assumes joy and success are limited, and if someone else succeeds or flourishes, then we become impoverished by default. Fortunately, I was aware of the nature of my mixed reaction, and I laughed about it to myself and with my friend. I was simply being human and getting caught up in my own anxiety, which expressed itself as jealousy.

This experience is universal. It can arise when a friend tells us they have met their perfect "soul mate" and are off to Hawaii for a romantic getaway. Or when a colleague receives a windfall in their end-of-year bonus. We can feel it when looking at people's seemingly ideal lives on Facebook or Instagram. We become both simultaneously happy *and* jealous, experiencing a twinge of contraction or fear that our lives are not enough. Or we may judge others, feeling they don't deserve their good fortune and we would be more worthy recipients.

Paradoxically, delighting in the joy of others is a potent way to increase one's own well-being. I discovered this in my twenties during a meditation course in New England. As soon as I heard about it, it made perfect sense. Why wouldn't we want to rejoice in the happiness of others, particularly if this fosters happiness in our own heart? This simple practice is a win/win with no downside. All it requires — along with all the practices in this book — is present-moment awareness, an open heart, and the intention to cultivate such things.

To practice sympathetic joy, simply turn your attention to others when things go well for them, whenever others are touched with joy or success. It is as simple as feeling happy for your partner's successful day at work. Or celebrating the accolades your child received at school. Or delighting when Olympic athletes dance with ecstasy as they receive a medal. Or appreciating a bumblebee who nuzzles its way into a foxglove and comes out soaked in pollen. Examples of joy and success are everywhere, including insects as they find their pots of powdered gold.

Appreciative joy frees the heart from the unnecessary burden of envy, comparison, and scarcity. To live without those qualities clouding the freedom of our being is liberating indeed. What would it look like to turn your attention to friends, family, colleagues, and strangers and delight in their successes, accomplishments, joys, and ordinary delights? How would it feel for you to simply enjoy their happiness and to hope it would only grow? To transform the heart from its prison of envy by delighting in the well-being of others is to live in an enchanted land.

• **PRACTICE** •

Celebrating the Joy of Others

Cultivating sympathetic joy can be an uplifting practice because you focus on the happiness, success, and good fortune of others. Start by sitting comfortably, closing your eyes, and sensing your body and your breath.

Call to mind a good friend. Choose someone who is currently happy and doing well, whether in relationships, at work, or generally in their lives. Take time to appreciate this person's joy, success, and good fortune. Visualize and sense their happiness or contentment.

The conduit for sympathetic joy is saying phrases that express your delight in their happiness. First, express this appreciation by saying, *I'm happy for you*, or *I delight in your happiness*. Next, offer them this wish: *May your happiness and good fortune (or success) continue to grow*. You may alter these words to fit the person or your particular wish for them, but keep the general spirit of these sentiments. As you hold this person in your heart or mind's eye, repeat the phrases slowly and meaningfully. Take time to genuinely feel this wish for them in your heart.

Next, call to mind someone else, a loved one or a colleague, and repeat the process for some minutes. If you wish to stretch your capacity, extend this wish to someone you don't know well, even a stranger, or call to mind someone you are in conflict with or are particularly envious of. Genuinely wish each person you call to mind, as much as you are able, continued joy and success.

While this is a delightful practice — and often the heart blooms with a sense of celebrating the well-being of others — it is not unusual for the opposite feelings to arise. The practice can trigger jealousy, envy, or a contracted state where we feel self-judgment for not having similar success or happiness. This is natural. In fact, this meditation is considered a purification practice, in that it can stir up whatever negative reactions get in the way of our being able to rejoice in the joy of others. As it does, we get to see the ways that our heart is not yet open fully, and continuing this practice is a way of working with that and of growing and stretching our heart's capacity to love.

If this happens, and you find certain people trigger too much reactivity, put them aside and focus on others. Go back to people with whom you can access this quality of sympathetic joy. Over time you will find that the heart is able to expand and move through the world genuinely wishing for the well-being of all others without the need to compare or judge. In this way, you significantly increase your own inner joy and happiness.

• • •

Chapter 29

Extending Compassion to Others

Be kind to every person you meet because each person has been asked to carry a great burden.

— REVEREND JOHN WATSON

This beloved quote by John Watson is one I try to live by. It encourages us to keep our heart open to others, rather than closing down out of fear, judgment, or resistance. No one gets through this life with a free ride. Even the most blessed, abundant person has to deal with stress, physical pain, and health issues. They are just part of the human condition.

However much we may love our families, every parent is challenged by raising children, and every child is challenged by growing up. We all lose friends and loved ones eventually. Walking life's path means, at times, losing things, like our health, our wealth, and our direction, and at times challenging even our faith. When I remember this, it helps me to turn toward others with a compassionate heart and loving spirit.

It is easy to make assumptions about people based on superficial appearances, perhaps on where they live, how they dress, or how they talk. A whole, complex world lives inside each and every person that is neither visible nor obvious from the outside. As a teacher, I meet people from all walks of life, and I get to scratch beneath the surface and hear what is really going on in the deeper currents of their lives — what is troubling their hearts and causing stress or anxiety.

I am often moved by the litany of woes that each person has to navigate: from a mother's loss of a child at birth to the pain of an elder whose life partner has Alzheimer's and has forgotten all sense of who they are. I see retirees who haven't recovered from the abuse they suffered as infants, while combat veterans struggle with the trauma from serving in Vietnam or Afghanistan. I've worked with beautiful models whose lives are riddled with anxiety about weight and struggles with bulimia. Single parents can barely make their monthly rent and worry about not having enough money for their children's college fees. Meanwhile, millionaires wrestle with guilt over inherited wealth, feeling unworthy and embarrassed at never having worked for it. This is just a snapshot of what might comprise a typical group on retreat, and it is a small sampling of the multitudes who struggle in their lives.

I have learned to never underestimate what someone might be going through. People are often coping with difficult challenges beneath the surface. Remembering this can inspire us to give people the benefit of the doubt, to be a little more patient and forgiving when they are grumpy, short-tempered, or neurotic. I was sharply reminded of this recently when I stopped to say hello to James, my neighbor. I usually have very little contact with James, who is often out of town, and lately when he was around, he seemed quite unfriendly. Then one day, I saw James alone, and something prompted me to ask how he was doing. After a little small talk, he shared that he had just lost his wife three weeks ago due to a brain tumor, which had been diagnosed only a month before she passed. I was stunned and felt deeply sorry for James, whose recent behavior I now understood in a whole new light.

Such moments remind us of the importance of infusing love into our practice of mindfulness, without which it is incomplete, or as one of my teachers calls it, "one-legged." Compassion arises when our open hearts meet suffering. It is the heart's natural response: to care and wish to find ways to relieve the pain of others. Compassion is sometimes referred to as the quivering of the heart, which resonates with the anguish of another. Though innate, compassion can be developed with practice, intention, and care.

History is replete with figures who have developed compassion to a high level, such as Mother Teresa and St. Francis of Assisi. They are shining examples of compassion that knows no limits, as is Desmond Tutu. During the brutal apartheid regime in South Africa, he endured a lot of suffering and had to bear witness as his people underwent decades of abuse and violence, yet he was able to find in his heart a place of compassion for those same oppressors. This is boundless compassion that rises above our personal, self-centered story.

We all have this potential. I think about the mass shooting in 2015 at the Emmanuel AME Church in Charleston, South Carolina, when a white supremacist opened fire during a prayer service in the church, killing nine people and injuring others. Despite these terrible murders, many in the congregation were able to find in their hearts the power of forgiveness. Nadine Collier, the daughter of seventy-year-old Ethel Lance, who was slain, stood up in court to face the attacker and said, her voice breaking with emotion: "You took something very precious from me. I will never talk to her again. I will never, ever hold her again. But I forgive you. And have mercy on your soul." This is a heart that has truly developed a compassion that knows no limits.

Other examples include Dr. Martin Luther King Jr. and participants in the U.S. civil rights movement. They confronted injustice, racism, and violence with an unstoppable power of love. It is hard to watch the film archives of those Southern marches in the

1960s, where nonviolent protesters were attacked with dogs, water cannons, and violent police brutality. Yet despite such aggression, they managed to hold their heads up high and look into the eyes of their oppressors without hatred or vengeance. Such courage is a testament to the power of the human heart to face adversity and overcome through peaceful means.

What supports the heart to open, and what closes it down? The first step on the path of compassion requires turning toward what is, particularly what is difficult. When we can attune to the suffering of another without judgment, reaction, or recoiling — when we can simply witness and acknowledge the pain — this allows the window of loving care to open. This movement in the heart allows us to feel *with* another and to ask the important questions: *How can I help, and what would serve this person?*

We can also explore what interferes with the heart opening. Often it is fear of feeling another's pain or worry about being overwhelmed by someone's distress. Other reasons might be judgments about someone's struggles or feeling too burdened by our own or the world's suffering to face more anguish. We need to honestly scrutinize the ways we turn from pain, as these can serve to numb the heart and lead to inaction.

We can observe and work with this dynamic anytime we meet someone who is hurting. A very common example is encountering the homeless on city streets. In San Francisco, where I work, homelessness is at epidemic levels, and every day, this intense suffering hits me in the face. It is heartbreaking to see so many people who are hungry, cold, and traumatized, or to see elderly people, thin and frail, trying to sleep on cardboard boxes, or young mothers with children in tow, begging for a few dollars so they can buy food or get a hot drink.

How open I am to their plight depends on many factors, and noticing these is key to understanding the heart's capacity. Sometimes, I am embarrassed to say, I am too busy, distracted, or hurried, and I either don't notice or don't want to slow down and take in someone's vulnerability. At other times, someone's predicament feels like too much to take in, so I avert my eyes. Almost always, homelessness is a problem that's beyond my ability to solve on an individual level, so I can easily feel overwhelmed, numb, and incapacitated.

At some point, everyone struggles in these ways. Whatever the reason, our heart shuts down to pain, and by doing so, we short-circuit our capacity to care, to be kind and responsive, which is the heart of compassion. What is required is pausing, taking someone in fully, and feeling the whole messiness of their situation. Once we can feel the pain of another, then we can ask the important question of how we can help and what we can do.

With regard to homelessness, I make sure I donate to homeless charities in the city. It doesn't solve the problem, but it is one small way I can make a difference, and it ensures my money goes directly to feeding and providing shelter to those I meet on the street. I also aspire to treat everyone humanely: to meet people's eyes and offer the simple kindness of a genuine smile and greeting. Often that human contact and acknowledgment seem the most important. I may not be able to solve homelessness, but I can relate kindly and with care to each person in the moment.

• PRACTICE •
Developing Compassion for Others

Compassion begins with the courageous turn toward pain and the desire to bring relief to it. Being open to the anguish of others is what motivates us to want to alleviate such suffering. It cannot be done in the abstract. This ancient practice is a way to open the heart and cultivate this beautiful quality.

Sit comfortably, close your eyes, and bring attention to your physical sensations. Become aware of the center of your chest, your heart area; feel your breath there. Now call to mind someone you care about deeply who is currently suffering. Take a moment to visualize this person and sense them as if they were with you. Recollect their particular woes and struggles, and let the person and their pain into your heart. Use your breath as a support both to feel the emotion and to soften the intensity of the feeling if it becomes too strong.

Then, silently offer wishes that express the heart of compassion, the sincere desire to relieve another's pain. As you hold a loved one in your heart and mind, repeat these phrases slowly and genuinely: *I care about you. May you be free of pain and suffering. May you hold your difficulty with ease and kindness.* This last wish is offered because, for many people, there may not be any immediate relief from anguish, particularly if they are dealing with loss or chronic pain or a terminal diagnosis. As you sense your loved one and their struggle, gently repeat these phrases, or similar ones, that express your heart's wish for the relief of their pain.

After some minutes, consider bringing another person to mind, perhaps a good friend who is in distress. Follow the same process: sense and visualize them first, open to the pain they are going through, and offer them the same wishes of compassion.

If you wish to stretch your capacity further, call to mind someone you may be in conflict with, or whom you find difficult or challenging, but whom you know is struggling. In the same way, repeat the process of offering them these wishes of compassion. Know that this is not necessarily easy to do but can help you heal the pain and contraction in your own heart as it relates to them.

If you are currently experiencing adversity or pain in your life, you might next apply this same practice of compassion to yourself. Sometimes we are least likely to turn this caring heart to our own suffering. Take some time to sense into your own particular afflictions, then with a kind heart, direct the phrases of compassion to yourself: *May I be free of pain and suffering. May I hold my burdens with kindness and ease.*

Last, turn your attention outward to the vast ocean of suffering in the world. Call to mind the pain of particular populations or of people in particular circumstances, such as the homeless, those living through warfare, or people suffering famine and poverty. Similarly, you can extend compassion to all creatures, such as livestock trapped in feedlots or species under threat of extinction. Whoever it may be, call these beings to mind, sense their pain, and offer your wishes of compassion to them.

As you end the practice, reflect on how you can take more active steps to help those in need. Ask: What is the need, how can I help, and how can I serve? Then let your response come from this tenderhearted place of compassion; listen to what action or initiative comes forth. Compassion is a dynamic force that can bring tremendous salve to any pain in life.

• • •

· SECTION 4 ·

FINDING PEACE
IN THE WORLD

Chapter 30

Mindfulness in Relationships

For one human being to love another, this is perhaps the most difficult
of human tasks, the work for which all other work is but preparation.
— RAINER MARIA RILKE

As the poet Rilke states, though few of us need reminding, human relationships, beautiful as they can be, are also one of the more challenging places to keep the heart open. We all need healthy human connection and meaningful positive social contact, yet that means dealing with the very thing we often find the most difficult: other people! When I teach the Search Inside Yourself Leadership Institute's program on mindfulness and emotional intelligence, there is a communication exercise where people are asked what they love about their work and what their biggest challenges are. Barely a workshop goes by without people reporting that "other people" fit both categories. Our colleagues are often the best and most-challenging aspects of our work life.

Many might say the same about families and intimate relationships. As the saying goes: "You can't live with them and you can't live without them." If you think you can escape this by becoming a monk or a nun and dropping out of society, think again. I have friends who have chosen a monastic life, and they agree that one of the hardest parts of living in a monastery is other people. Ironically, this dilemma is perhaps more challenging in a monastery because you have little choice over who lives with you — and in some cases, who shares your bedroom, dormitory, or cave!

Most people need only consider their relationship with their own parents to appreciate how difficult family dynamics can be. The spiritual teacher and former Harvard professor Ram Dass humorously suggests that, if you think you are enlightened, go home and live with your parents for a week, and then see how awake you feel after that! People often ask me why their buttons are so easily pushed when they go home to visit parents. I jokingly remind them that their parents are the ones who put the buttons there in the first place. They know where the triggers are.

One issue that usually creates the most difficulties in relationships is expectations. We sometimes have idealized or romantic notions about the way relationships should be. I know people who longed for years to have children and create a family, and they didn't appreciate till they had kids just how difficult parenting would be. Every life stage comes with its own challenges, from navigating the "terrible twos" to dealing with rebellious teenagers who resist everything you say, to grown children who can't hold down a job. Parenting can be joyful, except for all the havoc and heartache that comes with it.

This is perhaps even more challenging in the crucible of intimate relationships. Hollywood and modern culture peddle myths about romance and marriage that are impossible to live up to and that bear little resemblance to normal life. Everyone I know in a successful marriage freely admits the hard work it takes to stay connected, to cultivate and grow love, to work through conflicts, and to deal with being triggered by the person who knows you best.

We all need an ally in the journey of relationships. Without awareness, we can blindly react to others, say things we regret, and do things that hurt those we love. It takes presence and self-regulation to navigate, and not escalate, a heated discussion with a spouse. Mindfulness practice helps us develop the necessary self-awareness to communicate clearly and honestly, to understand our intentions, and to recognize and manage our own reactivity when others trigger us.

Nevertheless, there is no doubt that relationships are humbling. When we live with more awareness, we see how hard it is to live up to our ideals and principles. Take one simple quality like patience. How easy is it to lose patience with a spouse, child, or coworker who doesn't seem to listen to our requests, though we've repeated them a hundred times? Then, all of a sudden, harsh words come out of our mouth saying things we immediately regret. Or conversely, we take out our frustrations on others, unnecessarily nit-picking at some mannerism, just because we feel hurt, jilted, or unappreciated in some way.

However, it is important not to give up. A discerning self-awareness shines a light that reveals many of our foibles and blind spots. Hard as that is to see, we should rejoice rather than feel bad, since once such shortcomings are seen, we can begin to transform them. François Fénelon, a seventeenth-century archbishop and theologian, put it beautifully: "As the light increases, we see ourselves to be worse than we thought.... We are amazed at our former blindness.... But we are not worse than we were; on the contrary, we are better. While our faults diminish, the light by which we see them waxes brighter.... Bear in mind, for your comfort, that we only perceive our malady when the cure begins." The cure in this case is the wisdom of awareness.

In most interactions with people, we are not just dealing with the challenges of our present time, adult experience. Often our relationships mirror dynamics we developed with parents and caregivers in our formative years. Sustained observation can help reveal these patterns, such as when we have regressed and are acting out from a hurt or reactive place, reenacting dynamics from when we were young. These patterns are why relationships provide such potent ground for inner growth. They force us to work through unresolved childhood developmental issues. The key is whether we can stay conscious during this process so we can learn and heal. Otherwise, we risk simply repeating old dynamics and wounds.

For example, if someone felt invisible, ignored, or abandoned by their parents when they were young, they might be sensitive to signs that a romantic partner is becoming bored with the relationship or is more excited by other people or interests. With lightning speed, that person could be triggered by their partner's new work friendship or absorbing hobby. In a flash, the person may withdraw out of self-protection or lash out in anger, driven by a fear of rejection.

During those times when we feel the volcanic urge to protest, attack, or fly into a fit of righteous indignation, it takes discernment to remind ourselves to stop, breathe, and allow our nervous system to calm down before responding. I know firsthand how important it is to breathe first when I am triggered and not act out the urge to judge or provoke! I have, like countless others, learned that lesson the hard way, by watching what happens when we don't.

A recent story I heard from a colleague illustrates this well:

This morning at a train stop near the hospital, a man and his three young kids got on. The kids were loud and completely out of control, running from one end of the train car to the other. An annoyed passenger sitting next to me looked over at the man and fired off a snarky comment,

'Is there a reason you're letting your kids go nuts right now?' The man looked up with tears in his eyes and said, 'The doctor just told me their mother isn't going to make it. Sorry, I'm just trying to think before we all sit down at home to talk about this.' Of course, the annoyed passenger was speechless. And regretful. And yet how easily [it could have been] any one of us saying or thinking something similar in that situation.

With mindfulness, we can learn to monitor our internal experience, so that we are much less likely to be caught off-guard and cause harm when we don't intend to. Over time we become less prone to say or do something we later regret. That interior awareness allows us to sense when we are repeating old patterns or when reactivity distorts our perception or negatively affects what we say. We are also more likely to hold the pain of our reaction with kindness, which in itself helps soften the intensity and distress of that experience.

Equally important, we can all grow our heart and capacity to love. That moment-to-moment training, to meet experience just as it is, supports us to embrace others — including our partner, our parents, and strangers — just as they are, "warts and all." We tend to commit many subtle acts of violence when we demand that others conform to our likes, preferences, and desires. Yet the key to healthy relationships is the ability to profoundly accept people as they are. Awareness practice gives us the tools to learn how to do that.

This doesn't mean we can't ask for what we need and want; we certainly can't avoid having preferences. However, we can recognize our own attachments and expectations and release them when others don't agree or don't live up to them. It is like freeing others from a confining straightjacket. It is a beautiful gift to meet someone just as they are. From this more open place, others can feel seen, accepted, and loved. This creates the optimum conditions for any relationship to thrive. And like anything, it takes practice! Over time we can learn perhaps to live our way beyond division, or in the Sufi poet Rumi's words:

> Out beyond ideas of wrongdoing
> and rightdoing, there is a field.
> I'll meet you there.

• PRACTICE •
Radical Acceptance in Relationship

One of the hardest things in life is to simply accept another person just as they are. It doesn't sound hard, but in practice we meet all kinds of challenges when we try. Take a moment to reflect on the ways you may want, expect, or demand other people to be different than they are.

To begin, sit comfortably, close your eyes, and turn your attention to your breath to establish present-moment awareness. Then call to mind someone you are in a close relationship with, perhaps a spouse, parent, child, colleague, friend, or other family member. Visualize this person and imagine them in all the ways you know them.

Now reflect on the ways you already accept them for who and what they are. Pay attention to how that feels in your body and heart when you fully welcome and accept someone, including all their perfectly human imperfections. Notice if this brings up any resistance.

Next, contemplate things about this person that you wish were different, that you would like them to change, improve, or get rid of. How do you react when this person acts in ways you wish they wouldn't? As you reflect on these issues, imagine accepting or allowing these traits just as they are. This does not mean you have to like these particular habits, communication styles, or attitudes. But see if it is possible to invite a quality of openness toward them.

Ask yourself how much of the conflict, turmoil, and stress you experience in this relationship is related to your attachment to how you want the other to be. Radical acceptance is a doorway to letting people be as they are, no matter what they are like. This can bring about unexpected harmony and ease, which is what we often seek but rarely experience in relationships. This is not to say we must put up with or accept any inappropriate or harmful behavior. Such actions often require confronting and challenging. However, in this practice, simply look at the ways your preferences influence relationships.

As you leave the meditation, try to put this into practice in everyday life as you spend time with friends, relatives, colleagues, and your partner. Notice what happens when you access this quality of allowing others to be who they are rather than imposing your ideas, demands, or preferences. Others, too, will no doubt notice a shift in you, which often leads to openness in other, unexpected ways that can support your relationship.

• • •

Chapter 31

Freeing Ourselves
from Self-Centeredness

It's all about me!
— BUMPER STICKER SEEN IN NORTHERN CALIFORNIA

When I first started to meditate back in 1984, I was teased about it constantly. In the 1980s, none of my friends and family had much experience with meditation, never mind practiced it. They had all kinds of quirky ideas and faulty assumptions about what it actually meant. They asked me why I would want to do such a selfish activity. Wasn't meditation just self-indulgent navel-gazing? Those same people thought nothing of going on holiday to a beach resort in Spain and getting absolutely drunk for two weeks straight. Yet they considered my attempts to cultivate awareness and compassion self-absorbed! I couldn't help laugh at the irony of it all.

I hear their concerns and assumptions about meditation still repeated today. From the outside, meditation certainly seems to be self-centered or to reflect a preoccupation with oneself. But let us be honest: the number-one person in our life, most of the time, *is* ourself. That's what takes up most of our mental and emotional attention anyway, whether we meditate or not. Yes, we care deeply for our family, friends, and others, but most of our default-mode thinking is about the main player in our own movie: me, myself, and I.

I remember well when I started meditating. I was consumed with hopes and worries about my life. Like most people I knew, I spent a lot of time reflecting on what I was doing with my life and what direction I was heading. But I was also mired in self-judgment about not being good enough and in fears I wouldn't amount to anything. As I cultivated awareness through meditation, I shone a light on these obsessive thinking patterns and began to create some space inside, becoming less wrapped up in my thoughts and mental preoccupations.

Now, many years later, I see how much quieter my mind has become. In this way, meditation can help develop the very opposite of self-centeredness. Today, the inner critic makes few inroads, and the swirl of self-centered thoughts that used to consume so much of my attention is greatly reduced. Often people ask me what I am thinking when I am quiet, doing nothing in particular, perhaps looking out the window or sitting in the garden. They assume I must think about something. But I am often just watching the world go by with a fair amount of inner peace. This allows me to be much more aware of what is going on around me, with others, and with the world.

How do we reduce our myopic self-absorption? The practice of mindfulness shifts us from the ruminative default-mode thinking to a clear present-moment attention. We learn to unhook from the inner critic and the background narrative that is frequently playing in our heads. When we notice a hummingbird flying outside our window, it snaps us out of our daydreams or planning mind and whips us into the present. Similarly, when we walk by a coffee shop and smell freshly roasted coffee, awareness of our senses draws us out of our head's swirling thoughts. The same process happens when we focus on our breath, drawing us ever more in the present.

One facet of mindfulness is the quality of deep listening, and we can bring that attuned skill to listen genuinely to others. It can help restore the lost art of conversation. We have become a society of talkers, not listeners. Discussions at the office can be reduced to the loudest person being heard, where people constantly interrupt and talk over one another. We multitask on our devices and rarely give anyone our full attention. Most communication now happens digitally, which is fraught with misunderstanding. In addition, most conversations are self-referential, seeking help for our problems and support for our perspective.

Through practice, we develop and offer this gift of attentive presence to others. By training our attention, we learn to hone that capacity, get out of our own heads, and become more attuned to people. Instead of immediately relating what others say back to ourselves and what it means for us, we practice asking with genuine curiosity about someone else's life, without judgment, correction, or self-concern.

For instance, Dipa Ma was a renowned Indian Vipassana teacher who was legendary for the depth of her meditation and concentration. When she brought that honed quality of attention to listening to others, it had a powerful impact. Despite having gone through a challenging and difficult life, she talked to others as if nothing else existed for her except the conversation and the person in front of her. You became the center of her laser-focused and penetrating presence. Her decades of mind training had refined that skill. The impact of that was tremendous for the recipient, often life changing.

Of course, like preferences, self-centeredness is almost impossible to avoid, and some argue that we shouldn't let it go. Some

246 • From Suffering to Peace

question how we could succeed in business or how we would take care of our family if we didn't focus on ourselves and our immediate concerns. Isn't it important to practice self-care? To a degree, this is valid, but mindfulness reveals how painful it can be when we are so caught up in our own drama and focus narrowly on ourself. This is the basis for so much neurosis and anxiety in our consumer-oriented, materialist, and some may say narcissistic culture today.

Recent research supports this. We experience greater happiness when our life is less wrapped up in self and instead is oriented to helping others, to being generous and kind. Though Darwin is renowned for popularizing the term "survival of the fittest," he also wrote about how the success of species was also due to their ability to cooperate. In fact, some say his research is better summarized by the phrase "survival of the kindest."

Our well-being is interdependent with that of others. Of course, we must take care of ourselves, but if we try to do this at the expense of others, we can actually thwart our own well-being. Conversely, helping others benefits us in the long run, even though that may not be our initial intention. Just think about the most altruistic and generous people you know. They are often also the happiest.

As I reflect on my own thirty-five-year journey in meditation practice, I see that this training has increased my ability to look beyond my own self-interest, to get out of my own way and genuinely take in the reality of others. I find this particularly true in my teaching work when I listen to the challenging plights of students. Such attunement to others inspires the desire to help.

Meditation is not the only way to cultivate this. There are many professions and skills that hone the capacity to orient to others. For example, therapists, social workers, nurses, and teachers have to get out of their own way, to refine their ability to focus on others in order to do their work well. Parenting also supports this understanding, since parents often have to put their own needs aside on a daily basis to prioritize their children. Mindfulness simply supports developing this orientation in every area of life, and from that comes greater responsiveness. It supports the heart to engage with others in a meaningful way.

I once heard a story that beautifully illustrates what can happen when we put aside self-absorption and become responsive to others. Jenny, a single mother from Illinois, had been out of work for some time and was running out of money. Despite that, she understood the importance of generosity and helping others around her.

One cold autumnal evening in Chicago, Jenny was standing and waiting at the bus stop. Along came a small older man, barely dressed, wearing a hospital gown, and with no shoes and few possessions. He shivered with cold. Jenny asked him where he was going and why he didn't have any warm clothing. The man told her he had gotten really sick with AIDS and lost his job and the lease on his apartment. He had been in the hospital recovering from his illness and was just discharged, but had no money. Because he was not from Chicago, he did not know anyone in the area. He was heading downtown to find a shelter for the night.

As her bus pulled up, Jenny spontaneously took off her jacket and gave it to the man. Looking down at his feet, almost blue with cold, she noticed they had similar size feet and took off her tennis shoes and gave them to him. He protested, asking what she was going to do without her shoes. She replied that she was not far from her apartment, and she would feel much better knowing he had a warm coat and shoes to get him through the cold night. She also gave him what little money she had in her purse so he could get some warm food.

As Jenny boarded the bus, the bus driver said with a wink and a twinkle in his eye that in general he didn't let people onto the bus who weren't wearing shoes. Then a well-dressed man in a business suit called her over and asked her to sit down. The gentleman asked Jenny: "I want to know who this person is that just did the most generous thing I have ever seen to a stranger."

Jenny recounted the man's story and shared about her own struggle to find work. As it turned out, the man was a human resources director in a large health care company. He suggested Jenny come to see him the following week, as he might just have a position open for her. And so the gift of generosity continued, as it often does when our attention is attuned to others, rather than being caught up in our self-absorbed world.

• **PRACTICE** •

Examining Self-Centeredness

The purpose of this practice is to observe how much of your mental machinations are taken up with thoughts, plans, and rumination about yourself. Don't judge these thoughts; simply observe how deeply ingrained self-absorption can be. Find a comfortable sitting posture that you can maintain for at least ten to fifteen minutes. Attune to the sensations of your breath to focus your attention.

You will probably find that your attention wanders from the breath many times during meditation, perhaps hundreds of times in a single sitting. That is normal. However, in this meditation, rather than noticing thoughts and returning attention to the breath, observe the content of each thought and note how often the focus is yourself: your worries, concerns, plans, memories, dramas, and so on. Don't be surprised if such thoughts comprise more than 90 percent of all mental content. If thoughts are not directly about you, they often are by inference, like about your work, family, or relationships.

In the same way, during everyday life, be attentive to self-centered thoughts when you talk to others. How often are the topics of conversation about you? Do you direct discussions to focus on yourself, or do you guide discussions toward the other person or a different subject? Who does most of the talking? Is it an equal back and forth, or do you tend to dominate? Do you love to have an audience, particularly to share extensively about yourself? Do you tend to inquire about other people, focusing on their experience, or do you prefer to be the principal object of the conversation?

As in the meditation, observe this without judgment. Everyone is self-focused to one degree or another; this is a universal phenomenon. The point is to reveal what supports genuine happiness and well-being for everyone. With self-awareness we can wake up to our own patterns of self-centeredness and free ourselves from that onerous habit. In this way, we develop an orientation to others that is both fulfilling and genuinely more satisfactory for all.

• • •

Chapter 32

We're All in This Together

In a real sense all life is interrelated. All are caught in an inescapable network of mutuality.... Whatever affects one directly, affects all indirectly.... This is the interrelated structure of reality.
— DR. MARTIN LUTHER KING JR.

During the U.S. civil rights movement in the 1950s and 1960s, Dr. Martin Luther King Jr. spoke eloquently about how, when one segment of society is downtrodden, the whole of society is impoverished. This radical notion asks us to step outside of the limited perspective of our tribal loyalties — which can limit our empathy and concern to only a narrow sector of people like us — and instead feel our shared humanity. It asks us to see ourselves not just as separate individuals, families, and nations but as interconnected, interdependent communities sharing one world. When we do that, compassion and care are more likely natural outcomes.

With that said, it is natural and healthy for marginalized communities who experience discrimination to identify with those who share their identity (however it's defined) and to seek safety and refuge within that community. The challenge for all people, as Dr. King expressed, is to do both: to care for one's own "tribe" while acknowledging our shared humanity.

To stretch one's capacity for inclusivity to include all of humanity, as Dr. King encouraged, is not an easy thing to do, either for individuals or for communities or nations. For instance, in recent years, many countries have struggled to cope with surges in immigration, especially by those fleeing war in their home countries. Across Europe, refugees of wars in Syria, Iraq, and Afghanistan have sought protection, acceptance, and help establishing a new life on foreign soil. National debates over whether to allow immigrants and how to treat them reflect how people characterize our common humanity. Some open their homes to refugees, providing food and shelter, and so exemplify Dr. King's expression of mutuality. Others would keep immigrants out and characterize these people as different, problematic, and even a dangerous threat to the fabric of their nation.

Interestingly, when one looks at history, most nations were formed, at least in part, by migrations of people no different than the ones occurring today. However, these complex social issues are rooted in a core dilemma that each of us faces: the sense of separateness or connectedness that defines our individual lives, our worldview, our political persuasions, and our social actions.

Such issues are also impacted by our evolutionary heritage, which has hardwired us to look for difference rather than perceive similarity. We are programmed to orient to our "in group": our family, tribe, and people. With awareness, we can become aware of how this perspective can fuel bias and unconscious prejudice. In addition, our brain creates a perceptual illusion of separation, which we tend to believe most of the time. We see ourselves as separate individuals, and we carve up reality into dualities: this and that, self and other, us and them. This misperception feeds a sense of disconnection. We can look out across a sea of people in a busy city street or at a party and feel alone, isolated, as if we existed separately from others and even from life. A tree seems to have nothing to do with us, but it helps create the oxygen we inhale. The clouds above seem remote and unrelated, but the water they release helps sustain us.

So when we look deeply, we can see through that cognitive illusion and discover just how deeply intertwined everything is. We can move beyond our limited perception, as Einstein wrote: "A human being is part of the whole, called by us 'Universe'; a part limited in time and space. He experiences himself, his thoughts and feelings, as something separated from the rest — a kind of optical delusion of his consciousness." The Vietnamese mindfulness teacher Thich Nhat Hanh has described speaking in a similar way when he asks students what they see as he holds a piece of paper in the air. They, of course, say they see paper. He replies that they are also seeing rain, forests, sunlight, oxygen, and the cycles of the moon. Everything is interconnected.

Through words and actions, Dr. King asked us to see through this illusion of separation. When we believe we are separate, we are more likely to suffer because we feel lonely, isolated, and overwhelmed by the scale of the world's problems. When we understand our connection with all life, we sense how embedded we are into the fabric of the world. From that perspective, nothing we do is insignificant. We realize we are part of a whole, something much greater than our small, separate ego self. Our lives are inherently intertwined with everyone else's lives, and so tackling societal and global problems is part of how we take care of our own lives, and vice versa. Our actions can affect much more than our own lives because we are all in this together.

In 1955, when Rosa Parks engaged in civil disobedience by sitting in the white section of a segregated bus, she sat alone, but she acted as part of the broader civil rights movement, which demanded inclusion, acceptance, and equal rights, not separation. In 1930, when Gandhi undertook his famous Salt March to the Indian

Ocean, he wasn't just reclaiming the right of Indian people to make salt. His act was a symbolic protest against British colonialism in general and all the ways Indian people were being oppressed. Social justice movements are rooted in interconnection. They propose that it's not enough for some to succeed at the expense of others; all of society must flourish as one. This was particularly true for the Occupy movement that rose up in 2011 to demonstrate against social and economic inequality. When Dr. King was assassinated, some think it was because he was organizing and connecting the civil rights movement with America's labor movement, which was too much of a threat to the established order.

Another vivid example of how separation is an illusion is when we look at ecology. Climate change and the planet's mounting environmental catastrophes threaten all people and all species alike. These issues reveal our intimate connectedness on a daily basis. Fossil fuels burned in the Northern Hemisphere create atmospheric conditions that melt ice sheets in Antarctica, raise sea levels in the Mediterranean, and threaten Pacific Ocean islands. The world's economies are similarly linked: a meltdown in the Japanese economy can affect the lives of Chilean soybean farmers and Icelandic fishing communities.

Homo sapiens were once wholly tribal. In his book *Sapiens*, Yuval Noah Harari describes how, as a species, we evolved in small roaming bands of hunter-gatherers with a maximum size of 150 people. We survived by responding to immediate threats and opportunities, moving with the seasons. Today, you could say all people live in a global village, one connected by technology, transportation, and communication. We are profoundly interdependent: local problems reflect global problems, and local solutions can radiate out, with far-reaching consequences. In essence, global circumstances now ask us to wake up to a reality that we were not evolutionarily designed for. People worldwide are being asked to see beyond the immediate concern of themselves and their country and beyond the limited timescale of their own life span to include countless future generations. The question for our species is whether we can adapt in time to respond quickly enough to the looming crisis that now faces everyone.

Humanity has proven that it can come together to respond effectively to global problems. For example, in 1987, the growing hole in the ozone layer caused by CFCs (and other chemicals) was effectively thwarted by passage of the pioneering Montreal Protocol, which banned these chemicals worldwide. Such collective vision and action is necessary again to solve the even greater challenge of climate change. This requires radical action by all nations, whether or not they currently feel the full brunt of the consequences of global warming. The 2016 UN-sponsored Paris Agreement was one attempt to take collective action, but so far this isn't enough to make any significant impact on the heating of the atmosphere. In essence, the technological know-how is there; the political will and urgency and the ability to see beyond our immediate concerns are not. At least not yet.

Whether humans, political entities, and corporations can resolve such global issues depends on whether we can collectively create a vision that connects us, not just with the wider global community, but also to future generations. Taking into account such a broad scope of time is something humanity has yet to do successfully. Time will tell whether we can do so now.

Understanding the prison of our individualized consciousness and the limitations of our tribalistic perspective can nudge us toward a large vantage point. As an example of how awareness practice can help with this, I want to share a letter that Jared, a meditation student, sent to me. He wrote:

I was in the middle of a three-month meditation retreat at Tassajara, a Zen monastery in central California. As I was meditating for the sixth or seventh hour one day, a new, life-altering awareness arose in me. I realized that I was not who I had always thought I was. I was not the star of my own Shakespearean drama. I was actually everyone and everything in the whole universe. To try to be even more precise, I'll share some wisdom from the founder of my school of Zen, Dogen Zenji. He said, "The truth is, you are not it. It is you." In other words, what became clear wasn't that I was the universe, but that the universe was me.

At that time, the US was bombing Iraq, deforestation was rampant, and estimates were that humans were sending about two hundred different species into extinction every day. I thought about all that and more, and I cried. I don't have the words to express how sad it made me to see how much suffering is born from the delusion that we are disconnected from one another and the Earth.

When the meditation ended, I glanced around at the other practitioners. It was like I was the left hand and they were the right hand of the same body. And in the same way that the left hand tends to the right hand without hesitation if it needs help, when I felt their emotional pain and the pain from their aching bodies, love poured out of me. I would have done anything for them. And what dawned on me is possibly the most important lesson that we have to learn in today's day and age: When we become aware of who we really are, our love gets unleashed.

At the end of the day, with our planet in ecological crisis, and people worldwide suffering from poverty, war, and inequality, the only solutions are communal. There can be no "out group" anymore because what affects one part of the planet affects all the others. Pollution is the obvious example, but immigration is another.

If all places valued healthy environments and social justice, perhaps there would be no mass movements of people from one place to another. We only have one small planet, and everyone has to go somewhere. If we don't realize how utterly interdependent we are on one another and this planet, we will literally drown under rising seas, which will breach whatever wall we erect to keep people out.

During a meeting with Joanna Macy, a scholar and elder in the environmental movement, about how we should respond to the pressing ecological crisis, she emphasized how essential it is for people to not act alone. She said it is vital to engage with others in a shared goal. She added that it matters more that people work together, engaging and supporting one another, than succeed in any particular project. Doing nothing leads to alienation, hopelessness, and numbness. Acting in collaboration means making positive impacts in the world and within ourselves, as we erode the corrosive sense of separation that is at the root of so many of our problems.

• PRACTICE •

Developing Interconnectedness

To sense interconnection requires a cognitive shift, as well as a movement, an opening or expansion of the heart. We tend to perceive things at face value, to see only what is immediately in front of us, and so we often miss the deeper weave of connection. This is particularly true when we consider the ecological impact of our actions and choices.

In this contemplation, consider simple everyday activities in your life: driving your car, taking baths, playing golf, flying for work, eating exotic food in restaurants, buying produce from other countries. Then reflect on all the causes and consequences of such simple actions. With each activity, think about all the impacts they have, including resources, other creatures, and the planet.

For example, if you enjoy taking long hot baths, reflect on where your water comes from, the energy to transport and heat the water, and the environmental impact of those things. Likewise, if you love eating strawberries year round, consider the distance these fruits must travel and the ecological impact of that. If you drive a car, consider the factories that make that car, the people working on the production line, the gas it uses, the pollution it causes, the activities it allows, the roads it requires, the consequences to human health, and so on. In the same way, reflect on the effect when you decide to have lentil soup for lunch rather than a burger. That simple choice, if followed by millions around the world every day, affects methane levels, deforestation, and precious lives. Everything is connected. Every action has a consequence. Everything we do affects others and the earth and its limited resources. Awareness of those connections helps us to not take them for granted.

This reflection is not meant to foster judgment or guilt. Not every connection or impact is negative. But each action we take is woven into an interconnected tapestry that literally includes every being on the earth. Environmentalists remind us that if everyone lived at the same standard of living as North Americans, we would need several planets to handle the demand for resources. In this contemplation, as you reflect on this, notice what arises in your heart and mind, and throughout your day, continue to consider how the ways you act and live affect the welfare of all life, including your own.

• • •

Chapter 33

Service in the World

*Too often we underestimate the power of a touch, a smile, a kind
word, a listening ear, an honest compliment, or the smallest act of
caring, all of which have the potential to turn a life around.*

— LEO BUSCAGLIA

All spiritual traditions encourage engaging in selfless service
to help improve the lives of others. One inspiring example of
this is Dr. A. T. Ariyaratne's work in the Sarvodaya Shramadana
movement in Sri Lanka. His work has brought to life the Sanskrit
meaning of *sarvodaya* — "the welfare of all" — and redefined the
term to reflect another ideal important in that country: "the awakening of all."

This grassroots movement has helped uplift tens of thousands
of villages in rural Sri Lanka and improved the lives of over ten
million people by providing comprehensive development and conflict resolution programs. This began simply by Dr. Ariyaratne
helping an outcast village improve its own living standards.

Dr. Ariyaratne regards this selfless service to others as a way
for people to turn their consciousness into a more awakened and
compassionate state. He posits that selflessness is brought about
through the service that is done through Sarvodaya Shramadana,

which results in both personal and societal transformation. This is a beautiful example of how the shift from a self-centered focus to a selfless orientation benefits one and all.

Movements like this stand in stark contrast to the consumerism that drives much of modern society. For example, in the United States, the baby boomers were first dubbed the "me generation," but a case could be made that in each decade since, people have only become more self-absorbed. Social media and materialist consumer culture seem to perpetuate this myopic self-centered focus. The underlying premise or expectation is that pleasure-seeking consumption will make us happier. But is this true? Depression, anxiety, and suicide rates are sadly skyrocketing among all age groups. A genuine contented life seems ever-elusive despite billions spent in the self-help, cosmetics, and consumer industries.

On the other hand, for millennia, spiritual traditions have taught that a life devoted to the welfare of others is the secret ingredient to genuine happiness. Putting other people's well-being before our own brings a genuine satisfaction and lasting joy that a life of pleasure-seeking just cannot yield.

Martin Seligman, often referred to as the father of positive psychology, corroborates these ancient perspectives. He researched what helps people create a meaningful life and discovered three basic avenues for happiness: pursuing a life of pleasure, of engagement, and of purpose. Seligman found that a life dedicated to pleasure fails to deliver on the promise of satisfaction for the simple reason that pleasure habituates. One bite of cake may be delicious, but the fifth or tenth bite fails to maintain the same punch.

The life of engagement refers to using our skills, talents, and strengths to learn, work, and overcome challenges. This does provide some satisfaction, but not to the same degree as a life of purpose, which means putting your strength and skills to work in service of something greater than yourself. The life of purpose turns out to be the most impactful as a support for well-being, since the shift from "me" to "we" provides the basis for a truly fulfilled and genuinely happier life.

Sadly, consumer culture encourages people to fixate on and maximize pleasure. America has come to epitomize this orientation, and yet it often has some of the highest rates of mental health disorders. Despite being the wealthiest country, it sadly ranks eighteenth on the UN World Happiness Report, an index initiated by the United Nations to measure real happiness of people across the world. Norway, Denmark, Iceland, and Switzerland rank highest on all the main factors found to support genuine happiness: caring, freedom, generosity, honesty, health, income, and good governance.

On a personal level, how does one shift from this self to other orientation? The simplest avenue is to find a way to serve, to prioritize the needs of others. This is not done out of self-negation; service benefits the giver and the receiver and is to flow naturally from the heart. Neem Karoli Baba, an esteemed Indian saint, told his devotees: "Love people and feed them." That encouragement is found across religions, and feeding the hungry and needy is often the most obvious first step in service. Glide Memorial Church in San Francisco serves over sixty thousand meals a month to the homeless and hungry on the streets. The joy and delight that pervades those who show up to offer their time and energy to help prepare and cook all that food is a potent testament to the well-being that service brings.

But service goes beyond that. At a deeper level, it is about seeing through the illusion that we are separate. As soon as we orient to something larger than our small selves, we tap into a greater sense of purpose that brings its own well-being. Some of the great leaders we admire, both past and present, in public service, business, and government, exemplify this level of functioning.

When leaders let go of their own self-interest and genuinely act for the greater good of others, something transformative can happen both for the individual and for the organization or state. When we cease to act from a small separate self, when we get out of our own way, then energy, dynamism, and flow happen. Service becomes effortless effort. As the Tao Te Ching says: "A leader is best when people barely know he exists. A good leader, who talks little, when his work is done, people will say, 'We did this ourselves.'"

Nelson Mandela symbolized this kind of leadership and the power of a wise, generous heart. Despite imprisonment for twenty-seven years in cramped, confined conditions in Robben Island prison, Mandela emerged from the dismantling of the apartheid regime without bitterness, hatred, or desire for vengeance. Further, Mandela's loving magnanimity and visionary guidance allowed the country not to be torn apart by violent retribution; instead, he helped usher a peaceful transition to a democracy none thought possible. His living example of being kind, caring, and generous, even with people, like his prison guards, who saw him as an enemy, transformed the hearts and minds of so many.

What helps with this transformation is being aware of when we get caught up in ourselves or lost in self-interest, which ultimately serves neither ourselves nor others. The paradox of mindfulness is that one initially turns attention inward to become more self-aware and self-conscious, but as Dogen, one of the most significant teachers in Zen and founder of the Soto Zen lineage, taught: "To study the Way is to study the self. To study the self is to forget the self. To forget the self is to be awakened by all things."

Through mindfulness practice, we cultivate an intimate awareness of inner experience. Yet as Dogen suggests, that introspection allows us to understand and untangle ourselves from our mental processes, which keep us bound in self-referential loops. It helps us find freedom from the reactive patterns of our thoughts and feelings. As that occurs, we become less wrapped up in our inner processes. Our heart and mind become quieter, more at ease, and so require less attention and management. This frees up attention and energy to be more aware of life around us and liberates energy to help others.

Another way to shift self-centeredness is to cultivate generosity. Being generous shifts us from thoughts about ourselves to how we can serve and help. I remember well when I first encountered the teaching of generosity as a support for awakening. What struck me was the understanding that to give, by necessity, entails we let go and release attachment to things like money, possessions, and one's time and energy. We relax the tendency to grasp and hold on, which is one of the causes of painful constriction in the first place. Being generous is like exhaling; it is both a release and a letting go.

Research shows that when we are generous, the areas in the brain associated with happiness light up; dopamine fires in our brain's reward center. We naturally feel good when we give, when we share and care for others. Perhaps it is because we are both physically vulnerable and social creatures, and mutual generosity was originally necessary for our survival. Whatever the cause, the fact that being generous brings about well-being both for ourselves and others is good enough reason to practice it. This shift from self-centered preoccupation to being generous and caring for others is one of the hallmarks of the freedom that comes with practice.

One of the first techniques I undertook with generosity was to follow through on the first impulse to give. The feeling of generosity can arise in many moments, such as when we hear of a natural disaster like a tsunami affecting thousands, when a friend talks to us about the hard times they are in, or when we see a cold, hungry homeless person in the street. Our hearts often respond immediately with natural generosity or a desire to help even in small ways, such as giving money, food, or at least the warm comfort of our attention. I have learned it is helpful to trust that first impulse.

All too often, however, that altruistic impulse is quickly followed by the scarcity mind, which offers all sorts of reasons and rationales for not acting on that generosity. I might worry that I'm too busy to call my friend who is having a hard time. I may believe the fear thought that I don't have enough money to give to a disaster relief effort, that I shouldn't donate my old winter jacket since I might need it again, or more cynically, that the homeless person will use my money to buy drugs and not food or shelter.

Whether or not there is any truth to these fears, they are expressions of the small self, which is conditioned to conserve and preserve its own narrow interests. Thus, if we act on our first generous impulse, we can avoid and overcome the fearful thoughts that undermine our expressions of caring. This is a great practice if you wish to stretch beyond just giving only to those closest to you. It is a way of expanding our ambit of concern to include a wider swathe of life. Putting others first, we soften the painful hold of self-centeredness.

There are innumerable ways to serve. One obvious path is parenting. This is perhaps the most universal way that humans stretch beyond themselves to serve another. This beautiful, challenging practice requires us to constantly attend to and prioritize our children's needs often ahead of our own. Sometimes this is experienced as a burden, but when approached wholeheartedly, it illuminates the profound effect generosity has on our heart and well-being. Of course, this is easier to feel when we are not suffering from days of sleepless nights when our children are infants! However, even people without children can experience this when their parents age or become sick. Then the situation reverses, and children may be asked to provide a similar form of selfless service.

Joining a service organization is another way to practice generosity. In *Blessed Unrest*, Paul Hawken and his team chronicle a global movement oriented to serving others; he found that more than 1.7 million organizations worldwide — including nonprofits, for-profits, and NGOs — are dedicated to improving the lives of others and benefiting communities, creatures, and the environment. Uncounted millions of people are helping perhaps billions of people, not to mention other species and the planet. Service within and as part of a community offers benefits that go beyond the actions we take.

A sign of a mature mindfulness practitioner is taking one's practice from the safe confines of the meditation cushion out into the world and putting into practice the integration of love and awareness. Now more than ever, this is essential for the welfare of ourselves, for underserved and vulnerable communities, and for the planet itself. The way to start, and the place to look, is within your own life, with whatever is in front of you.

The close relationship between spiritual practice and service is beautifully illustrated in a story about Hafiz, a wise Sufi master. A spiritual seeker experienced visions of God, and he sought confirmation of his mystical awakening with Hafiz, his teacher. Hafiz listened to the student's excited report and then asked him a range of questions: "Do you take care of your parents? How do you look after your servants? Do you tend with care to your animals? Do you feed the birds in winter?" The spiritual seeker was incredulous. He wanted to discuss his mystical revelation, but all Hafiz cared about was how he was conducting himself with others in his life. Hafiz responded: "You ask me if your visions of God are true. I say they are if they make you more kind and more caring to every person and creature that you meet."

Hafiz could not have made his case more clear. Helping others is both the grit and the fruit of spiritual practice.

• **PRACTICE** •

Cultivating Generosity

Generosity is a beautiful expression of a loving and caring heart, and you can cultivate generosity through intention. This practice is very simple: take a few minutes to reflect on one way you would like to express generosity, then do it.

Try to follow through on this intention immediately if you can or as soon as it's appropriate. There are endless ways to give, but listen to your heart and trust the first impulse of generosity that arises. Then be aware that fear can arise in the mind that may cause you to second-guess or doubt that impulse. For this time at least, try to put that doubt aside and follow the original urge.

As the chapter describes, you might focus your generous act on a friend or family member who needs help, even if that help is simply emotional support and being a kind listener. You might help a stranger on the street, or you might support or join a service organization. You might offer money, time, or particular skills.

After completing your act of generosity, reflect on how you felt while helping and how you feel once it's done. Observe if you experienced any gladness in the moment or if your spirit feels uplifted. Generosity is a mutually beneficial process, and sometimes it can be hard to know who is the giver and who is the receiver. Be curious: Did the act of giving soften a sense of separation or isolation you may have had?

To extend this practice, try to do it daily. Then notice how small, everyday acts of service not only cultivate your own well-being but bring happiness and joy into the world.

• • •

Chapter 34

Waking Up to Unconscious Bias

It is not our differences that divide us. It is our inability to recognize,
accept, and celebrate those differences.
— AUDRE LORDE

We are all conditioned by and subject to a host of impressions from our culture, family, and society as well as from the vast tapestry of our personal experience. Such influences inevitably affect the ways we see the world and one another. Mindfulness practice teaches us to see more clearly the reality of experience. This means becoming cognizant of the various filters that can occlude our perception. These filters are like glasses we don't realize we are wearing that color the world and make it seem a certain way. Filters are the implicit bias we develop, and this affects our understanding, perceptions, and decisions. How do we become aware of such biases, particularly if they are unconscious and implanted at an impressionable age?

One answer is by simply being aware that everyone develops bias, and then, through mindfulness practice, paying attention to how we are influenced by such predispositions. This is an ongoing process, one that never fully ends, since distortions of perception will always arise. For instance, in a well-known study by Daniel Simons, participants were asked to watch a video of a basketball game and focus on how often players in white shirts passed the ball. Participants became so engrossed in the task that over 50 percent of viewers failed to see a large gorilla walk across the field of play in the center of the screen! We see what we either want to see or are conditioned or told to see. I watched the same video and was amazed that I also did not see the gorilla on first view. Only after I knew to look for the gorilla did I actually see it.

While bias develops with all sorts of things — age, gender, social status, fear of strangers and people from different cultures, and so on — one of the more insidious distortions is conditioning around race and ethnicity. Becoming aware of our own racial bias is a necessary part of practice and essential for avoiding unconscious racism, unintended discrimination, and the immense pain this can cause. For example, I have been conditioned to see race from the perspective of my upbringing as a white male in northern England. Growing up, white Anglo-Saxon culture was considered the norm against which all other ethnicities were unconsciously measured, often negatively. Because of my conditioning, even when I moved to London, which is a very multicultural city, I was barely self-conscious of my race and my identity as a white person.

On the other hand, in the 1980s, I was in a relationship with Yvon, a black woman of Caribbean descent who wore a large afro. Her experience was almost the opposite of mine. Traveling around London, she was constantly aware of race, as barely a day went by when someone didn't look at her in a derogatory way or express some insulting racial remark or gesture. Though today there is more awareness and education of these issues, people of color today still experience the negative bias and racism inherent in white-dominant cultures.

In America, the Black Lives Matter movement has highlighted

how such racist conditioning negatively influences the way the police and the courts treat men and women of color. For example, minorities and black people are killed by police at disproportionate rates. In 2012, while black people made up 13 percent of the U.S. population, they accounted for 31 percent of people killed by police; meanwhile, racial minorities made up about 37.4 percent of the general population, but they accounted for 62.7 percent of unarmed people killed by police. Similarly, African American men are more likely than white men to suffer mistreatment by police, and innocent black men are far more likely to be selected for committing a crime by witnesses. These are just a few of the innumerable ways racial bias continues to distort perception and thus influence actions with grave consequences.

Waking up to such bias means paying attention to how our perceptions are influenced by conditioning. In America, long-standing cultural and media stereotypes persist that black men are more violent and more likely to commit criminal acts, and this can condition people to discriminate even when such stereotypes are proved false. Unearthing these distortions can be like trying to see one's own shadow or like a fish trying to see the water it swims in. It takes ongoing work, study, and help from others, since the roots of such prejudice run deep, but the negative effects of unconscious bias are real.

For instance, an African American acquaintance of mine was on a silent retreat at a meditation center in Oregon, and he decided to take a walk in the nearby forest. When he returned, a staff member confronted him and asked what he was doing at the retreat center. The man said he was attending the meditation course and wished to not have his silence interrupted. The woman apologized, but after the course, the man confronted the staff person and asked whether she would have accosted him if he had been white. She admitted it was unlikely, and in fact, the staff person had recently undergone training about undoing bias. This is just a small example of how our filters can influence us even after we become aware of them or been educated about them.

Undoing internalized racism, bias, and conditioning is an ongoing process. We must be vigilant and maintain awareness of how it emerges in small and insidious ways. Of course, our personal bias depends on our particular conditioning and circumstances. Such bias is not limited to how we perceive race. It affects how we perceive gender and gender identification, sexual orientation, age, physical ability, and economic status. It also impacts how we perceive others who may have a different mother tongue, lower level of education, a different body shape, a different home country, or a different religion.

For instance, when you go for a medical exam, do you doubt the competence of your physician if they are not the gender you expect? If you walk past a group of people from a different socioeconomic class, do you relate to them differently? What assumptions do you make when you see people of different physical ability? What arises when you see two men or two women holding hands in the street or when a transgender person is elected to public office? If someone trains you who is twice your age, or half your age, what thoughts or feelings arise? How we think, feel, and react to such circumstances indicates how much conditioning or bias is alive within us.

From a mindfulness perspective, the key is not to judge our conditioned responses but to become aware of them and see how they affect our perceptions, thoughts, and actions. With awareness, we have the power to choose to act differently. We can recognize our own bias and the distortion it creates and avoid causing unintended harm. And we can start to educate ourselves about our own conditioning and the limitations it places on our perceptions. We can also learn to become an advocate and ally for those groups and people who are routinely discriminated against or marginalized because of their differences and who may not have had the privilege of being part of a society's predominant cultural group. This is the beginning of undoing the suffering of bias in ourselves and in the world.

• **PRACTICE** •

Mindfulness of Bias

Being mindful of what we do not ordinarily see is not easy. This practice asks you to look at your life as you are living it right now and identify how your conditioning creates implicit bias in all sorts of ways. Consider the people in your life, the places you feel safe or comfortable, the place of worship you attend, the type of neighborhood you live in, the kind of school your kids go to, and the activities you like or engage in. Reflect on the following questions and observe what they bring up for you:

- Are your closest friends the same ethnicity as you?
- What is the racial makeup of your neighborhood or your kids' schools, and do particular populations make you comfortable or uncomfortable?
- If you are followed in a store by security, what assumptions might you make about why you are being targeted?
- Does race factor into your thinking when it comes to who to befriend, date, or hire?
- Does the gender or race of a doctor, teacher, or lawyer make any difference to you when you seek their help?
- How would you feel if your new next-door neighbors were a gay couple, if you were to work under a

manager who was transgender, or if one of your children or grandchildren told you they were gay?

- How do you feel toward a child who feels they are a different gender than their own physical body?

- Do you ever consider how someone who is less physically able may navigate the obstacles, stairs, or other challenges in your office or home?

- What effect does it have on you when you hear that one in five children lives in poverty in the United States?

- When you buy Band-Aids or bandages, do you ever think about whose skin color they are most likely to match?

- If a traffic cop pulls you over, do you ever wonder if you have been singled out because of your race?

Reflecting on these and similar questions can help unearth our unconscious bias toward people. Once you discover possible bias, reflect on what steps you can do to understand the limitation or distortion of this perception or conditioning. In what ways can you educate yourself so that these distortions can be uprooted? Commit to learning about the perspectives of people who are not part of the dominant culture or who don't fit the cultural norms and stereotypes of the society you live in.

• • •

Chapter 35

Waking Up to Nature as Teacher

When the eyes and ears are awake, even the leaves on the trees
read like pages from the scriptures.

— KABIR

Nature is a supreme support for developing mindfulness. Mystics and meditators for millennia have sought refuge in the mountains of the Himalayas and in desert caves, in the serenity of lakes and streams and in the stillness of forests. These are places that help awaken our minds and hearts. People tend to naturally be more attentive when outdoors. Nature allures our curiosity. Our sensory awareness becomes more awake in an aromatic rainy forest or by the crashing waves of the ocean. Nature is one of the few things that can pull us away from our screens, out of our thinking minds, and into the present moment. Think about the last time you were really present. Did it involve nature? Perhaps you were watching a beautiful sunset, listening to morning birdsong, swimming in a lake, tending to flowers in the garden, or playing with your cat. It becomes easier to cultivate mindful presence when our attention is allured fully in the natural world.

The body and its senses are always in the now; sensory stimuli are portals to present-moment awareness. Our homes, offices, and cars are designed to reduce external stimuli. They temper the extremes of heat, cold, wind, and rain. Living indoors, our sensory awareness can go to sleep, since there is minimal input from fragrance, breeze, movement, or sound. To compensate, we watch action movies and high-drama TV to stimulate our deadened nervous system.

How different it feels when we step out of our air-conditioned office and take a walk in a park. The fresh oxygen literally wakes our brain cells. We inhale the fragrance of the trees after a recent rainfall and feel the humidity moisten our skin. A north wind blows, ruffling our hair, and we feel a refreshing cool breeze on our face. The sun peeks out from behind the clouds and drenches us in warm light. We step out onto grass and feel the soft ground underfoot. A cacophony of chirping arises as a flock of starlings takes flight in unison. A gray squirrel busily scurries around oak trees collecting acorns. How easy to pay close attention to this rich tapestry of experience.

Not only does nature support awareness, she offers a doorway to insight and understanding. It is hard to walk for more than a few steps without seeing signs of the reality of change. Plants, grasses, and trees are emerging, flourishing, decaying, and slowly becoming nutrients for the soil. A hillside of flowering lupines includes some in full bloom and others already withered, full of their own unstoppable decay. Impermanence, the truth that every living thing is transient, broadcasts loudly as we stroll outdoors.

In nature, no two moments are the same. Something always changes: a shift in sunlight, a breeze rustling leaves overhead, a bird's song rising and falling. We are often mesmerized by changing landscapes, gazing for hours at the restless ocean as waves perpetually crash and recede on the shore. We can lose ourselves in the vast cloud-filled sky. I personally relish watching the rain sweep across the hillsides or the wind blow tall grasses in the valleys of Northern California. With intimacy and insight, we dwell in the naturalness of transience, part of the fabric of life, and are invited to release rather than hold experience, which continually slips through our fingers.

Similarly, we encounter the naturalness and beauty of death everywhere we go. Even in death, an old oak tree, leafless, its dignified, sturdy trunk soaring to the skies, retains its gracefulness. Perhaps we encounter a bleached deer skull lying in tall grasses and are reminded that death's hand is never far away. Similarly, when I teach retreats in Baja, California, the coastline is littered with the skeletons of crabs and starfish, a graveyard of bones from countless sea creatures. Life's transience is everywhere, inviting us to wake up to each precious and passing moment.

As we live our individual lives, cut off from one another in our cars, cubicles, and condos, it is easy to feel distant from the truth that our lives are intimately interconnected. In the outdoors, however, we can sense the matrix of life, in which everything is interwoven with everything else.

When I take groups to Alaska on a kayaking retreat, we swim in an intact ecosystem, where humpback whales, herring, bald eagles, spawning salmon, and black bears interact as they have for millions of years. We are at risk of destroying such ecological balance through pollution, the use of chemicals, and countless other human impacts. In our ignorance, we risk harming all life. We must understand and honor just how intricately our lives and the consequences of our actions affect the web of life. Immersion in nature helps wake us up to the delicateness of this balance and reminds us of the necessity to live in harmony with all creatures.

Nature can also teach us about simplicity and peace. In his poem "The Peace of Wild Things," Wendell Berry writes of being stressed about his children's lives and how nature is a salve for that anxiety: "I come into the presence of wild things / who do not tax their lives with forethought / of grief.... / For a time / I rest in the grace of the world, and am free." When surrounded by the natural world, we see how preoccupied we get with future thoughts and worries. Nature reminds us of the peace that is available when we orient to the present rather than get lost in a swarm of future concerns. Immersing ourselves in such landscapes strengthens our ability to abide in the grace of the present.

Bringing mindfulness outside can also help us step out of clock time and into natural rhythms. We get so caught up in busyness and a lack of time, which causes us to rush anxiously through life. Outdoors, we adjust to nature's clock, which moves slowly, organically, everything happening in its proper time.

Along Utah's Green River, the high canyon walls are up to three hundred million years old, which provides a different scale of time entirely. Rafting the river on a nature meditation retreat, I realize how silly and unnecessary all my rushing and angst about deadlines are. Our hurry creates so much extra stress and burden. Instead, nature invites us to slow down, to sense the vastness of time and the intimacy of this moment, if we are present enough to notice.

Perhaps the most significant lesson is how nature can take us out of our myopic self-centered absorption. Indoor living can accentuate a self-focus and a preoccupation with the details of our life. The further we roam from our human-centric world, the more we foster a sense of spaciousness and perspective. Immersing ourselves in nature, absorbing its rhythms, distancing ourselves from egocentricity, our sense of self naturally softens and relaxes. It is as if our psyche can breathe.

On my nature meditation retreats, many students report how the constricted sense of self easily dissolves while spending quiet time outdoors. It is like shedding a tight-fitting suit, and without such constriction, a natural sense of peace emerges. This easing of the tightly wrapped sense of self can be both insightful and life-changing. We see how the self, to which we cling so tightly, is like all things transient and ephemeral. With that we can access a natural lightness and freedom that can profoundly transform how we live in this world.

• **PRACTICE** •

Gleaning Wisdom from Nature

This practice involves going outside to a nearby park, meadow, woodland, or coastline and immersing yourself in a natural environment for half an hour or more. Once you arrive, take time to meander around and take in the elements of the setting. Then find a place to sit comfortably, whether against a tree, on a rock, in a shady grove, or even on a park bench.

Notice how the natural world allures your attention. Notice colors, shapes, forms, movements, smells, and textures. Let the movement of wind, the sound of waves, or a flight of birds capture your curiosity. See how awareness spontaneously becomes attentive to the rich, dynamic landscape compared to the relative flatness and lack of stimulation in our homes and offices.

Now attune to your senses and notice the fluctuating flow of experience. Observe how no two moments are the same. Observe the waterfall nature of the sensory world — how sounds, sensations, temperature, sights, smells, and touch ceaselessly change. This is also true of inner experience. Can you sense how this is occurring all the time, though we often fail to notice?

In the same way, notice how everything in nature embodies both growth and decay. Consider the grasses, trees, flowers, or even the fresh falling snow. Notice how life is disintegrating and emerging in myriad ways. What happens when you take in that dynamic aspect of transience?

Next, attune to the interconnected flow of life. Notice how everything is interdependent. Notice how temperature shifts with the movement of the sun and breeze or how the fragrances of the forest emerge after rains. Animals, plants, insects, weather, and landscape exist in an interwoven dance that moves to the daily rotation of the planet and the yearly orbit around the sun. Be curious how your inner world of feelings and moods follows similar cycles, how inner and outer landscapes impact each other, how everything is interwoven — body, mind, heart, and world.

Finally, notice how you can lose all sense of self when you are fully absorbed in nature. These moments of "self-forgetting" can allow us to merge or dissolve into something greater. Our limited, contracted sense of self can drop away, and instead we open to a sense of vastness, awe, wonder, and profound silence. Be open to such moments arising. They most often occur when you least expect them! Yet they point to a truth about our own nature.

• • •

Chapter 36

Being a Steward of the Earth

The earth will not continue to offer its harvest,
except with faithful stewardship. We cannot say we love the land
and then take steps to destroy it for use by future generations.
— POPE JOHN PAUL II

When I started my own meditation journey, people told me that meditation was too introspective, little better than self-focused navel-gazing. Now, several decades later, I have seen how both the practice and the fruits of mindfulness could not be more different than those critical assertions. Mindfulness frees us from our emotional reactivity, mental confusion, and personal suffering, giving us more energy and clarity. We see clearly our interconnectedness, that if one part of life is not flourishing, we cannot fully flourish. We come to understand that the joys and sorrows of all beings are intricately interwoven with our own well-being. As George Bernard Shaw famously wrote: "I am of the opinion that my life belongs to the whole community, and as long as I live, it is my privilege to do for it whatever I can."

Thus, mindfulness practice ultimately motivates us to engage, to make our life be a force for goodness, for improving the welfare, health, and well-being of life, people, creatures, communities, and the earth itself. In this closing chapter, I want to speak to this motivation to help and serve as it relates to being better stewards of the planet. However, it could equally inspire us to campaign for social justice or prison reform or to serve anyone who is less fortunate than ourselves, such as those living in poverty, who are homeless, or who suffer in any of the ways people can.

The industrial world is only just beginning to wake up to the mystery and complexity of the natural world. In recent times, scientific research in the fields of biology, botany, and zoology have begun to penetrate just how sophisticated organic life is. Despite these breakthroughs, we know very little about life and how it evolves. Why does a monarch butterfly create such complex wing patterns out of its soupy chrysalis? How does a lotus flower evolve such perfection out of muddy waters? We still don't know what gave birth to life on earth in the first place nor how gravity really functions and keeps us tied to this blue-green planet floating in space.

Until only recently, *Homo sapiens* assumed in their hubris that they were the only species that could reason, have complex communication, use tools, and feel compassion. Recent discoveries in the life sciences disprove these ignorant notions. Research continues to reveal how an increasing number of species, from whales to mycelia, have sophisticated mediums of communication, capable of signaling warnings to one another and sending signals across thousands of miles of ocean or under the soil. Octopuses are now understood to have complex personalities. Even some fish have been shown to use simple techniques, similar to sea otters, to break shellfish. Mammals like dolphins and whales express self-awareness and show empathy and compassion, including rescuing humans in distress or at risk from sharks.

Such findings challenge how we relate to other species. New Zealand was the first government to grant animals the same rights as humans. Other countries are following suit. Yet human society has changed the earth's landscape in unprecedented ways with devastating impact for the majority of the world's creatures.

Farm animals now make up 60 percent of the world's mammals. Another 36 percent of mammals are humans. That means wild mammals make up only 4 percent. Birds have not fared much better. Sixty percent of all birds are poultry, mostly kept in inhumane conditions on factory farms. Populations of birds and their sweet song are sadly disappearing rapidly from the planet. Climate change and habitat reduction threaten to kill 50 percent of all large mammals living in the wild by 2050. These are hard times to stay present for.

The U.S. Endangered Species Act of 1973 was a landmark bill that sought to preserve the vast array of species that were close to extinction due to human activity. This was a beautiful example of what can happen when people wake up to the fragility of life and see the consequences of our actions on other species. This legislation galvanized collective action to save humpback whales, California condors, brown pelicans, alligators, and many others from the brink of extinction. However, these noble efforts are not sufficient in themselves. So much more is required if we are to save the world's threatened species. Actions to restore habitats, fisheries, and breeding grounds are just some of the many measures necessary to support the vulnerability of life.

My Awake in the Wild meditation retreats involve taking people into nature and the wilderness for a profound immersion in the natural world. What is unique about these programs is how people learn to enter a wild landscape with a contemplative awareness. The programs are held in silence, which supports a receptive and often reverential relationship to nature. My intention with these retreats is to create the conditions for people to have an intimate connection with the inner and outer wild.

When we abide in nature in that way, it inevitably touches and opens the heart. It is hard not to feel moved by gentle wildlife, delicate flowers, rugged mountains, and the silent mystery that touches and moves us in the desert or in virgin forests. My aspiration is that, as people fall in love with the beauty and biodiversity of flora and fauna in the forests, oceans, and deserts, they become more active in their compassionate care and stewarding of nature.

It is only through love of nature that we become passionate enough to protect it. Just ask any parent about the force of love and its drive to protect what we care for! This responsiveness of the heart is what may help save this earth from irreversible ecological destruction. Love manifested through concrete action is a powerful force that can move mountains. Being inspired by that heartfelt love for the sacredness and preciousness of the natural world may help guide humanity to live in harmony with the abundance of life and other species on earth.

Of course, that love has to be conjoined with wisdom to be complete and fully effective. We now understand the impact of our collective actions on climate change, on species extinction, and so on. Understanding that intellectually is one thing, but when we go into nature with mindful awareness, it allows our heart to be touched, moved, and inspired, which fuels the necessary work to bring about a radical transformation in how we live sustainably on this planet.

When I led a sunrise meditation recently on farmland as part of a nature teacher–training retreat, a herd of cows and their calves came to stand right in front of us. They looked at us with their beautiful deep black eyes, curiously wondering what these strange two-legged creatures were doing sitting still as the sun rose. After this intimate encounter, two people in the group said they could no longer eat meat and became vegetarians. Such responses are common when the heart is touched by nature.

Similarly, snorkeling among tropical fish and octopuses in a coral reef can convince us not to order calamari or baked haddock afterward. During such close encounters with wildlife, we can't help but marvel at the beauty, sensitivity, and vulnerability of these creatures. Similarly, when we see the vast amounts of plastics floating among the coral, it may inspire us to become an advocate for the oceans and to rid society of single-use plastic. An open heart can incline us to protect rather than harm the very nature we behold.

We need to integrate this compassionate attitude with the wisdom of awareness to have optimal impact in the world. What is asked of humanity now is that we shed the distorted view that our actions, like burning fossil fuels, aren't having a catastrophic impact on climate change and rising sea levels. When our eyes and hearts are open, we recognize the harm we are inflicting on untold species and the poorest of humanity through our collective actions. It also kindles the urge to engage in immediate compassionate action.

When our everyday lives are separated from nature, news of clear-cut forests, drained wetlands, and extinct species can feel distant, abstract, and disconnected from us. However, as mindfulness grows, our sensitivity and awareness extend beyond ourselves. We become attuned to the beauty and uniqueness of the natural world. We are both moved by its precious fragility and feel grief and rage at its loss.

My meditation students often ask me what to do in response to the ecological crisis and how to hold such an overwhelming situation. I respond by saying it is necessary to first feel our response to the tragedy, to allow the grief, sadness, anger, and whatever is there to be felt. Only by processing such emotions with a kind awareness can we then utilize those feelings to galvanize us into action. This clarity then informs a wise response to whatever situation we meet.

I also stress the balance necessary between staying informed versus being overwhelmed by news of an ecological crisis. To be paralyzed from listening to endless alarming reports on climate change is of no help to anyone. Joanna Macy, an environmental activist and scholar, has said that a significant risk facing the earth is numbness. This happens easily when we listen to too much negative environmental or political news. I instead point to taking in the wealth of positive actions that millions of citizens around the world are engaging in to save species, take carbon out of the air, develop green energy, eat plant-based diets, and clean up the oceans by banning plastics. My Facebook page, entitled "We Protect What We Love," is an expression of that. I choose to post only positive news that may inspire others to engage in similar ways. That phrase is the basis of all my contemplative nature work: connection and action inspired by love.

Rather than drown in media overload and overwhelming data, it's better to connect with others who are engaged in constructive actions. This helps stave off isolation and despair about the current catastrophe. Macy noted that even if our particular actions fail, such collective action galvanizes our energy and helps us see we are not alone, which is essential. Earth Day, which began in 1970, is an example of what can happen when millions of people come together to raise awareness and act to protect the earth. Given the urgency of the current environmental crisis, we need to see every day as Earth Day. To lose sight of that is to risk the very earth that sustains us.

Finally, I like to remind people of the need to spend time in nature, to allow oneself to be moved and inspired by all the beauty that still abounds. The irony is that environmental activists, working hard in offices to campaign for ecological justice, need this perhaps more than anyone. Let your heart and soul be nourished by walking in a snowy forest, wading by a babbling brook, or gazing at migrating geese flying overhead.

No matter what problems arise, never forget the renewal that awaits in nature. In spring, the bluebells emerge to share their beauty, the swallows return to dance in the skies, and the mountain streams flow with icy clear waters. In these difficult times, it is essential that we take time to absorb the earth's beauty and drink in the goodness that exists.

In conclusion, through the journey of mindfulness, as we become more aware, we begin to wake up, personally and collectively, to our common humanity and our shared responsibility. With this awareness, we see our interconnectedness and understand that our role, in part, is to be stewards of our community and our world. Our goal is to embody an awakened caring, so that we leave to future generations a society and a planet that are sustainable and healthy in all ways. The clarity that comes from practice helps us realize that life is short and that what we do, think, and say makes a difference. The time to act is now, but with mindfulness, we can do so with balance, wisdom, and compassion. This is the fruition of a life of awareness, which expresses itself as love in action, borne out of concern for the welfare of all life.

The heart of the poem "School Prayer" by Diane Ackerman speaks beautifully to the fruition of the intentions that arise from this practice:

> I swear I will not dishonor
> my soul with hatred,
> but offer myself humbly
> as a guardian of nature,
> as a healer of misery,
> as a messenger of wonder,
> as an architect of peace....
> I will honor all life —
> wherever and in whatever form
> it may dwell — on Earth my home,
> and in the mansions of the stars.

286 From Suffering to Peace

• PRACTICE •

Protecting What We Love

This practice is simple and always available: spend time in your favorite natural environment, whether that's the ocean, the woods, the mountains, or the grassy meadows of a local park. Even in cities, the natural world is never far. You can connect with it by looking up at the skies, clouds, and stars. You may feel it as the wind that blows through city streets or the trees that blossom in your neighborhood. Try to connect with and enjoy the landscape and its creatures. Take off your shoes, put your feet in a stream, rise early to listen to the dawn chorus of birds. Take a stroll in a city park. Every day, in some way, immerse in natural beauty.

When you do, reflect on the fragility or vulnerability of the landscape. Do you notice fewer butterflies, birds, or insects? Are all the trees and plants healthy? Have extreme weather conditions, whether droughts or storms, impacted the environment and taken a toll?

Let your heart be touched by the struggles of the natural world, and consider how you might help, support, or protect the places, species, communities, and habitats you treasure. If you were to engage in some action, what would it be? Be open to whatever suggests itself: perhaps donating resources to environmental organizations, volunteering to support a certain habitat, or calling your local representatives in government to express your concerns.

The more time we spend in nature, the more we will value it and want to protect it. Allow your heart to be touched, and be open to the possibility that, at some point, you will feel called to act on the earth's behalf.

• • •

Acknowledgments

F irst, I wish to thank New World Library for kindly agreeing to publish this work; Jason Gardner for guiding the book along; and Jeff Campbell for patiently and thoughtfully editing.

No meditative practice happens without a lot of support and guidance from teachers, colleagues, and centers that preserve and nurture the teachings and practice of mindfulness and wisdom. For that, I have deep respect and appreciation for the teachers and practitioners in the Buddhist tradition who have carefully preserved, taught, and developed the body of mindfulness teachings these past 2,600 years. And of course, profound appreciation for Siddhartha Gautama, who originally birthed this revolutionary practice of mindfulness in the forests of northern India.

In particular, I have much gratitude for my teachers who have taught me the range and depth of mindfulness practice as a path of wisdom and awakening. They include my Insight Meditation teachers Christopher Titmuss, Joseph Goldstein, Jack Kornfield, and Sharon Salzberg; my teachers from the Thai Forest tradition; Stephen Batchelor for his original perspectives on the teachings; Analayo for his lucidity around Satipatthana practice; and Sangharakshita, who first opened the door to meditation practice for me. Lastly, deep appreciation for Martin Aylward, my dear friend and cocreator of the Mindfulness Training Institute, for his friendship and for creating with me a worldwide teaching community that has guided my understanding of the needs of mindfulness teachers and students in the United States, Europe, and beyond.

Many thanks to those who supported me to write this book, giving suggestions and guidance along the way as well as reading earlier drafts, including Hugh Delaney, Lori Schwanbeck, Sharda Rogell, Dawn Mauricio, Gokce Bulgan, Kelly Boys, Bob Licht, Leslie Butterfield, and others.

Special thanks to my beloved partner, Lori, most of all for her love and generous heart, but also for her suggestions and continuing support, wisdom, and guidance as I walk this path of teaching, writing, and training.

Finally, I'd like to express my ongoing appreciation for all the students who have studied with me around the world — from the wilderness of Baja, Mexico, to the tranquil abode of meditation centers, to hospitals, clinics, prisons, and boardrooms. Some of their stories of how mindfulness has supported them in life are peppered throughout this book, and I wish to thank all those who shared anecdotes. It is for these students that I have written these words, and I hope that this book will both serve their deeper understanding of mindfulness and support their fuller awakening.

Endnotes

Introduction: Understanding Mindfulness

p. 7   *In a 2010 study at Harvard, psychologists concluded*: Steve Bradt, "Wandering Mind Not a Happy Mind," *Harvard Gazette*, November 11, 2010, https://news.harvard.edu/gazette/story/2010/11/wandering-mind -not-a-happy-mind.

Chapter 1: Living with Embodied Awareness

p. 20   *In a 2008 study, researchers found that, after only eight weeks*: J. Carmody and R. A. Baer, "Relationships between Mindfulness Practice and Levels of Mindfulness, Medical and Psychological Symptoms and Well-Being in a Mindfulness-Based Stress Reduction Program," *Journal of Behavioral Medicine* 31, no. 1 (2008): 23–33, https://www .ncbi.nlm.nih.gov/pubmed/17899351.

Chapter 2: Listening and Tending to the Body

p. 29   *In one 2010 study, researchers found that increased practice of mindfulness*: Desleigh Gilbert and Jennifer Waltz, "Mindfulness and Health Behavior," *Mindfulness* 1, no. 4 (2010): 227–34, https://www.researchgate .net/publication/225152897_Mindfulness_and_Health_Behaviors.

Chapter 3: Working Carefully with Physical Pain

p. 33   *Cohen wrote: "People sometimes ask me where my own healing energy"*: Quotes by Darlene Cohen are from her book *Turning Suffering Inside Out: A Zen Approach to Living with Physical and Emotional Pain* (Boston: Shambhala Publications, 2000).

p. 35   *Research has shown that mindfulness practice helps reduce anticipatory fear*: J. Lutz et al., "Mindfulness and Emotion Regulation—An fMRI Study," *Social Cognitive Affective Neuroscience* 9, no. 6 (2014): 776–85, https://www.ncbi.nlm.nih.gov/pubmed/23563850.

p. 35   *Similarly, a 2008 pain study considered older adults with chronic low back pain*: N. E. Morone et al., "'I felt like a new person': The Effects of Mindfulness Meditation on Older Adults with Chronic Pain: Qualitative Narrative Analysis of Diary Entries," *Journal of Pain* 9, no. 9 (2008): 841–48, https://www.ncbi.nlm.nih.gov/pubmed/18550444.

Chapter 5: Meeting Aging with Kind Awareness

p. 50   *This extract from a poem by Carmelene Siani speaks beautifully about meeting*: Carmelene Siani, "A 73-Year-Old Woman's Ode to the Art of Aging Gracefully," *Elephant Journal* (blog), November 8, 2015, https://www.elephantjournal.com/2015/11/a-73-year-old-womans-ode-to-the-art-of-aging-gracefully-poem.

p. 52   *In a 2014 research study using fMRI scans, findings revealed*: E. Luders, N. Cherbuin, and F. Kurth, "Forever Young(er): Potential Age-Defying Effects of Long-Term Meditation on Gray Matter Atrophy," *Frontiers in Psychology* 5 (2014), https://www.ncbi.nlm.nih.gov/pubmed/25653628.

p. 52   *Similar findings by Lutz and others have shown that long-term meditators*: A. Lutz et al., "Attention Regulation and Monitoring in Meditation," *Trends in Cognitive Sciences* 12, no. 4 (2009): 163–69, https://www.ncbi.nlm.nih.gov/pmc/articles/PMC2693206.

Chapter 6: Embracing Death's Invitation

p. 59   *In the poem "When Death Comes," Mary Oliver wrote about confronting*: Mary Oliver, *New and Selected Poems: Volume One* (Boston: Beacon Press, 1992).

Chapter 7: Riding the Waves of Pleasure and Pain

p. 64   *Or as the poet Jack Gilbert writes in his poem "A Brief for the Defense"*: Jack Gilbert, "A Brief for the Defense," *Refusing Heaven: Poems* (New York: Alfred A. Knopf, 2005); copyright © 2005 by Jack Gilbert.

Chapter 8: Understanding the True Nature of the Body

p. 70 *As Rilke once wrote in* Letters to a Young Poet: Rainer Maria Rilke, *Letters to a Young Poet* (New York: Norton and Company, 1962).

Chapter 9: Working with the Thinking Mind

p. 79 *The National Science Foundation posited that we can think upwards*: George Dvorsky, "Managing Your 50,000 Thoughts," *Sentient Developments* (blog), March 19, 2007, http://www.sentientdevelopments .com/2007/03/managing-your-50000-daily-thoughts.html.

Chapter 12: Identifying the Judging Mind

p. 99 *In one 2008 study, researchers investigated the impact of mindfulness*: Paul A. Frewen et al., "Letting Go: Mindfulness and Negative Automatic Thinking," *Cognitive Theory Research* 32 (2008): 758–74, https://contextualscience.org/system/files/Frewen,2008.pdf.

Chapter 13: The Illusion of Time

p. 106 *An illuminating radio series on National Public Radio called* Serial: NPR, *Serial* (podcast, 2014), https://serialpodcast.org/season-one.

Chapter 16: Learning the Wisdom of Letting Go

p. 124 *In* Man's Search for Meaning, *Viktor Frankl wrote about his experiences in the Nazi concentration camps*: Viktor E. Frankl, *Man's Search for Meaning* (Boston: Beacon Press, 1959/2006).

p. 125 *Ajahn Chah, a renowned Thai meditation master, once said: "If you want a little peace"*: Ajahn Chah, *Being Dharma* (Boston: Shambhala Publications, 2001).

Chapter 17: Freedom from Attachment

p. 133 *The Third Zen Patriarch, a famous Chinese Chan meditation master of the fifth century, wrote*: Seng-T'san, "The Third Patriarch of Zen Hsin Hsin Ming,"Age-of-the-sage.org (no date), https://www.age-of-the-sage .org/buddhism/third_patriarch_zen.html.

Chapter 19: Releasing Mistaken Identity

p. 147 *Astoundingly, over half our body weight is made up of microorganisms*: http://www.sciencealert.com/how-many-bacteria-cells-outnumber -human-cells-microbiome-science.

p. 148 *In Apocalypse, D. H. Lawrence hypothesized poetically almost a century ago*: D. H. Lawrence, *Apocalypse* (New York: Penguin Classics, 1931/1995).

p. 154 *Wes Nisker, a colleague and meditation teacher, gave this solution to the problem*: Wes Nisker, *Buddha's Nature: A Practical Guide to Discovering Your Place in the Cosmos* (New York: Bantam Books, 1998).

Chapter 20: The Causal Nature of Everything

p. 161 *Researchers in Canada have found that, over the past twenty years, the average human*: Kevin McSpadden, "You Now Have a Shorter Attention Span Than a Goldfish," *Time*, May 14, 2015, http://time.com /3858309/attention-spans-goldfish.

Chapter 21: Exploring the Nature of Awareness

p. 167 *A text called* The Flight of the Garuda *by Shabkar Tsogdruk Rangdrol*: Keith Dowman, *The Flight of the Garuda: The Dzogchen Tradition of Tibetan Buddhism* (Somerville, MA: Wisdom Publications, 2014).

Chapter 22: Opening to Vulnerability with a Kind Heart

p. 176 *In the United States alone, more than sixteen million children go hungry each year*: Katie Dupere, "6 Startling Facts about Child Hunger in the U.S. — and How You Can Help," Mashable, July 14, 2016, https://mashable .com/2016/07/14/child-hunger-united-states/#BulroaaoYaql.

p. 176 *Up to 20 percent of the U.S. population is on some kind of mental health medication*: Sara G. Miller, "1 in 6 Americans Takes a Psychiatric Drug," *Scientific American*, December 13, 2016, https://www.scientificamerican .com/article/1-in-6-americans-takes-a-psychiatric-drug.

p. 176 *Suicide rates, perhaps an expression of many people's inner struggles, are also increasing*: National Institute of Mental Health, "Suicide," last updated May 2018, https://www.nimh.nih.gov/health/statistics/suicide .shtml.

Chapter 24: Cultivating Self-Compassion

p. 191 *Kristin Neff, a psychologist and leading researcher on self-compassion, talks about three key components necessary to foster self-compassion:* https://self-compassion.org/the-three-elements-of-self-compassion-2/.

Chapter 26: Embracing Loss

p. 203 *The Palestinian American poet Naomi Shihab Nye speaks of the inseparability of loss:* Naomi Shihab Nye, *Words under the Words: Selected Poems* (Portland, OR: Eighth Mountain Press, 1995); copyright © 1995 by Naomi Shihab Nye; excerpt from "Kindness" reprinted with the permission of Far Corner Books.

Chapter 27: Living with a Steady Heart

p. 213 *They remind me of a poem by the Russian poet Anna Akhmatova:* Anna Akhmatova, *Poems of Akhmatova: Izbrannye Stikhi*, ed. Stanley Kunitz (Boston, MA: Houghton-Mifflin, 1997).

p. 214 *In one 2007 study, researchers found that people who had even minimal experience:* J. Kingston et al., "A Pilot Randomized Control Trial Investigating the Effect of Mindfulness Practice on Pain Tolerance, Psychological Well-Being and Physiological Activity," *Journal of Psychosomatic Research* 62, no. 3 (2007): 297–300, https://www.ncbi.nlm.nih.gov/pubmed/17324679.

Chapter 29: Extending Compassion to Others

p. 227 *Nadine Collier, the daughter of seventy-year-old Ethel Lance, who was slain:* Marc Maxmeister, "Gratitudes: Small Acts in Defiance of Hate, in Service of Love," *Chewy Chunks* (blog), December 18, 2016, https://chewychunks.wordpress.com/2016/12/18/gatitudes-small-acts-in-defiance-of-hate-in-service-of-love.

Chapter 30: Mindfulness in Relationships

p. 237 *François Fénelon, a seventeenth-century archbishop and theologian, put it beautifully:* François De Salignac De La Mothe-Fénelon, *Spiritual Letters of Archbishop Fénelon* (Germany: Hansebooks, 2012).

p. 240 *or in the Sufi poet Rumi's words: "Out beyond ideas of wrongdoing"*:
Coleman Barks, trans., *The Essential Rumi* (New York: HarperCollins,
2004).

Chapter 31: Freeing Ourselves from Self-Centeredness

p. 246 *Though Darwin is renowned for popularizing the term "survival of the
fittest"*: Christopher Kukk, "Survival of the Fittest Has Evolved:
Try Survival of the Kindest," NBCnews.com, March 8, 2017,
https://www.nbcnews.com/better/relationships/survival-fittest
-has-evolved-try-survival-kindest-n730196.

Chapter 33: Service in the World

p. 261 *Despite being the wealthiest country, it sadly ranks eighteenth on the UN
World Happiness Report*: J. Helliwell, R. Layard, and J. Sachs, *World
Happiness Report 2018* (New York: Sustainable Development Solutions
Network, 2018), http://worldhappiness.report/ed/2018.

p. 262 *Dogen, one of the most significant teachers in Zen and founder of the Soto
Zen lineage, taught*: Jay L. Garfield, *Engaging Buddhism: Why It Matters
to Philosophy* (New York: Oxford University Press, 2015).

p. 263 *Research shows that when we are generous, the areas in the brain associated
with happiness*: Ana Sandoiu, "How Does Generosity Benefit Health?
Brain Study Sheds Light," *Medical News Today*, August 31, 2018,
https://www.medicalnewstoday.com/articles/322940.php.

p. 265 *In* Blessed Unrest, *Paul Hawken and his team chronicle a global move-
ment*: Paul Hawken, *Blessed Unrest: How the Largest Social Movement in
History Is Restoring Grace, Justice, and Beauty to the World* (New York:
Penguin Books, 2007).

Chapter 34: Waking Up to Unconscious Bias

p. 268 *For instance, in a well-known study by Daniel Simons, participants*: D. J.
Simons and C. F. Chabris, "Gorillas in Our Midst: Sustained Inat-
tentional Blindness for Dynamic Events," *Perception* 28, no. 9 (1999):
1059–74, https://www.ncbi.nlm.nih.gov/pubmed/10694957.

p. 269 *For example, minorities and black people are killed by police at disproportionate rates*: German Lopez, "There Are Huge Racial Disparities in
How US Police Use Force," *Vox*, November 14, 2018, https://www

.vox.com/identities/2016/8/13/17938186/police-shootings-killings
-racism-racial-disparities.

Chapter 35: Waking Up to Nature as Teacher

p. 275 *In his poem "The Peace of Wild Things," Wendell Berry writes*: Wendell
Berry, *The Selected Poems of Wendell Berry* (Berkeley, CA: Counterpoint, 2010).

Chapter 36: Being a Steward of the Earth

p. 281 *Climate change and habitat reduction threaten to kill 50 percent of all large
mammals*: Paul Brown, "An Unnatural Disaster," *Guardian*, January 8,
2004, https://www.theguardian.com/science/2004/jan/08
/biodiversity.sciencenews.

p. 285 *The heart of the poem "School Prayer" by Diane Ackerman speaks beautifully*: Diane Ackerman, "School Prayer," *I Praise My Destroyer* (New
York: Vintage Books, 2000). Used by permission of Random House,
an imprint and division of Penguin Random House LLC. All rights
reserved.

Index

About the Author

Mark Coleman is an inner and outer explorer who has devotedly studied mindfulness meditation practices for over three decades. He is passionate about sharing the power of meditation and has taught mindfulness meditation retreats worldwide for the past twenty years. Mark is a senior meditation teacher at Spirit Rock Meditation Center.

Mark likes to share the fruits of meditation with wider audiences, so he founded the Mindfulness Training Institute, through which he has brought mindfulness programs to companies and the nonprofit sector across North America and Europe. Through the Institute, Mark leads professional mindfulness teacher trainings in the United States and United Kingdom annually. Mark is also a trainer for the Search Inside Yourself Leadership Institute, developed at Google, and teaches in its teacher trainings.

Mark is an unabashed nature lover, and through his organization Awake in the Wild, he shares his passion for integrating mindfulness, meditation, and nature. He leads wilderness meditation retreats from Alaska to Peru, taking people on inner and outdoor adventures. Through Awake in the Wild, Mark also leads yearlong meditation-in-nature teacher trainings in the United States.

Mark is the author of *Make Peace with Your Mind: How Mindfulness and Compassion Can Free You from Your Inner Critic* and *Awake in the Wild: Mindfulness in Nature as a Path of Self-Discovery.*

He holds an MA in clinical psychology and draws on his extensive experience in working with people and organizations as a coach and consultant.

Mark lives in Marin County, California, and enjoys spending his free time in nature, hiking, backpacking, biking, and kayaking.

NEW WORLD LIBRARY is dedicated to publishing books and other media that inspire and challenge us to improve the quality of our lives and the world.

We are a socially and environmentally aware company. We recognize that we have an ethical responsibility to our readers, our authors, our staff members, and our planet.

We serve our readers by creating the finest publications possible on personal growth, creativity, spirituality, wellness, and other areas of emerging importance. We serve our authors by working with them to produce and promote quality books that reach a wide audience. We serve New World Library employees with generous benefits, significant profit sharing, and constant encouragement to pursue their most expansive dreams.

Whenever possible, we print our books with soy-based ink on 100 percent postconsumer-waste recycled paper. We power our offices with solar energy and contribute to nonprofit organizations working to make the world a better place for us all.

Our products are available wherever books are sold. Visit our website to download our catalog, subscribe to our e-newsletter, read our blog, and link to authors' websites, videos, and podcasts.

customerservice@newworldlibrary.com
Phone: 415-884-2100 or 800-972-6657
Orders: Ext. 10 • Catalog requests: Ext. 10
Fax: 415-884-2199

www.newworldlibrary.com